The Creative Suffering of the Triune God

ACADEMY SERIES

SERIES EDITOR
Kimberly Rae Connor, University of San Francisco

A Publication Series of

The American Academy of Religion
and
Oxford University Press

INCARNATION AND PHYSICS
Natural Science in the Theology of Thomas F. Torrance
Tapio Luoma

OF BORDERS AND MARGINS
Hispanic Disciples in Texas, 1888–1945
Daisy L. Machado

YVES CONGAR'S THEOLOGY OF THE HOLY SPIRIT
Elizabeth Teresa Groppe

HSIEH LIANG-TSO AND THE *ANALECTS* OF CONFUCIUS
Humane Learning as a Religious Quest
Thomas W. Selover

GREGORY OF NYSSA AND THE CONCEPT OF DIVINE PERSONS
Lucian Turcescu

GRAHAM GREENE'S CATHOLIC IMAGINATION
Mark Bosco, S.J.

COMING TO THE EDGE OF THE CIRCLE
A Wiccan Initiation Ritual
Nikki Bado-Fralick

THE ETHICS OF ANIMAL EXPERIMENTATION
A Critical Analysis and Constructive Christian Proposal
Donna Yarri

PAUL IN ISRAEL'S STORY
Self and Community at the Cross
John L. Meech

CROSSING THE ETHNIC DIVIDE
The Multiethnic Church on a Mission
Kathleen Garces-Foley

GOD AND THE VICTIM
Traumatic Intrusions on Grace and Freedom
Jennifer Erin Beste

THE CREATIVE SUFFERING OF THE TRIUNE GOD
An Evolutionary Theology
Gloria L. Schaab

AAR

The Creative Suffering of the Triune God

An Evolutionary Theology

GLORIA L. SCHAAB

WITH A FOREWORD BY
ARTHUR R. PEACOCKE

OXFORD
UNIVERSITY PRESS
2007

OXFORD
UNIVERSITY PRESS

Oxford University Press, Inc., publishes works that further
Oxford University's objective of excellence
in research, scholarship, and education.

Oxford   New York
Auckland   Cape Town   Dar es Salaam   Hong Kong   Karachi
Kuala Lumpur   Madrid   Melbourne   Mexico City   Nairobi
New Delhi   Shanghai   Taipei   Toronto

With offices in
Argentina   Austria   Brazil   Chile   Czech Republic   France   Greece
Guatemala   Hungary   Italy   Japan   Poland   Portugal   Singapore
South Korea   Switzerland   Thailand   Turkey   Ukraine   Vietnam

Published by Oxford University Press, Inc.
198 Madison Avenue, New York, New York 10016

www.oup.com

Oxford is a registered trademark of Oxford University Press

Library of Congress Cataloging-in-Publication Data
Schaab, Gloria L.
The creative suffering of the Triune God : an evolutionary
theology / Gloria L. Schaab ; with foreword by Arthur R. Peacocke.
     p. cm.
Includes bibliographical references and index.
ISBN 978-0-19-532912-4
1. Suffering of God.   2. Trinity.   3. Religion and science.
4. Theology, Doctrinal.   I. Title.
BT153.S8S45 2007
231'.8—dc22   2006102005

9 8 7 6 5 4 3 2 1

Printed in the United States of America
on acid-free paper

To

Arthur R. Peacocke

1924–2006

in thanksgiving for his scholarship, faith, courage,
and spirit of inquiry
that have inspired so many like myself.

Foreword

Sometimes the terminology of theology sits ill at ease with the spiritual instincts of those who deploy it. The sense of God's prevailing immanence in the world that is the locus of divine creation is not, for example, well served by the term *panentheism*, whose definition is "the belief that the Being of God includes and penetrates the whole universe, so that every part of it exists in Him, but (as against Pantheism) that His Being is more than, and is not exhausted by, the universe." This sense of divine transcendence-in-immanence has long been impressed on me through the recognition that contemporary science unveils a world in which self-organization and self-complexification, coupled with natural selection, are apparently the means, inter alia, whereby in the natural world there have been evolved new forms of matter—both nonliving and living, both insentient and conscious, both sensitive and self-conscious. No wonder that in the seventeenth century, which saw the birth and efflorescence of natural science, as we now call it, into a new realm of human creativity a priest-poet could exclaim,

> The WORLD is unknown till the Value and Glory of it is seen,
> till the Beauty and Serviceableness of all its parts is
>   considered.
> When you enter into it, it is an Unlimited field of Variety
>   and Beauty

where you may lose yourself in the multitude of Wonder and
   Delights,
But it is a happy loss to lose oneself in admiration at one's own
   Felicity:
and to find God in exchange for oneself, Which we then do when
   we see
Him in his Gifts and adore his Glory.
[Thomas Traherne, *The Centuries of Meditations*, 1670]

Today the sciences have massively delivered a natural, continuous scenario from the "Hot Big Bang" to the intricate and fruitful web of life spun by the DNA structure in all living forms, a scenario evoking a sense of wonder and even awe. Such a response occurs, indeed, not least in those who do not attribute the existence of this process to an Ultimate Reality, supremely rational, "that than which nothing greater can be conceived," as Anselm famously defined "God." It is a theme of this book, and of my own work, that these considerations today constitute an imperative to view the world from the perspective of panentheism and also from an emergentist monism and a theistic naturalism.

Apart from the obvious dissonance of panentheism as a word, it has its drawbacks from earlier and other associations, and I trust that the reader will lay these aside when reading Gloria Schaab's book. In it, she has been able to expound accurately and fruitfully—by never detaching the Trinity of God from the God-world relationship—the many ways in which I and others have been able to suggest that this conception of God and of God's relation to the world enriches and deepens our understanding of God as transcendent, incarnate, and immanent. Indeed, this tighter involvement in an emergentist naturalistic panentheist perspective of God with the world—yet maintaining the ontological distinction of God from the world—helps to illuminate the ways in which the freedom, autonomy, and self-creativity of the cosmos may be integrated with the ubiquity of pain, suffering, and death, for the Triune God can be seen to suffer in, with, and under the creative processes of the cosmos, not least in those inherent to the exercise of human creativity.

I am indebted, as will be the reader, to Gloria Schaab for her lucid exposition of such themes, which, I hope, will show that to see the world through scientific spectacles is to delineate with a sharper focus than ever before (we are a fortunate generation) that Triune God who is so creative in nature and in humanity.

—Arthur R. Peacocke
June 29, 2006

Acknowledgments

No one successfully sets out, travels, or completes the journey of scholarly research without the companionship of a community of support and love. I am deeply grateful to Sister Patricia Kelly, President, and Sisters Merilyn Ryan, Anne Myers, Anna Louise Schuck, Mary Barrar, Mary Dacey, and Dorothy Urban, members of the General Council of the Congregation of the Sisters of Saint Joseph of Chestnut Hill, Philadelphia, from 1999 to 2005, whose personal, prayerful, and financial generosity in the name of the congregation enabled the expeditious and felicitous completion of this manuscript. I am also grateful to the Graduate School of Arts and Sciences of Fordham University and to the Department of Theology, whose award of the Alumni Dissertation Fellowship provided the opportunity for me to devote myself full time to the completion of the dissertation that formed the basis of this book. I also thank my colleagues in the Department of Theology and Philosophy at Barry University who journeyed with me along the road to its final publication.

I am especially grateful to Elizabeth A. Johnson, my mentor, whose professional, scholarly, and personal example continues to inspire and inform my growth in these very areas. I dearly thank Margie Thompson, SSJ, my closest friend and colleague, whose loving, unfailing, and unconditional belief in me and in my potential encouraged, enlightened, and emboldened me throughout this undertaking. Her affirmation of the meaningfulness of many of my proposals about the mystery of God in suffering to those whom she encounters in her ministry of spiritual direction has validated the pastoral efficacy of this work. I am grateful as well to Jeannine Hill Fletcher and Aristotle Papanikolaou, whose invaluable insights, guidance, and patience helped to bring this project to scholarly fruition. I also extend my thanks to the staff of the Walsh Library of Fordham University, Rose Hill, who graciously and skillfully aided me in locating and acquiring resources through Walsh Library.

I am immensely grateful to the Sisters of Saint Joseph of Saint Anastasia, Teaneck, New Jersey: Sisters Adrienne Bradley, Clare DiGregorio, and Susie Thornton; and of Divine Shepherd, Erdenheim, Pennsylvania: Sisters Joan Dolores Boyle, Margaret Burns, Constance Gardner, Marjorie Mayle, and Margie Thompson. Their interest, affirmation, and flexibility inspired confidence and good cheer at every stage of the process.

Finally, I am profoundly thankful to my father, Albert R. Schaab, who died during the final months I spent writing this book, and to my mother, Gloria H. Schaab. Their abiding love and support through all the seasons of my life and their personal example of dedication, tenacity, and creativity uniquely prepared me to engage this endeavor. Little did I know when I began this inquiry into the mystery of God and suffering that it would end in the midst of so much suffering in the lives of our family. Nonetheless, in the unfolding of its understandings, Mom, Dad, and I have found both challenge and consolation.

Ad majorem Dei gloriam!

Contents

Abbreviations

The Creative Suffering
of the Triune God

Introduction

In every era, the ubiquity of pain, suffering, and death, endemic within the cosmos and endured by its creatures, has provoked poignant and perplexing questions. This is especially the case for those who attempt to fathom and to reconcile such experiences with belief in an all-loving and all-powerful God. How shall one speak rightly of God in the midst of a suffering cosmos? Invoking the vagaries of cosmic existence, the consequences of human freedom, or the ineffable omniscience of God, many theologians throughout the centuries have developed responses to these questions in terms of sophisticated theodicies that attempt to shore up the delicate balance between the experience of cosmic tragedy and belief in an all-good and almighty God. While such theodicies are theoretically successful in preserving the attributes of divine omnipotence and benevolence, they frequently do so at the cost of commending the concept of an immutable and impassible God untouched by cosmic tragedy and unaffected by cosmic angst. Other theologians, however, perceive the persistent suffering that has reached global proportions and cosmic potential in the twentieth and twenty-first centuries and ask how God the Creator can comprehend the pain, sufferings, and death of creation and yet remain unmoved. Among theologians who profess the Christian tradition, many have answered this question by affirming that the God of Jesus the Christ does not remain unmoved. Rather, the God who is Love, who is *hesed*, is a suffering God, not only familiar with suffering but also burdened by cosmic grief.

Christian understandings of the concept of the suffering of God stem from the theological heritage that Christianity shares with its ancestral tradition, Judaism. As proclaimed in the revelation of the Hebrew Scriptures, the intense pathos of the God of the Jews is largely unquestioned. While particular passages communicate a sense of the immutability of God, the overwhelming propensity of biblical revelation is to proclaim a God who is a living, dynamic agent in intimate relationship with a covenant community. Biblical anthropomorphisms and anthropopathisms for the Divine are central to the message of God's interaction with the chosen people. The Torah includes incidences not only of God's passibility but also of God's mutability in passages that refer to a change of attitude or intention on the part of the Divine. Furthermore, the prophetic books of the Hebrew Scriptures chronicle an amazing range of divine pathos revealing the essentially personal nature of the God of Israel through bold and nonspeculative language. For Christians, this pathos of God became incarnate in the person and ministry of Jesus of Nazareth. Rooted in and enlivened by his intimate and loving relationship with the God whom he called Abba, Jesus' person, life, and ministry radiated radical love and unconditional compassion toward those plagued by the suffering and angst of the human condition, a suffering and angst that he himself endured.

When the early Christian community came into contact with the influence of Greek philosophy, the notion of God changed decisively, particularly concerning divine mutability and passibility. The Stoic quality of imperviousness, the Platonic notion of perfection, and the Aristotelian concept of the Unmoved Mover fashioned a deity incapable of pain with a primary quality of permanence. Hence, rather than aroused by covenant and compassion, God's nature was characterized by *autarkeia* (self-sufficiency) and *apatheia* (immunity to outside forces), because, for the Greeks, rationality rather than relatedness was the measure of perfection. Gradually, the dynamic and impassioned God of Israel and of Jesus the Christ became the ultimate term of an arduous Greek philosophical analysis, which produced a modification of the Christian theology of God.

In the last decade of the nineteenth century, increasing criticism of the doctrines of divine immutability and impassibility arose, particularly in England and Germany. Among the most prominent factors contributing to this critique were developments in biblical theology, in praxical and political theology, in contemporary metaphysics, and in an ecological and evolutionary view of science. These factors restored the notion of God as an active participant in history, as immanent in the evolutionary struggle, and as suffering in, with, and under the affliction ubiquitous in the cosmos and its creatures. Moved by such insights, as well as by the escalating violence demonstrated by twentieth-century events such as the Holocaust and the atomic bombing of Hiroshima and Nagasaki, some contemporary theologians such as Jürgen Moltmann have appropriated the passion narratives of the Christian Scriptures to affirm a "crucified God." Others like Jon Sobrino have emphasized praxis toward the liberation of the oppressed of Latin America to proclaim a God who suffers with the victims of history. Daniel Day Williams and others have embraced the metaphysics of process philosophy to speak of the effect of cosmic events on the consequent nature of God, and others like Sallie McFague have construed the God-world relationship in terms of the world as the body of God to image divine participation in the travail of the cosmos.

Although each of these approaches has viability and fecundity within its particular hermeneutical perspective, each also has limitations that restrict its applicability within the lives of contemporary Christians shaped not only by Scripture and tradition, world events, and culture but also by a scientific worldview. In my own attempt to advance a theology of the suffering of God, therefore, I sought a theological approach that would include salient elements of these alternative perspectives, address their limitations, and be judged credible by Christians informed by the understandings of evolutionary cosmology and biology. I required an approach that is Christian, praxical, relational, cosmocentric, and contemporary in its worldview. I found such an approach in the evolutionary theology of scientist-theologian Arthur R. Peacocke.

Arthur Robert Peacocke, Anglican Canon, Doctor of Science and Doctor of Divinity, received a doctorate in physical biochemistry as a scholar at Exeter College at Oxford in 1948. For the next eleven years, he taught at the University of Birmingham and was part of a research team associated with the University of California at Berkeley that identified the helical properties of the newly discovered DNA molecule. He returned to Oxford as a fellow and tutor from 1959 to 1973, having pursued the study of theology at Birmingham. He received his Diploma in Theology and Bachelor of Divinity degree from Birmingham in 1971 and was ordained a priest of the Church of England that same year. This merging of Peacocke's interest in science and theology resulted in the publication of his first interdisciplinary book on study of science and theology, *Science and the Christian Experiment.* In 1972, Peacocke promoted this interdisciplinary integration that has characterized the latter years of his scholarly activity by founding the Science and Religion Forum of the United Kingdom, which later expanded to the whole of Europe.

From 1973 through 1984, Peacocke served as Dean of Clare College, Cambridge, and then returned to St. Peter's College at Oxford, where he earned a Doctor of Divinity degree in 1982. He taught both biochemistry and theology and possessed the distinction of being the only theology faculty member of

Oxford University to hold both a Doctor of Divinity degree and a Doctor of Science degree during his tenure. In this period, Peacocke became the founding director of the Ian Ramsey Centre at St. Cross College, Oxford, for the Interdisciplinary Study of Religious Beliefs in Relation to the Sciences and Medicine in 1985, a position that he held until 1988. In addition, he became an Academic Fellow at the Institute on Religion in an Age of Science in 1986. As a result of his convening an international group of those interested in the interaction between science and theology in 1984, he was a primary catalyst behind the founding of the European Society for the Study of Science and Theology. Peacocke served as Honorary Chaplain of Christ Church Cathedral, Oxford, from 1989 through 1996, a post that enabled him to more fully engage his interdisciplinary research, and he resumed directorship of the Ian Ramsey Centre in 1995 and held that post until 1999.

In more than thirty years of interdisciplinary work in science and theology, Arthur Peacocke produced more than eighty essays for scholarly journals and edited volumes. His ten books include the aforementioned *Science and the Christian Experiment*; *Creation and the World of Science*; *Intimations of Reality: Critical Realism in Science and Religion*; *Theology for a Scientific Age*; *God and the New Biology*; and *Paths from Science Towards God: The End of All Our Exploring*. He edited and coedited a number of books on select topics integrating science, theology, and philosophy, including *The Sciences and Theology in the Twentieth Century*; *Evolution and Creation: A European Perspective*; *Chaos and Complexity: Scientific Perspectives on Divine Action*; and his most recent effort, *In Whom We Live and Move and Have Our Being: Panentheistic Reflections on God's Presence in a Scientific World*. As a result of his work in science and theology and with the philosophical questions that attend such inquiry, Peacocke won acclaim for his scholarship through the prestigious 1973 Pierre Lecomte du Noüy American Foundation Award, an international tribute for *Science and the Christian Experiment* as the best book toward reconciling science and religion; the 1995 Templeton Foundation Prize for *Theology for a Scientific Age* as the outstanding book on theology and natural science; and the 2001 Templeton Prize for Progress in Religion. He presented the 1978 Bampton Lectures at Oxford University; the 1984 Mendenhall Lectures at DePauw University in Indiana; the 1993 Gifford Lectures at the University of Edinburgh; and the 2001 Christian Culture Lecture Series at Saint Francis Xavier University in Nova Scotia. Made a member of the Order of the British Empire in 1993 by Queen Elizabeth II, Arthur Peacocke served as Warden Emeritus of the Society of Ordained Scientists, an ecumenical religious order that he founded in 1985; Honorary Canon of Christ Church Cathedral in Oxford; and an international lecturer and scholar.

In addition to the many publications that he himself wrote, Arthur Peacocke and his scholarship have also been the subjects of others' scholarly work, including the book *Scientists as Theologians: A Comparison of the Writings of Ian Barbour, Arthur Peacocke and John Polkinghorne,* nearly two dozen essays, five dozen book reviews, and six doctoral dissertations. Although these numerous studies have investigated and evaluated Peacocke's scientific theories and epistemological perspectives, no analysis of the understanding of the suffering of God exists that grounds itself specifically in Peacocke's evolutionary theology. Furthermore, although Peacocke is arguably a leader in the field of science and theology, no one has yet written at length about his theological work. Therefore, this book clearly addresses a lacuna in the critical scholarship on the work of Arthur Peacocke and witnesses to the potential of his theological insights for right speech about God in an evolutionary cosmos. Moreover, with the death of Arthur Peacocke on October 21, 2006, I offer this work in testament to the enduring vitality and efficacy of his contributions to the theology-science dialogue and in gratitude for the gift of his encouragement, indulgence, and good humor throughout my research. I sadly regret that he did not live to see its publication. May he grant each of us a double portion of his spirit that we may not cease from our exploring until we arrive at Where we started and know the Place for the first time.

My primary objective in this work is to plumb the critical question of speech about God in the midst of a suffering cosmos. I begin my inquiry into the mystery of the suffering of God by examining the state of the question of divine passibility in contemporary theology. After reviewing some of the contemporary critiques of a theology of the suffering of God, I recount and analyze several representative proposals toward a theology of the suffering of God that are distinct in their hermeneutical approaches: the biblical theology of Jürgen Moltmann, the liberation theology of Jon Sobrino, the process theology of Daniel Day Williams, and the feminist-ecological theology of Sallie McFague. Despite the viability of each of these proposals within their specific hermeneutical perspectives, there are limitations in each of these proposals for the theology of the suffering of God. I sought an approach that can speak to individuals on a broader basis than that of biblical revelation, to be truly cosmocentric rather than anthropocentric, to have consistency with the Christian doctrine of the triune nature of God, and to preserve essential distinctions between the Creator and the creation. It is this very approach that I found encapsulated in the evolutionary theology of Arthur Peacocke.

In probing Peacocke's evolutionary theology toward an affirmation of the suffering of God, I follow four principles on which Peacocke founds his theological proposals. Through these principles, Peacocke expresses his conviction that God is Creator of the cosmos as creation; that the entities, processes, and structures of creation are revelatory of the nature, attributes, and purposes of God as Creator; that the nature and attributes of its Creator are inferable from the nature and attributes of the creation; and that these inferences must be articulated in terms of tentative, yet viable metaphors and models that express the cosmic revelation of the mystery of God. Guided by these principles, I explore the epic of an evolving universe in order to understand the entities, structures, and processes that disclose the nature, attributes, and purposes of its Creator. This exploration investigates insights regarding the origin of the cosmos in a transcendent Ground of Being. It engages scientific theories that challenge classical conceptions of the God-world relationship and focuses on Darwinian and neo-Darwinian theories of cosmic being and becoming that suggest an ongoing creativity immanent in the cosmos itself. Through a consideration of this immanent creativity, my exploration probes the interaction of law and chance that suggests freedom and autonomy inherent in the evolving cosmos and that raises questions concerning the operation of divine omnipotence and omniscience in relation to cosmic events. Arriving at the conclusion that such cosmic freedom and autonomy implies an intrinsic measure of risk, pain, suffering, and even death for its creatures and its Creator, this exploration finds itself in an inexorable movement toward the inference of the suffering of God in, with, and under the suffering of the cosmos.

But how does one authentically express insights concerning the ineffable mystery of God and suffering? Neither science nor theology can speak uncritically as if a one-to-one correspondence existed between the meaning of their words and the realities to which they refer. However, neither can they speak instrumentally as if their words were simply useful fictions bearing no intrinsic connection to their referent. Rather, each discipline must speak in terms of a critical or skeptical realism, employing certain concepts, analogies, metaphors, or models to signify something akin to the entity to which its words refer. This approach to scientific and theological language is consistent with Peacocke's fourth principle and leads to the methodology of inference-to-the-best-explanation. This methodology aims not at certainty but at intelligibility, not at finality but at fecundity, not at immutability but at emergence with regard to its metaphors and models.

Having thus pursued Peacocke's principles through their practical expressions in terms of science, epistemology, and methodology, I reach the heart of my theological investigation. I examine the impact of Peacocke's evolutionary cosmology, biology, epistemology, and methodology on Christian theology and demonstrate how these insights come to fruition in an understanding of a Triune God. Not surprisingly, there is a particular model concerning the God-world relationship that emerges from the interaction of these insights. The model is pan*en*theism, which, in broad terms, denotes that the Being of God includes and penetrates the whole universe—a universe pervaded by pain, suffering, and death—but is not exhausted by the universe itself. Within this panentheistic paradigm, the Triune God is the transcendent Ground of Being who is immanently creative under the groaning of the cosmos, and who becomes incarnate in the cruciformity of the cosmos with its ubiquitous suffering.

While many elements of evolutionary science contribute to this affirmation of divine suffering in, with, and under the cosmos, certain key concepts provide primary grounding. Hence, I explore six elements that factor significantly into a proposal of divine passibility: the costly process of evolution, the reality of cosmic indeterminacy, God-world interaction through whole-part influence, the notion of the anthropic universe, the transcendent and immanent creativity of God, and the panentheistic paradigm of God-world relationship. I then analyze each one specifically in terms of its impact on a theology of the creative suffering of the Triune God.

It is obvious to the reader at this point that this work addresses more than the question of right speech about God in the midst of a suffering cosmos. In view of its approach through evolutionary theory, it also speaks strongly to a variety of issues and themes associated with the contemporary encounter between theology and science. At a fundamental level, this book demonstrates that evolutionary science and Christian theology need not be in conflict and that a mutually illuminative and integrative relationship between the two is not only possible but also authentic and valuable. Hence, it belies the clash that particular Christian hermeneutical traditions claim exists between divine and evolutionary creativity. Furthermore, it reveals a variety of novel, persuasive, and viable interpretations of the Christian tradition based on the data of contemporary human experience and scientific discovery. One such interpretation is the understanding of divine creativity as originally and continuously operative in, with, and under the processes of an evolving cosmos. A second is the insight that such divine creativity is the working of the transcendent, immanent, and incarnate presence and action of God in the cosmos. Third, coupling this insight with a panentheistic notion of God-in-relation to the cosmos inspires a compelling interpretation of God as Trinity that authentically reconstructs the classical understanding of the Triune God in terms consistent with evolutionary creativity, emergence, and transformation. This conception of the Trinity in panentheistic relation to the cosmos provides a critical and efficacious response to the question of the mystery of God and suffering in the cosmos and its creatures. For a God who exists in enduring transcendent, immanent, and incarnate relation to the world inevitably bears its sufferings and yet effects its liberation.

Finally, this work contributes to the renaissance of a practical theology of Trinity by delineating some positive implications of its evolutionary theology of the suffering God for feminist, ecological, and pastoral concerns. It proposes a female panentheistic-procreative paradigm of the creative suffering of the Triune God through female images of God drawn from biblical and rabbinical traditions. In keeping with such a paradigm, it advances a model of midwifery as an approach toward ecological ethics. Finally, in view of the ubiquity and diversity of suffering in the cosmos and its creatures, it sets forth a pastoral model of threefold differentiation of suffering in God.

Though pregnant with the possibility for new and abundant life, these proposals are as so many developing embryos that require tending, nurturing, and guidance in order to develop to full flourishing. Hence, I bear the hope and the intention that my proposals and the entire work of this study will midwife new offspring of theological discourse and praxis. Moreover, I deeply desire that this book offers some measure of insight, encouragement, and compassion to those burdened by the suffering of this world. May each intimately experience the presence and action of the Triune God whose creative suffering moves always toward transformation, liberation, salvation, and fullness of life.

I

God in a Suffering Cosmos

Auschwitz. Hiroshima. Nagasaki. Rwanda. Vietnam. El Salvador. The Sudan. September 11. Iraq. Tsunami. Katrina. Such a litany provokes images of staggering atrocities, unmitigated violence, incalculable destruction, and inexpressible terror. Weapons of mass destruction—sophisticated, sinister, and covert—threaten the international community. The horrors of nationalistic genocide and terroristic suicide; the ravages of poverty, starvation, and AIDS; the prevalence of global, urban, and domestic violence; and the insidiousness of racism, sexism, and classism decimate human bodies and stun human sensibilities. Natural disasters, as well as pervasive and escalating exploitation and abuse, devastate and despoil the earth's ecosphere and atmosphere. Such is the strident litany of barbarous and senseless suffering echoed in diverse modes through the ages and amplified to global consciousness, scope, and impact in the twentieth and twenty-first centuries. Such is the plaintive litany that rises as a lament to God, straining to pierce the shadowy mystery of divine presence, responsibility, and responsiveness in the midst of a suffering world.

Clearly, the reality of suffering that attends existential and inflicted pain and death has demanded a reasonable and authentic theological response in every era and has persistently impelled theological debate concerning the relationship of God to suffering and the conceivability of the suffering of God. However, the global consciousness, scope, and impact of suffering, pain, and death in the twentieth and twenty-first centuries have often driven this debate to an acute pitch. Atrocities committed through multinational and multicultural conflicts and terrorism, aberrant human relations, and environmental devastation relentlessly provoke the question, "How can God rule over a world of such suffering and be yet unmoved?"[1] While in a former age, some may have looked to an omnipotent and impassible deus ex machina to provide a solution to worldly distress, the contemporary worldview directs theologians to reflections on a powerless and suffering God, a God who "allows himself to be edged out of the world and on to the cross . . . weak and powerless in the world, and that is exactly the way, the only way, in which he can be with us and help us . . . only a suffering God can help."[2]

The Rise of the "Orthodoxy" of the Suffering God

In his exploration of "The Suffering God: The Rise of a New Orthodoxy," Ronald Goetz proposes a rationale for the development of this "orthodoxy" of divine suffering in the twentieth century.[3] Citing scholars as diverse as Karl Barth, Hans Küng, Reinhold Niebuhr, Wolfhart Pannenberg, Rosemary Radford Ruether, James Cone, Pierre Teilhard de Chardin, Jürgen Moltmann, and Daniel Day Williams, Goetz contends that the development of this "open secret" of a suffering God potentially has an impact on every classical Christian doctrine that considered divine impassibility axiomatic. Expressing his uncertainty concerning the effect that this shift might ultimately have on systematic theology, Goetz discusses four historical factors that he believes have contributed to the rise of the concept of a suffering God: the decline of Christendom, the rise of democratic aspirations, the problem of suffering and evil, and the scholarly reappraisal of the Bible.

Associated with the phenomenon of Christian atheism, the factor of the *decline of Christendom*, according to Goetz, stems from the consciousness of many Christians that "the mighty acts of God" seem conspicuously absent in the contemporary world. While most Christians continue to assert the reality of God, the accomplishment of God's will and purpose for human history seems sporadic and occasional, revealing an eschatological potential at best. The *rise of democratic aspirations* contests the relevance of an immutable and impassible God to human freedom and agency in the world. Moreover, the *problem of pain, death, and evil*, related to Darwin's theory of evolution and exacerbated by the brutalities of two world wars, urges the question of God's complicity in and response to existential and deliberate events of pain and death, which appear to be a fundamental part of the unfolding universe. Moreover, the historical consciousness manifested in these factors effected a *scholarly reappraisal of the*

Bible, which clearly revealed in its turn that the God of Israel and of Jesus the Christ was by no means an unaffected deity, but one full of immense passion and anguish.

While acknowledging the other factors Goetz develops, I intend to focus on the rise of the notion of divine suffering in relation to the problem of cosmic suffering. Profoundly affected by the immensity and inexorability of such suffering, many twentieth-century theologians advanced a broad spectrum of proposals addressing the mystery of God's relation to the "barbarous excess" of "unmerited and senseless suffering" witnessed in this last century.[4] This problem of suffering and evil moves some theologians to theodicy, to the defense of an omnipotent, immutable, and all-loving God whose nature, attributes, and purposes must somehow be justified or justify the presence and purpose of suffering in response to pain, death, and evil in the cosmos. It causes other scholars to ascribe the presence of evil to other factors, such as human freedom or finitude.[5] However, the presence of such suffering and evil persuades many others to rethink the classical attributions that have been applied to God in relation to the world. Thus, as John Haught observes in *God after Darwin*, "The cruciform visage of nature . . . invites us to depart, perhaps more than ever before, from all notions of a deity untouched by the world's suffering."[6] Moved not to theodicy but to departure from "all notions of a deity untouched," I contend that the attribution of immutability, impassibility, and unmitigated omnipotence to God is no longer theoretically defensible, theologically viable, or pastorally efficacious in view of the insidious and multifaceted presence of pain, death, and suffering in the human and nonhuman cosmos. Rather, the poignant travail of the cosmos in toto and of sentient beings in particular demands an authentic and adequate theological response, a response that cannot be conceptualized in an unchanging, unfeeling, and unrelated Deity. In the chapters that follow, therefore, I intend to demonstrate that the most viable response to the ubiquity of pain, suffering, and death in the cosmos is the postulate of God's own intimate participation in and suffering from the effects of evil in the cosmos and to advance a theological affirmation of the Christian Creator God as so intimately related to creation as to participate in the very sufferings of cosmic being itself. This position, however, is not without its critics. Although theological proposals toward the suffering of God often seem to present compelling arguments for the renunciation of the impassible, omnipotent God of classical theism, other contemporary interpretations caution against too ready an attribution of suffering to God or too uncritical an affirmation of suffering in God. In the main, these cautions rise from a diverse chorus of voices representing feminist liberation theologies, with an incessant basso profundo from the classical Catholic tradition.

Critiques of the Concept of the Suffering of God

While by no means harmonized in their conclusions, a chorus of feminist theological voices concurs that, as interpreted within the patriarchal tradition of Christianity, the image of the crucified Christ, the suffering servant of God, tends to glorify violence and abuse and to commend freely chosen suffering as an example to be emulated. Moreover, classical Christologies of sin, atonement, and redemption communicate the message that suffering is salvific in itself and that self-sacrifice effects the salvation of the world. A forerunner in the feminist critique of such interpretations is theologian Mary Daly, who indicts the image of the crucified Christ as a "scapegoat image" who bears the guilt and the blame for the failures of the dominant societal group.[7] Building on Daly's foundation some twenty years later, Rebecca Parker and Joanne Carlson Brown mount a critique of the notion that Jesus suffered in accord with God's will. They indict such a notion as an example of "divine child abuse" perpetrated by a "divine sadist," in which death is lauded as salvific and the suffering child represents the hope of the world.[8]

Rather than taking their critical approach through Christology, many Catholic theologians have charted a course through the classical theological tradition concerning the divine nature and attributes. Such theologians maintain that the attribution of suffering to God only exacerbates the problem of evil. It entangles God in time, inhibits divine freedom, and subjects the Creator to the created order. In turn, this attribution leads to an eternalization and universalization of suffering that may militate against resistance to injustice. Furthermore, these theologians note, the affirmation of divine suffering radically contests notions of divine immutability and impassibility and of omniscience and omnipotence, which relate logically within the classical system. Hence, the assertion of suffering in God looms as a potential liability to every classical Christian doctrine that considers these philosophical and theological predicates axiomatic.

Notable among the Catholic voices raised in this critique is that of theologian Edward Schillebeeckx, who flatly maintains, "We cannot look for the *ground* of suffering in God."[9] For Schillebeeckx, God as "Being Itself" must be conceived as "pure positivity," the "benevolent, solicitous 'one who is against evil,' who will not admit the supremacy of evil and refuses to allow it the last word."[10] Maintaining that the Christian message does not attempt to justify evil or the history of suffering, Schillebeeckx rejects both the "sadistic mysticism of suffering" that claims that God required the death of Jesus and the "false trail" trod by Jürgen Moltmann and others who eternalize suffering in God through interpreting the cross as an event within God's own self.[11]

Johann Baptist Metz is also critical of those theologians who see suffering as an event within Godself in order to epitomize God's intimate involvement with the world or to divert the charge of apathy from the Divine. According to Metz, such a theological position is *"too much* of a response . . . too much of a speculative, almost Gnostic reconciliation with God behind the back of the human history of suffering."[12] In a series of questions that clearly outlines the major theological and philosophical objections to the notion of suffering in God, Metz relentlessly challenges this theological move:

> How is the discourse about a suffering God in the end anything more than a sublime duplication of human suffering and human power-lessness? How does the discourse about suffering in God or about suffering between God and God not lead to an eternalization of suffering? Do not God and humanity end up subsumed under a quasi-mystical universalization of suffering that finally cuts off the counterimpulse resisting injustice?[13]

The Position of This Work

Mindful of these critiques, this present work nevertheless contends that "for any concept of God to be morally acceptable and coherent . . . we cannot but tentatively propose that God suffers in, with, and under the creative processes of the world with their costly unfolding in time."[14] In support of this position, I begin with an exploration and analysis of several contemporary Christian theologies that affirm the notion of suffering in God through a variety of theoretical approaches. These affirmations include the biblical theology of Jürgen Moltmann, the liberation theology of Jon Sobrino, the process theology of Daniel Day Williams, and the ecological theology of Sallie McFague. In response to this exploration and analysis, I propose that the most defensible, viable, and efficacious proposal toward the suffering of God lies not in biblical, liberation, process, or ecological approaches, but in an evolutionary approach to the suffering of God, an approach presented through the lens of scientist-theologian Arthur Peacocke. Using his approach of Christian evolutionary theology, I propose with Peacocke, "if God is immanently present in and to natural processes, in particular those that generate conscious and self-conscious life, then we cannot but infer that God suffers in, with, and under the creative processes of the world with their costly unfolding in time."[15]

Approaching the Concept of the Suffering God

Jürgen Moltmann: The Crucified God

Profoundly moved by the experience of the Shoah and by the God of Jesus Christ revealed in Mark 15:34, German theologian Jürgen Moltmann grounds his assertion of the suffering of God in the Hebrew and Christian biblical traditions. Drawing on the prophetic tradition of Israel, the kenosis of Christ (Philippians 2:5–11), and the Pauline affirmation that "God was in Christ" (2 Corinthians 5:19), Moltmann's theology in the shadow of Auschwitz is most forcefully articulated in *The Crucified God*. Incontestably political and decisively Christian in his attestation of the cross of Christ as a fully Trinitarian event, Moltmann centers his reflections on God's revelation in the scriptures and in economy of salvation, rather than on the propositions of classical theism or the protests of modern atheism. He sets aside classical theism's "*apatheia* axiom" of a God who is physically unchangeable, psychologically insensitive, and ethically unaccountable as inconsistent with the biblical vision of the God of pathos as revealed by the prophets. Moltmann contends, "At the heart of the prophetic proclamation there stands the certainty that God is interested in the world to the point of suffering." Thus, for Moltmann, rather than being capricious or irrational, divine pathos "describes the way in which God is affected by events and human actions and suffering in history."[16] The prophets did not identify the pathos of God with God's being, but with God's free relationship to creation, to people, and to history that was framed in the notion of covenant. In this covenant relationship proclaimed by the prophets, God is passionately interested and invested in the history of God's people, both active on their behalf in absolute freedom and capable of suffering under humanity's disobedience. Beyond his critique of classical theism, Moltmann also criticizes its "brother," modern atheism, for rejecting a God who is no more than a mirrored image of "an unjust and absurd world of triumphant evil and suffering" and then proceeding to divinize humanity in God's stead.[17] According to Moltmann, the way beyond both theistic and atheistic responses to suffering is through a theology of the cross "which understands God as the suffering God in the suffering of Christ. . . . For this theology, God and suffering are no longer contradictions . . . but God's being is in suffering and the suffering is in God's being itself."[18]

Moltmann's point of departure for his theology is the cry of dereliction of the Markan Jesus from the cross to the God who has forsaken him (15:34). This cry of Jesus was his anguished plea for God to demonstrate divine righteousness and sovereignty, a plea that, by all accounts, received no answer. With no divine intervention forthcoming, the torment of Jesus increased, exacerbated by the intimate relation of mutual love that he had enjoyed with God, the love of a Son and his Father. At this critical moment, the Godforsakenness of the Son is visited on the Father, who stands indicted for the death of his beloved one. Consequently, "The Son suffers dying, the Father suffers the death of the Son."[19] The loving self-deliverance of the Son unto death is met by the grief-stricken and suffering love of the Father who has delivered his Son unto death. Moreover, while Moltmann understands what happened on the cross as an event within God's own self, because of the Trinitarian distinction of Persons, the Father's suffering is not the same as that of the Son.[20] "In the passion of the Son, the Father himself suffers the pains of abandonment. In the death of the Son, death comes upon God himself, and the Father suffers the death of his Son in his love for forsaken man."[21] According to Moltmann, therefore, the capacity of both Father and Son to suffer is eminently associated with the capacity of God to love. "God is unconditional love, because he takes on himself grief at the contradiction in man.... God suffers, God allows himself to be crucified and is crucified, and in this consummates his unconditional love that is so full of hope."[22]

This hope, nonetheless, is eschatological. Suffering in the present is assuaged solely by the recognition that God suffers with and in humanity. In Moltmann's Trinitarian schema, while the Father and the Son bear the suffering of humanity in their solidarity with the crucified of history, it is the Spirit who provides eschatological hope for the future transformation of human suffering into joy. The Spirit who proceeds from the loving communion of the Father and the Son "serves the history of God's joy... and his completed felicity at the end."[23] The Spirit creates love for forsaken humanity and, in the manner of the resurrection of the Crucified One, brings the dead to life. Because this event takes place in human history through the cross of the Risen Christ, it is part of the history of humanity and of God, into which human struggle, death, and evil are subsumed. Nevertheless, in the power of the Spirit, these human afflictions will be eschatologically transformed through the liberation of the unloved, the unrighteous, and even the dead from the midst of unrelieved and unrelenting suffering.[24]

In another work, *The Trinity and the Kingdom*, Moltmann offers his critique, retrieval, and construction of a doctrine of divine pathos in contrast to the tradition of the *apatheia* of God.[25] In opposition to classical alternatives regarding God and suffering, Moltmann proposes a form of active suffering, the suffering of passionate love. Moltmann develops this doctrine by retrieving several rare theological formulations to ground his perspective, including the doctrine of the *Shekhinah* and the notion of the sacrifice of eternal love.

Moltmann commences his construction with the insights of Abraham Heschel on the theology of the divine pathos. The experience of divine pathos opens human persons to respond to their historical situation with a sympathy born of the spirit that comes from God. This, according to Moltmann, signals a self-differentiation in God—an inference that he expands in his exploration of the rabbinic and kabbalist doctrine of the *Shekhinah*. The term *Shekhinah* is derived from the Hebrew *shakan*, meaning "presence" or "act of dwelling." In the early rabbinic sources, the *Shekhinah* "connotes the personification and hypostatization of God's presence in the world," of God's immanence and immediacy in a specific place on the earth.[26] One such place in which the *Shekhinah* is consistently considered to dwell is among the suffering and the poor of Israel. Countless tracts from the rabbinic and kabbalist literature affirm that, as the immanent and intimate presence of divine love and compassion, *Shekhinah* shares the joys and the afflictions of both the community and the individual person of Israel.[27] The *Shekhinah* is experienced as an ever-constant presence when Israel is in trouble, to the extent that the Divine feels the pain of the human. "When a human being suffers, what does the *Shekhinah* say? 'My head is too heavy for me; my arm is too heavy for me.' And if God is so grieved over the blood of the wicked that is shed, how much moreso over the blood of the righteous?"[28]

More than an isolated theophany, the *Shekhinah* literally walks in the midst of the people Israel, ever mindful of their sufferings, watching over them with love. In *Shekhinah*, God is carried into captivity with God's people into foreign lands, sharing their misery and "wandering restlessly through the dust" of their wanderings. Consequently, *Shekhinah* not only weeps for the suffering of her people, crying out when someone undergoes punishment, but also suffers their persecutions with them, "like Israel's twin."[29] This is, according to Moltmann, "the most moving potentiality" of the tradition of the *Shekhinah*—that it allows humanity to comprehend Israel's history of suffering as the history of the tortured *Shekhinah* of God.[30] Moreover, this doctrine symbolizes three movements of God in the history of the world: God's "self-humiliation" or condescension in the hypostatized and personified form of the *Shekhinah*, God's presence in exile and estrangement from Godself, and the restoration of union between God and humanity through *tikkun*, the prayer and good works of the people of the covenant, leading to the glory of God that is manifest in this reunion.

Next appropriating the work of C. E. Rolt, Moltmann explores the notion of God's eternal sacrifice of love, symbolized by the passion and death of Christ and indicative of the nature of God as self-sacrificial, suffering love. In Rolt's schema, suffering is characterized as the endurance of that which is contrary to one's own nature, which, in the case of God, is evil. In Rolt's formulation, the source of evil is in God's refusal to create evil; thus, in its nonexistence as that which is shut out from God, evil is that potential threat to creation that God endures in suffering love and ultimately transforms into glory through God's suffering acceptance. Related to Rolt's conception is that of Miguel de Unamuno in his theology of the sorrow of God. Grounded once again in the crucified Christ and in Christ's experience of *congoja* or the tragic sense of human life, Unamuno postulates that because God interpenetrates all that is living in love, God participates in the world's pain and tragedy and suffers in its suffering. Because of this, God, too, is in need of deliverance—an insight that relates to the exile of the *Shekhinah*. Hence, in the mysticism of the *Shekhinah*, the sacrificial love of the cross, and the tragic sense of human life, Moltmann finds a revelation of God "interested in the world to the point of suffering,"[31] who nonetheless draws humanity toward eschatological hope with both divine promise of consolation and divine protest against suffering.

ANALYSIS

Taking his starting point from the event of the cross and from the horror of the Holocaust, Jürgen Moltmann depicts a God intimately and actively involved in the travail of the created order. Grounded in a panentheistic perspective of the God-world relationship, Moltmann's God is a deity of pathos and passion immersed in history and involved in the dynamics of the cosmos. Unlike most other Christian theologians who discuss the mystery of God and suffering in predominantly monist or Christological terms, Moltmann situates his proposals squarely within the Triune mystery of God through his radical assertion that the event of the cross is an event within Trinitarian life itself. This movement in Moltmann's thought enables him to discuss different aspects of suffering in God, namely, the distinctive suffering of the Father and the Son in the event of the cross. Furthermore, it enables him to propose how it is that God might both suffer with creation and yet move it toward new life and ultimate liberation through the action of the third divine hypostasis, the Holy Spirit. Moreover, in his resourceful retrieval of the kabbalist doctrine of the *Shekhinah* to discuss the active, suffering love of God in the creation, participation, and transformation of the universe, Moltmann not only symbolizes from a Jewish perspective the threefold movement of God in Christ expressed in the Letter to the Philippians but also suggests a female image of divinity with potential for creative theological reflection and discourse.

Despite the significance of Moltmann's theological understanding for addressing the question of God in suffering, however, Moltmann's conception of divine suffering has several negative implications for the Christian image of God and the God-world relationship. In his strict reading of the biblical witness to the crucifixion in Mark 15:34, Moltmann clearly stresses the Father's deliberate subjection and abandonment of the Son on the cross, an emphasis that raises concerns from a pastoral standpoint and that opens Moltmann's proposal to the critique of Parker and Brown that the cross was an event of divine child abuse in which the Father sacrificed the Son according to the divine will. Moreover, the assertion that both Father and Son entered into this death pact out of love for a broken world subjects it to the charges of scapegoating powerfully framed in the work of Mary Daly. Thus, although Moltmann undeniably provides a suffering world with the image of a God who knows its affliction and who understands its pain, Moltmann risks the conclusion that the very God who suffers is the God who willed it so. Moreover, from its biblical and existential foundations, Moltmann's proposal moves in an eschatological direction that seems to imply God's inability to effect any historical change in the plight of the suffering in which God shares. In awaiting liberation as a pneumatological and eschatological event, Moltmann's crucified God risks remaining a victim of history in need of the redemption accomplished at history's end.[32] Hence, although Moltmann's concept of the crucified God offers suffering humanity empathetic companionship in its present affliction, salvation eschatologically delayed seems to be salvation existentially denied, which supplies little experiential respite and minimal motivation for action toward justice.

Jon Sobrino: The God of Solidarity

In *Jesus the Liberator: A Historical-Theological Reading of Jesus of Nazareth*, Latin American liberation theologian Jon Sobrino, like Jürgen Moltmann, situates his discussion of the suffering of God theologically in the cross of Christ and biblically in the passion narrative of Mark.[33] Existentially, however, Sobrino locates his insights on divine suffering in the travail of the oppressed persons of Latin America. Although Sobrino declares that the cross of Christ is a scandal, he insists that it is necessary that Christians dwell on the scandal of the cross and warns against relativizing its humiliation with a rush to resurrection that avoids the ambiguities concerning God and evil raised by the event of the cross. For Sobrino, to dwell on the scandal of the cross is theologically necessary because it proclaims the God in whom one believes. Moreover, focus on the cross of Christ is also existentially necessary, according to Sobrino, "because history goes on producing crosses . . . and not even God changes things."[34]

In his theological reflection on Mark 15:34 and on the image of the Son of God's dying abandoned by his Father, Sobrino illuminates two elements of discontinuity raised by God's alleged absence to Jesus at his crucifixion. The first discontinuity concerns the absence of any perceptible relation between Jesus' death and the Kingdom of God. However, the second focuses more pertinently on a disturbing discontinuity in Jesus' relationship with his Father. Sobrino suggests that the relationship between Jesus and the God whom he called Father was, throughout Jesus' life, a balance of mystery and intimacy. The "infinite distance" of the incomprehensible God was, by all Gospel accounts, accompanied by the "absolute closeness" of the God whom Jesus called Abba. This intimacy, however, seems to vanish on the cross of the Markan Jesus, whose life apparently ends shrouded in the silence and inactivity of God his Father. In the words of Edward Schillebeeckx, whom Sobrino quotes,

> Jesus was indeed condemned because he remained true to his prophetic mission "from God," a mission which he refused to justify to any other authority than God himself. In all this Jesus continued to rely on the Father who had sent him. The Father, however, did not intervene. Nowhere, indeed, did Jesus see any visible aid come from him whose cause he had so much at heart. As a fact of history, it can hardly be denied that Jesus was subject to an inner conflict between his consciousness of his mission and the utter silence of the One he was accustomed to call his Father.[35]

According to Sobrino, this sense of abandonment undoubtedly deepens the mystery of Jesus' own relationship with God. However, it also weighs heavily on the faith of each Christian who risks contemplating this mystery of abandonment because it is a mystery that unavoidably "transforms and questions our ideas about God" and inevitably raises the issue of who God is and what God does about suffering.[36]

Engaging the enigma of God in suffering, Sobrino indicates that, in the scriptures, individuals come to know God through God's words and deeds in history. Therefore, if it is the case that, on the cross of Jesus, God neither speaks to console nor acts to intervene, then one wonders how the absence of such divine word and deed may be a revelation of God. Such wonder has drawn a variety of theological responses; nevertheless, for his own part, Sobrino affirms the assertion of Jürgen Moltmann and contends, "There is no substitute for calling this God 'the crucified God.'"[37] If both biblical witness and experiential evidence indicate that, in the suffering and death of God's only Son and in the face of existential suffering, God by and large does not intervene, then Sobrino himself concludes that God participates in suffering, bears suffering, and thus reveals that suffering must be borne.

At this juncture in his argument, Sobrino cautions that any proposal concerning the way in which suffering affects God can be only reflective and speculative, arising from a particular theologian's own faith and "ultimate premises" concerning suffering and God. Returning to one of his own basic premises, Sobrino reiterates the Thomistic principle that one can speak of God only on the basis of something accessible to experience, linked to God as a matter of faith. On this point, Sobrino suggests that positive speech concerning God derived from human experience becomes accepted without much difficulty because it imposes no threat of limitation on the nature of God as understood by Greek philosophy.[38] However, Sobrino maintains, the event of the Incarnation introduced a radical novelty into the Christian conception of the nature of God. Within this radically novel perspective, Sobrino contends, "Jesus is neither only what 'God has become,' nor only 'the firstborn' who points to God's future, but also the one who suffered on the cross and suffered specifically abandonment by God."[39] This reality impels one to question the nature of God revealed on the cross and to consider suffering as a possible mode of God's being.

Like Moltmann, Sobrino notes that the writings of Paul intimate that God was present on the cross of Christ (2 Corinthians 5:19). Because this presence cannot be separated from the cross itself, the nature of the cross mediates the nature of God.

> It is a feature of the historical structure of revelation that the nature of the place in which God manifests himself is a mediation of God's own nature.... It is therefore likely that God's presence on the cross, insofar as it is a cross, reveals something of God.[40]

On the basis of this mediation, Sobrino concludes, "God suffered on Jesus' cross and on those of this world's victims by being their non-active and silent witness." Rather than implying negativity, cruelty, or impotence in God by such an assertion, Sobrino claims that this proposal must be seen "as a consequence of God's original choice, incarnation, a radical drawing near for love and in love, wherever it leads, without escaping from history or manipulating it from the outside."[41] This God, incarnate and crucified, reveals Godself as the "God of solidarity," the God who in a world of victims was prepared to become a victim in suffering love.

> On the positive side the cross presents a basic affirmation about God. It says that on the cross God himself is crucified.... This ultimate solidarity with humanity reveals God as a God of love in a real and credible way rather than in an idealistic way.[42]

Thus, from his stance in the midst of the suffering and oppressed of Latin America, Sobrino concludes, "If from the beginning of the gospel God appears in Jesus as a God *with* us, if throughout the gospel God shows himself as a God *for* us, on the cross he appears as a God *at our mercy* and, above all, as a God *like* us." Although theologians argue whether this symbol of a crucified God functions to sublimate and justify suffering or serves to mount the strongest possible protest and impetus against suffering, Sobrino maintains that the matter is not one of theory but one of praxis. According to Sobrino, the symbol of the suffering, crucified God

> makes clear in a history of suffering . . . that between the alternatives
> of accepting suffering by sublimating it and eliminating it from the
> outside we can and must introduce a new course, bearing it. However,
> we must also add that in bearing this suffering God says what side he
> is on, what struggles he is in solidarity with.[43]

Consequently, in a history of victimization, this image generates neither resignation nor despair, but hope and liberation. In the words of Leonardo Boff, "If God is silent in the face of suffering . . . it was not to make it eternal and leave us without hope, but because he wants to put an end to all the crosses of history."[44]

Accordingly, Sobrino contends that this theology of the suffering and crucified God necessitates a revised perspective on both revelation and divine transcendence. Anticipating the problems that arise in the attempt to synthesize and systematize the different elements of God's self-revelation in history, Sobrino suggests that the very inability to do so is the practical proof that one is in the presence of the mystery of God. Therefore, Sobrino proposes that the particular moment of God's revelation on the cross be situated beside other moments to yield "an open history of revelation that will reach its climax only at the end . . . without trying to find a finished synthesis of the reality of God in history."[45] As a consequence, this eschatological revisioning of revelation entails a redefinition of transcendence that adequately expresses the radical discontinuity between God and creation. Rather than being associated exclusively with the greatness of God in relation to creation, divine transcendence for Sobrino is also mediated, often scandalously, in the small, the suffering, and the negative in history. According to Sobrino, access to God on the cross occurs *sub specie contrarii*, as "power in impotence, speech in silence, life in death," and demands more than intellectual analysis and explanation.[46] The revelation of the crucified God demands that one take a stance of hope and action in relation to its reality, a movement toward the " 'more' that leaves hearts forever restless, questioned and questioning."[47]

Sobrino summarizes his proposals concerning the suffering of God by affirming, "Knowledge of God always has a material setting, and the place where the crucified God is known is on the crosses of the world." He references Dietrich Bonhoeffer's poem "Christians and Unbelievers" to illustrate his conviction that it is the victims of the world who make God known, for in them "the Godhead hides."[48] It is in the victim that Christians "find him poor and scorned, without shelter or bread, / Whelmed under weight of the wicked, the weak, the dead."[49]

Acknowledging the shadow of Auschwitz as the "material setting" in which Bonhoeffer writes, Sobrino reflects on the contemporary movement toward doing theology in the global climate "after Auschwitz." While granting the impact of the event of the Shoah on Christian theology, he contends that in Latin America at least, one does not do theology after Auschwitz. Instead, in Latin America, one continually does theology *during* Auschwitz and, in point of fact, "Inside Auschwitz," still "laden with reason, weeping and blood / immersed in the daily death of millions."[50]

ANALYSIS

Although affirmations of suffering in God generally tend to diverge along Catholic and Protestant lines, a significant exception to this generalization is Catholic liberation theologian Jon Sobrino, who acknowledges his debt to Protestant theologian Jürgen Moltmann and his discourse on the crucified God. Moltmann's influence is particularly evident in Sobrino's own reflections on the cry of derelictions from the cross based on Mark 15:34, as well as in his own interpretation and extension of the Pauline notion that "God was in Christ" (2 Corinthians 5:19), which figures prominently in Moltmann's reasoning. However, it is in his discussion of this Pauline affirmation that Sobrino demonstrates the influence of classical Thomistic philosophy and avoids the theological and pastoral pitfalls of Moltmann's reading as he interprets this biblical statement through the hermeneutic of the historical structure of revelation. Like fellow Jesuit theologian Karl Rahner, as well as Edward Schillebeeckx, Sobrino maintains that the historical structure of revelation is such that "God's revelation is sacramental in character, and not just deductive, when it becomes present in historical phenomena."[51] Thus, Sobrino deftly combines the biblical and philosophical perspectives to arrive at his affirmation of the notion of the God who suffers in solidarity with the victims of history—an affirmation rarely made in Catholic theological tradition.

Because of his eclectic theoretical approach, Sobrino's model of God has the means by which to propose a God disclosive in history and participative in suffering with the potency to save within time. Nevertheless, the experiential context of Latin America's history of oppression and suffering leads Sobrino to the problematic conclusion that divine solidarity with suffering offers not the option of eliminating suffering or sublimating suffering but only the option of bearing suffering. Although this conception demonstrates God's solidarity with history's victims, represents God's portion of the suffering necessary for history's liberation, and signals God's intention of ending history's crosses, it remains, by Sobrino's own admission, fragmentary and paradoxical, unfinished and lacking in synthesis within history. Thus as long as crosses still rise up in history, so long is the liberative act of God delayed. Because such an eschatological approach risks failing to inspire hope and commitment, Jon Sobrino issues an explicit challenge to Christians to commit themselves to justice and to solidarity with the victims of history. Sobrino points to the example of Jesus Christ and urges a Christian discipleship that bears the portion of necessary suffering that accompanies the quest for justice, a suffering borne by God's incarnate self in the historical struggle for liberation.

Daniel Day Williams: The Vulnerable God

North American process theology has long stressed God's involvement in history, an involvement that entails risk on the part of God and that acknowledges the capacity for suffering in God. In its own reconception of transcendence and immanence, process theology contends that God participates immanently in world events through God's consequent nature, yet transcends history in God's primordial nature. This notion of the dipolar nature of God provides for the conditioned, temporal, mutable becoming of God (consequent), while maintaining the eternal, absolute, and immutable being of God (primordial). The consequent nature of God responds receptively and actively to the concrete situations of the world, while God's primordial nature lures and persuades the world by means of possibilities that the world can accept, reject, or modify in the occasions of its becoming. According to North American Protestant theologian Daniel Day Williams, this process theological perspective "makes it possible for the Living God, the God who acts, the caring, saving God of the Bible, to be made intelligible."[52] Within this perspective, Williams and other process theologians like him have consistently argued for the passibility of God, grounded in God's immanent relationship with and participation in history. Although Williams takes care to connect his theological propositions with classical biblical sources in both the Hebrew and Christian Scriptures, his work is principally phenomenological. In *The Spirit and the Forms of Love*, Williams presents an analysis of human love to reason analogously to the suffering love of God.[53] While admitting that all human analogies ultimately fail in describing the love of God, Williams, nonetheless, calls for a "revolution in ontological thinking" on the presumption that there must be some elements in common between human and divine being, based on biblical and religious language, as well as on the "analogy of being."

Williams formulates several categories in interpersonal human love through which to reason to the love of God, including individuality, freedom, action, and suffering. In moving to assertions about God's love based on these categories of human love, Williams acknowledges the difficulty of carrying through the analogy of being in a way that does justice to the human structures of experience and that allows for the proper transmutation of these structures to the being of God. However, Williams contends that because God has constituted humanity in such a way that love can be real and that love between humanity and divinity can be actualized, this suggests that human categories have analogues in the being of God. This is not to say that God's being has exactly the same relations to time, space, and change as human being, in that "God's being is that on which all being depends." Nevertheless, Williams asserts, "God . . . can be involved in the changes in the world where there is coming into being and passing away."[54]

Because of the assertion that God loves, God's *individuality* is understood in relational terms, as one in communion with others. Relating to others in a "communality of being," God not only can love but also can be loved and can be addressed as an "other." Williams admits that it may be difficult to conceive of individuality in one who is characterized as "Being itself" and who is not simply one being among many. His response, however, is to suggest that "Being itself" is an inadequate expression for God. His preference is "Being which is the source of the community of being," which has Trinitarian inferences as well.[55]

In terms of *freedom*, Williams asserts, "God is the supreme instance of freedom to love." Although, in sublime freedom, God never refuses to love, God nonetheless risks the refusal of love in willing human freedom. This capacity of God to love, moreover, requires a rejection of God's impassibility. "To love is to be in a relationship where the action of the other alters one's own experience. Impassibility makes love meaningless." Hence, if God is subject to the *action* of another in a relationship of love, God consequently is subject to *suffering*. On this point, Williams reiterates the analogical nature of his analysis. Although suffering in the human being suggests and often includes destruction or threat to one's being, it cannot be regarded similarly in God. Suffering in God is "the acceptance in the divine of the tragic element in the creation, a patience and bearing with the loss and failure, and ever-renewed acceptance of the need for redemptive action."[56]

There are several conditions in Williams's assertion of suffering in God. Although suffering never threatens God's being, Williams suggests that it may jeopardize God's purposes in a particular situation. While a significant aspect of human suffering is the incapacity to know the full consequences of a situation, Williams asserts that God's being does include a knowledge of all conceivable outcomes of human free decision, though not in future specificity. Therefore, although God participates in human suffering, God does so without the limitations experienced by finite sufferers. In proposing this, Williams admits that he comes precipitously close to implying that God does not truly suffer. However, Williams insists that God's being is enacted in and through those who suffer and who are in turn occasions for God's own suffering.[57]

Having concluded that these categories suggest alternatives to the classical way of speaking about God and the communication of God's love, Williams, like the other Christian theologians previously discussed, extends these insights to the mystery of the suffering of God disclosed in the suffering of Jesus. Although traditional doctrine in classical theism contends that the Father did not suffer in the death of Jesus, Williams maintains that the inevitable consequence of such a position is to characterize the suffering and death of Jesus as a price exacted for God's forgiveness. This, however, cannot survive the analysis of love that Williams presented. If the Being of God is inseparable from the love of God, as both analogy and biblical testimony affirm, then the Being of God and the suffering of God are inseparable on the same basis. Jesus Christ reveals the love of God "which does not shirk from suffering." The essential nature and meaning of the suffering love of God remains a mystery, but Williams asserts that it is "consonant with his deity and with the integrity of the divine spirit." Although one must speak "with the greatest restraint" regarding God's suffering, it is crucial to do so in view of the biblical testimony and human experience that "God is Love." Hence, "if God does not suffer then his love is separated completely from the profoundest human experiences of love, and the suffering of Jesus is unintelligible as the communication of God's love to man." Ultimately, the affirmation that God suffers does not reduce God's stature to that of humanity but elevates human understanding of God to the level of faith that avows that God is truly revealed in Jesus Christ.[58]

ANALYSIS

Daniel Day Williams's phenomenological approach to the attributes of the God of love through the attributes of human beings who love relies heavily on the presuppositions of process philosophy and on the notion of the analogy of being. Although Williams supports his well-reasoned conclusions with biblical and religious references, his proposals concerning the capacity of God to suffer are principally extensions of his existential observation and analysis of a particular dynamic of finite relationality, namely, that the human love of free and finite creatures invariably involves suffering. If those who love in the human dimension cannot do so without the eventual experience of suffering, reasons Williams, then God, who is by nature infinite love, must necessarily suffer as well and to an infinite degree. Despite the ontological distance between the subjects of his observation and the Subject of his discourse, Williams's formulation nonetheless has the advantage of being intelligible and reasonable to the individual living in the contemporary world influenced by the social and empirical sciences. His formulation effectively communicates the image of a God who is vulnerably involved and operative in finite creation, yet who is invulnerably creative and transformative in infinite love. Moreover, his proposal has the capacity to foster the virtues of fidelity and forbearance with their potential to inspire and support ethical choices within interpersonal relationships.

The principal theoretical problem raised by the phenomenological approach in interaction with the notion of the analogy of being is expressed by Williams himself. In his caveat concerning the applicability of conclusions reached with finite beings to the infinite being of God, he, like many theologians who rely on a similar analogical approach, tends to advance his conclusions "in fear and trembling" with much dissembling about the limits of discourse and the incomprehensibility of the Divine. Citing the principles of scholars through the ages, Williams acknowledges that, while the Creator may be known through the creation, the effect is but a pale reflection of its cause and differs ontologically in both substance and nature. Thus, he cautions, anthropomorphic and anthropopathic language used of God is used inappropriately, as a strategy of last resort, in order to express the inexpressible and conceptualize the ineffable. Moreover, such discourse about God is of the nature of both conjecture and confession, a speculative interpretation derived by finite persons based on finite experiences within and toward the Infinite Horizon of religious faith. Although Williams's proposals remain contingent on the Thomistic distinction between the infinite form signified (*ratio significationis*) and the finite style of signifying it (*modus significandi*), between divine perfection and creaturely likeness, his theological understandings nevertheless have the ring of existential truth. Reflecting the dialectical reality of love and suffering so common in human relationships, Williams's insights concerning the suffering of the God who is Love retain the ability to be reasonable to the human intellect, consistent with human experience, and responsive to human freedom.

Sallie McFague: The God at Risk

Expanding the existential context of the God-world relationship beyond that of human love, North American Protestant theologian Sallie McFague focuses on the poor, oppressed, and ravaged of the world in her discussion of the suffering of God. For McFague, the poor, oppressed, and ravaged include not only humanity but also nonhuman creation and indeed the earth itself. McFague discusses this understanding in two groundbreaking works in ecological theology, *Models of God: Theology for an Ecological, Nuclear Age* and *The Body of God: An Ecological Theology.*[59] In each work, she grounds her theological reflections in significant moments in the paradigmatic life of Jesus of Nazareth. Locating her proposals within the framework of metaphorical theology and setting them forth as "likely accounts" of the God-world relationship, McFague's Christological starting point concerning the God-world relationship in *Models of God* is the resurrection of Jesus, which she interprets not as the resurrection of a particular body or bodies, but rather as the sign of God's promise to be with the world always in an incarnate way. In *The Body of God*, McFague's point of entry shifts from the resurrection to the mystery of the Incarnation itself as she invites one "to imagine 'the Word made flesh' not as limited to Jesus of Nazareth but as the body of the universe, all bodies . . . [as a] metaphor for both divine nearness *and* divine glory."[60] In this radically incarnational vision of the God-world relationship, McFague, like Jon Sobrino, emphasizes that all of creation mediates divine reality and communicates the way in which God and the world relate.

Having set forth her proviso that her metaphorical approach to theology is heuristic and imagistic, rather than definitive and descriptive, McFague in *Models of God* frames her proposals within a monist, panentheistic perspective.[61] Based on her interpretation of the resurrection, she suggests that God's relation to the world is analogous to the relation of the human person to the body. However, McFague contends that her model of the world as the body of God does not identify God with the world any more than a human is strictly identified with the body.[62] According to McFague, the mere fact that one can speak objectively of one's body precludes the assumption of total identity. Accordingly, she submits that her model of the world as God's body does not limit or reduce God ontologically, because it is the body of the universe that remains finite, while God as animating Spirit transcends the world's limitations.

Nevertheless, "though God is not reduced to the world, the metaphor of the world as God's body puts God 'at risk.'" If one follows the ramifications of this metaphor, McFague contends, God, like a human person, is "made vulnerable" by God's body, the world.

> God will be liable to bodily contingencies. The world as God's body may be poorly cared for, ravaged, and . . . essentially destroyed. . . . In the metaphor of the universe as the self-expression of God—God's incarnation—the notions of vulnerability, shared responsibility, and risk are inevitable.

Although this metaphor underscores the readiness of God to suffer for and with the world, a readiness enfleshed in "the inclusive, suffering love of the cross of Jesus of Nazareth," it nevertheless has for McFague the unavoidable consequence of identifying God's being with the evil and suffering in the world.[63] From her monist position, "The evil in the world, all kinds of evil, occurs in and to God as well as to us and the rest of creation. Evil is not a power over against God; in a sense, it is God's 'responsibility,' part of God's being."[64] God's involvement in evil notwithstanding, this position also serves to affirm that God is "profoundly, palpably, personally involved, in suffering . . . the pain that those parts of creation affected by evil feel God also feels and feels bodily. . . . One does not suffer alone." In the context of the cross, this leads McFague to propose an eternalization of suffering in God. According to McFague, "God's suffering on the cross was not for a mere few hours . . . but is present and permanent. As the body of the world, God is 'forever nailed to the cross,' for as the body suffers, so God suffers."[65] In her later Trinitarian treatment of God as Lover whose mode of relationship with the world is healing, McFague tempers this appraisal by maintaining that this divine identification with suffering is secondary to a primary divine resistance to suffering and warns that conceiving identification as primary results in an acceptance of the status quo and a romanticizing of suffering.[66] In this way, McFague is able to affirm that God is not helpless against evil and that the same radical, inclusive love that raised Jesus from the dead is at work in the world. Nevertheless, her monist, panentheistic understanding of the immanence of God tends to leave God irredeemably complicit in suffering and evil, as well as suffering and evil inextricably elemental in God.

Informed by revised biblical and Christological points of departure and by contemporary advances in the scientific understanding of evolutionary processes, McFague, in *The Body of God*, fine-tunes and develops her model of the God-world relationship in such a way as to address the problematic concerning God, evil, and suffering created in her earlier book. Approaching her theological reflections from the "backside of God," the mystery of the Incarnation, and the evolutionary understanding of the operation of chance within lawlike systems, McFague succeeds in presenting a balanced treatment of divine immanence and transcendence, as well as a modified understanding of the relationship of God to suffering and evil that is viable within the Christian tradition.[67] "Were we to imagine," McFague suggests, " 'the Word made flesh' as not limited to Jesus of Nazareth but as the body of the universe...might we not have an...awesome metaphor for both divine nearness *and* divine glory?"[68] According to McFague, this "awesome metaphor" results in a radicalization of divine immanence and transcendence. Rather than conceiving divine transcendence as a disembodied notion, in the model of the universe as the body of God, divine transcendence is "radically and concretely embodied...*in* the differences, in the concrete embodiments, that constitute the universe."[69] Thus, it is a transcendence-in-immanence that McFague proposes. As a result of God's embodied transcendence, God is immanently present in and through all bodies, a motif prevalent in both the Hebrew and Christian traditions that take seriously the mediation of God by the world.[70] Because of the age, the size, the diversity, and the complexity inherent in the history of creation, therefore,

> At one level our model—the universe as God's body—moves us in the direction of contemplating the glory and grandeur of divine creation...while at another level it moves us in the direction of compassionate identification with and service to the fragile, suffering, oppressed bodies that surround us.[71]

Because of its core doctrine of Incarnation, McFague considers Christianity uniquely suited to embrace the model of the world as God's body, understood in shape and scope through what McFague terms "the Christic paradigm." Based on the story of Jesus of Nazareth, this paradigm suggests that the direction of creation is "toward inclusive love for all, especially the oppressed, the outcast, the vulnerable" and that *the shape of God's body includes all, especially the needy and outcast.* Moreover, according to McFague, in an ecological age, the oppressed, the needy, and the outcast must include the "new poor," that is, nonhuman beings and the cosmos itself. It is at this stage of her argument concerning the body of God and suffering of the world in the Christic paradigm that the influence of contemporary science becomes evident.[72]

McFague echoes her earlier contention that a deistic or monarchical model construes the notion that God suffers with creation quite differently than does the organic model of the universe as God's body. However, rather than maintaining that these different models result in different notions of complicity on the part of God concerning evil and suffering—a complicity unavoidable in a monist model within lawlike evolutionary processes—McFague points out the shift in perspective that develops "if we take seriously the contemporary scientific picture of reality," the picture of evolutionary processes as an interplay of chance events within a lawlike system, resulting in a view of reality that denies an interventionist interpretation of divine activity in history.

> In neither model is God the cause of these human tragedies, but in the
> deistic and monarchical models, God is not involved in the conse-
> quences either, for God is external to and distant from the world. But
> this is not the case in the organic model: God is involved—in fact, is
> not only involved but feels the pain of all who suffer within the body.[73]

Hence, the insights of contemporary science enable McFague in her Christic
paradigm to maintain that whatever suffering happens in creation happens
to God as well. Nevertheless, McFague balances the suffering Christ in her
Christic paradigm with the resurrected Christ, the Cosmic Christ, "freed from
the body of Jesus of Nazareth, to be present in and to all bodies." The resurrection promise of God to be with creation always, which was the starting point
of McFague's reflections in *Models of God,* comes to fruition in this notion of the
Cosmic Christ as the scope of the body of God. It is this movement in Mc-
Fague's thought that is able to effectively counteract the notion of the eternalization of suffering in God, as "New Testament appearance stories attest to the
continuing empowerment of the Christic paradigm in the world: the liberating,
inclusive love of God for all is alive in and through the entire cosmos."[74] Hence,
the concept of the Christic paradigm assures the cosmos of God's suffering love
and presence with the human and nonhuman victims of exploitation, despoliation, and death in the body of the world. At the same time, the concept of the
Cosmic Christ assures creation of God's radically transcendent immanence
in "the incognito appearance of Christ whenever we see human compassion for
the outcast and the vulnerable . . . when and where the oppressed are liberated,
the sick are healed, the outcast are invited in."[75]

ANALYSIS

Sallie McFague's feminist ecological theology has the distinction of being the
sole theology reviewed here that explicitly develops female images of God and
the God-world relationship and includes the suffering of nonhuman creation
within the aegis of its concerns. In discussing the holistic paradigm of the
world as the body of God through which she envisions the world and the task of
theology, McFague both critiques the androcentric and hierarchical traditions
of Western religion and raises consciousness about the plight of the nonhuman creation of God. In so doing, McFague clearly demonstrates that it is not
enough to be concerned for the fulfillment of humanity alone; it is critical to
adopt an ethic of care for the earth, the giver and sustainer of human life.

From her feminist and ecological standpoint, theology and its discourse
must be for McFague responsive to the historical circumstances in which,

about which, and to which it presumes to speak. Therefore, constructions based on antiquated circumstances, language, thought forms, models, or paradigms are inadequate for a contemporary age affected by new and complex issues, informed by different cosmological and scientific discoveries, and threatened by heretofore-inconceivable ecological crises. Because McFague's interest is in inspiring an ethic that will motivate the Christian toward justice, healing, and companionship of the earth, she willingly sacrifices the classical attributes of God. She purposefully asserts that, in terms of the God-world relationship, God does suffer, God is in need, and God does depend on humanity for the fulfillment of the divine intention for the cosmos. Therefore, regarding the ethical capacity of these proposals, McFague's theology demonstrates pastoral effectiveness as it insists on the intrinsic value of embodiment and of all embodied creatures. Such valuing prompts the participation of all members of the body of God in action for justice and for the liberation of bodies in history.

McFague's proposal in *Models of God*, which links God and evil in a monist, panentheistic model, tends to be problematic in its implications for the nature of God and the God-world relationship. Although the theory of chance within necessity in McFague's *Body of God* somewhat alters this conception of God, the suspicion that God is somehow the source of evil or a silent bystander in the world haunts her panentheistic paradigm. McFague succeeds in countering this suspicion by presenting a viable Christian response, framed within the interplay of the Christic paradigm, which incarnates the suffering body of God, and the Cosmic Christ, which represents redeemed and transformed creation. Moreover, McFague's model of God rooted in the life, death, and resurrection of Christ ably acknowledges both the God immanently capable of suffering and the God transcendently able to save. Despite the pervasive and persistent reality of suffering and death endemic in the cosmos, in McFague's organic and ecological model of the world as God's body, each incidence of solidarity, of compassion, of liberation, of healing, and of welcome is a sign of God's transcendent immanence. Each is an in-breaking of the Cosmic Christ and a prolepsis of the fullness of creation yet to come. Each is a sign, however vague and fragmentary, that gives reason to hope and grace to endure.

Approaching the Suffering of God through Evolutionary Science

A review of this sampling of theological proposals concerning the concept of suffering in God clearly indicates the diverse and mutually critical nature of the arguments posed by these varied hermeneutical positions. Rather than an impediment to theological and pastoral efficacy, the theoretical and critical diversity of these responses offers rich possibilities for authentic insight, hope, and transformation in the unique and diverse lives of persons who ache for comfort, who yearn for respite, and who endure in faith. Nevertheless, I suggest that these approaches provide insufficient grounding for the task they seek to undertake: the task of speaking rightly about God in a cosmic context beset by suffering and informed by contemporary worldviews. A strictly biblical approach offers too narrow a point of entry in a religiously and theologically pluralistic world, and a strictly liberationist approach is frequently anthropocentric in its application. The approach through process philosophy is theologically inconsistent with the Trinitarian tradition of Christianity, and the ecological approach that conceives of the world as the body of God risks a pantheistic identification between creation and its Creator.

Assets of an Evolutionary Approach to the Suffering of God

Into this chorus of theoretically, theologically, and pastorally diverse voices, I invite the distinctive voice of evolutionary science as holding the most promise for the fruitful unfolding of an affirmation of suffering in God. Employing the science of evolutionary cosmology and biology to ground my theological affirmation of the suffering of God supports the aims of my project in several ways. First, evolutionary science extends the theoretical basis of this project beyond the revelation, philosophy, and metaphysics employed by the bulk of classical and contemporary theological thought. Second, this wider scientific compass permits an approach that assumes a cosmocentric perspective, rather than a narrow anthropocentric viewpoint. Third, a scientific approach provides a basis for proposals grounded in observable, empirical, and emerging data concerning the entities, structures, and processes of the cosmos, rather than dependent on essentially metaphysical or logical principles. Fourth, the use of the understandings of evolutionary science increases the theoretical defensibility of my proposals for persons who live in an age in which science as much as religion or philosophy shapes the personal and social consciousness of humanity concerning itself and the cosmos of which humanity is an integral part.

The Evolutionary Theology of Arthur Peacocke

In pursuing a course toward the affirmation of suffering in God through the paradigm of evolutionary science, I was guided by the work of one of the most compelling theorists and prolific spokespersons for this viewpoint, that of scientist-theologian and Anglican Canon Arthur Peacocke. Peacocke was Warden

Emeritus at the Society of Ordained Scientists and Council Member of the European Society for the Study of Science and Theology, and he demonstrated the viability and the necessity of regarding theology and science as interacting approaches to reality during more than forty years of scientific and theological scholarship. In so doing, he produced creative, insightful, and thought-provoking resources for the reinterpretation and reconstruction of theological models of God and the God-world relationship compatible with evolutionary science.

Grounded in Thomistic theology and guided by his scientific study of biological evolution, Peacocke had affirmed that the postulate of God as the Creator and Ground of all being remains a respectable response to questions of cosmic existence. He cautioned, however, that accounts of the universe offered by evolutionary science differ from the classical or mechanistic accounts that dominated theological exposition for centuries. Because of this difference, theology must now reckon with a God truly in relation to a continually developing world. Consequently, as evolutionary scientists consider both the "being" of the world (what is there) and the "becoming" of the world (what is going on), theologians must think of God in terms of Divine Being, that is, who or what God is in Godself, and Divine Becoming, that is, what God does in interaction with the cosmos. As a result, God's relation to the world involves both differentiation and interaction. In Divine Being, God is differentiated from the world in ontological otherness; in Divine Becoming, God is intrinsically creative in, with, and under the evolutionary processes of the cosmos.

Informed by the evolutionary theology of Arthur Peacocke, I submit that the concept of a suffering God is theoretically supportable, theologically viable, and pastorally crucial in a universe beset by pain, suffering, and death. Mindful of the limitations of other approaches set forth earlier in this chapter, I follow Peacocke's approach for several reasons. First, in developing a theology of Divine Being and Divine Becoming, Peacocke clearly evidenced the integration of classical and contemporary Christian theological insights. In so doing, he demonstrated his knowledge of and respect for a tradition whose insights have validly informed theological discourse for centuries, as well as a capacity to reenvision and reinterpret the principles of this tradition in ways responsive to contemporary understandings in theological anthropology and in the biological and social evolutionary sciences. Second, by focusing his conception of God and the God-world relationship through a panentheistic paradigm, Peacocke revisioned a balanced, interactive, and dialogical relationship between divine transcendence and divine immanence, one in which the cosmos mediates and communicates the ultimately ineffable mystery of God. Through this revisioning, he ably addressed the imbalance often arising from deistic or theistic understandings of God and the God-world relationship that stress the transcendent otherness of God in distant, impassive, and unrelated isolation. Conversely, his perspective also addressed the pantheistic alternative, which, in its emphasis on the radical immanence of God, identifies the Creator with the created order and obscures the ontological distinction between the two.

Third, by developing his theological proposals in dialogue with evolutionary science, Peacocke demonstrated the appropriateness and viability of using an alternate paradigm and worldview in which to frame theological analysis concerning the suffering of God. His paradigm validated ongoing creativity and transformation within cosmic history. As such, it suggested an interpretation of suffering that is dynamic rather than static, one that includes the potential for hope even in the depths of despair, and newness of life within the shadow of death. Although this does not negate or justify the reality of suffering, it does imply that suffering is not an end in itself but an experience within a dynamic process of ongoing creativity and growth. Through the wide-angle lens of this evolutionary scientific paradigm, the vision of this book has the potential to be comprehensibly cosmocentric, rather than narrowly anthropocentric, which enables it to address the ubiquity of ecological devastation and death, as well as biological and social suffering and death.

Fourth, in adopting the epistemological stance of critical realism, Peacocke grounded his theology in experiential and observable reality. This stance acknowledged the limitation of theological discourse derived from the created order, reiterated the analogical nature of theological language, and ultimately asserted the attributive validity of human speech about God. Such a stance supported the validity and value of human and nonhuman experience as fertile ground for theological reflection and discourse, rather than restricting theological foundations to solely metaphysical principles. Moreover, it affirmed the enduring philosophical conviction that an analogy exists between contingent being and Ultimate Being. This led to the understanding that categorical reality has the capacity to mediate Infinite Reality and to be revelatory of the Divine through the action of grace. Therefore, although faltering and fragile, the possibility of human speech about God remains conceivable and creative within a stance of critical realism. It is a stance that both recognized the inability of human discourse to adequately express the inexpressible mystery of God and upheld the human desire and capacity to voice its experience of the gracious Reality encountered in the heart of cosmic being.

Fifth, Peacocke formulated his insights concerning the divine nature and attributes in terms of the Triune God of the Christian tradition, the context of my research. In so doing, he was able to explore the variously nuanced ways in which the Triune God as Transcendent, Incarnate, and Immanent in the cosmos reveals Godself and the God-world relationship. Moreover, while acknowledging the richness and diversity of theological images within the Christian tradition, Peacocke's critical realist approach enabled alternative possibilities for imaging the Triune God and God-world relationship that arise from human experience and from a continually creative cosmos. In particular, Peacocke strongly advocated the appropriateness of female images, underrepresented in the Christian biblical and theological tradition, to communicate the creative suffering of the Triune God, the concept that focuses this exploration.

For these reasons, the approach through cosmological and biological science guided by Peacocke's evolutionary theology has captured my theological imagination as I seek to contribute to the ongoing theological discussion of the mystery of the Christian God in relation to cosmic suffering. In so doing, I seek to draw attention to the creative, insightful, and thought-provoking resources that evolutionary theology offers to theological interpretation and discourse. Ultimately, I want to probe these resources to discover their ramifications for the concerns of feminist theologies, ecological ethics, and pastoral ministry as each strives to confront and alleviate cosmic suffering in its innumerable life-shattering forms.

2

Scientific Foundations of an Evolutionary Theology

Profoundly moved by the suffering of creation and its creatures that results from ubiquitous pain, suffering, and death within the cosmos, I join my voice with those who contend that the most theologically coherent, morally acceptable, and experientially efficacious Christian response to this travail lies in affirming the concept of the suffering of God. Acknowledging the viability of biblical, liberation, process, and ecological approaches to the concept, I nonetheless choose the interdisciplinary path of evolutionary science and Christian theology toward an affirmation of divine suffering, and I do so along the particular route constructed by scientist-theologian Arthur Peacocke. Informed by his evolutionary theology and grounded in the panentheistic paradigm of God-world relationship, I contend that the concept of the creative suffering of the Triune God is theoretically defensible, theologically viable, and pastorally crucial in the midst of a suffering world.

In exploring the fertile territory defined by the theology-science dialogue, I follow four fundamental principles that serve as the basis for Peacocke's evolutionary theology and for my theological proposals. First is the primary conception of God as Creator of an evolving cosmos. Hence, the cosmos in turn is conceived as creation. Second, if God as Creator has given the evolving cosmos as creation the kind of being it manifests in its entities, processes, and structures, then these cosmic entities, processes, and structures are revelatory of God's nature, attributes, and purposes. It follows as a third principle that concepts of the nature, attributes, and purposes of God *in se* cannot be separated from concepts of the nature, attributes, and purposes of God in relationship to an evolving cosmos characterized by both unity and diversity, law and chance, simplicity and complexity, fecundity and extinction, delight and suffering, pleasure and pain, birth and death. Fourth, to be expressible, intelligible, fruitful, and efficacious, this self-revelation of God through the cosmos must be articulated in terms of appropriate models and metaphors that yield defensible, viable, and efficacious ways of articulating the God-world relationship in the midst of the suffering of the world.

Because the Christian tradition provides the framework of my research, I, too, affirm the principle of God as Creator and the cosmos as creation. In response to the principles concerning the revelatory character of creation in relation to its Creator, I focus on the evolutionary cosmology and biology from which Peacocke derived his understanding of natural being and becoming. This understanding served as the basis for the inference of the Being and Becoming of God that ultimately includes the capacity for creative suffering in the Divine. In this focus, I explore varied insights regarding the origin of the cosmos that point beyond the scientific horizon to a transcendent Ground of Being for the universe. I examine the understandings of Newtonian physics that once led to inferences about God as deistic Creator of a clockwork universe or as theistic Creator unrelated to the universe. This examination leads to the evolutionary, relativity, and quantum theories that have since challenged both mechanistic understanding of the physical world and deistic and theistic conceptions of a separated and unrelated Deity. I then narrow my focus to Darwinian and neo-Darwinian theories of biological evolution and survey the scientific picture of cosmic being and becoming afforded by these positions. This focused survey reveals a cosmos in the process of ongoing transformation and emergence of life that suggests not only the original but also the ongoing activity of God as Creator of life, an activity that is immanent in the creativity of the cosmos itself.

This immanent creativity of the cosmos, however, operates through the mutual interaction of both law and chance. This interplay implies a freedom and autonomy inherent in the evolving cosmos that challenges notions of unmitigated divine omnipotence and omniscience in relation to cosmic events. It involves an intrinsic measure of risk for the Creator and entails a ubiquity of pain, suffering, and death in the ordinary and extraordinary circumstances of its history.

Although pain itself is an odious physical sensation, suffering implies the "conscious endurance of pain or distress"[1] or the awareness of "the disruption of inner harmony" that results from physical, mental, emotional, and/or spiritual forces.[2] It is the experience of sentient creatures and conscious persons that is "induced by the loss of integrity, intactness, cohesiveness, or wholeness" or by the destruction and frustration of purposive behavior. Moreover, not only can one differentiate the experience of pain from that of suffering but also one can distinguish two sources from which they derive. The first source of pain, suffering, and death in the cosmos is the free and autonomous process of the self-creativity of the cosmos, especially in relation to the evolutionary pattern of natural selection, the operation of chance in the cosmos, and the indeterminacy of events at the quantum level. A second source of pain, suffering, and death in the cosmos derives from the free and autonomous exercise of human volition, in choices and actions that inflict deleterious effects on both human and non-human life in the cosmos. Although Peacocke recognized and distinguished these two sources of pain, suffering, and death in the cosmos, his focus centered on the capacity of humanity to consciously inflict injurious experiences on creation and on the degree to which humanity is able to thwart or disrupt the unfolding of divine purpose and intention in the universe through this capacity. He did not distinguish them according to the measure of pain, suffering, and death experienced from these different sources. Neither did he contend that the emergence of novel forms of life as a result of evolutionary pain, suffering, and death serves as a mitigating factor in the experience of this pain, suffering, and death in creatures or in their Creator. For Peacocke, *if* God as Creator suffers, then it is because God is in transcendent, incarnate, and immanent relationship to a suffering cosmos and its creatures.

The reality of such risk to the Divine and of pain, suffering, and death in the cosmos leads to the inevitable question of what these aspects of creation might disclose about the Creator. *If* risk, pain, suffering, and death are essentially inherent within the creative processes of an evolutionary cosmos and inflicted by the actions of its most highly evolved beings, and *if* the Christian God is not to be conceived as deistically separated from or theistically unrelated to creation, and, finally, *if* this Creator God radically affirms the intrinsic value of each and every aspect of the created order, *then* "for any concept of God to be morally acceptable and coherent ... we cannot but tentatively propose that *God* suffers in, with, and under the creative process of the world with their costly unfolding in time."[3]

Scientific Bases of Evolutionary Theology

There was God. And God was All-That-Was.
God's Love overflowed and God said:
"Let Other be. And let it have the capacity to become what it might be—

> *and let it explore its potentialities."*
> *And there was Other in God, a field of energy,*
> *vibrating energy but no matter, space, time or form.*[4]

Thus begins, in poetic form, the epic of evolution that is so sufficiently well established within the natural sciences that it is neither conceivable nor possible for theology to operate solely within the biblical understanding of the genesis of the universe that has shaped its cosmology and its doctrine of creation for two millennia. Although scientific perspectives have often been perceived as challenging and, at times, threatening to biblically based cosmology, anthropology, and theology, scientific understandings represent a critical stimulus and opportunity for Christian theology to become more encompassing, more inclusive, and, in fact, more credible in the twenty-first century in which it proclaims its message. Suggesting that this scientifically informed period presents Christianity with the most fundamental challenge to its system of beliefs in its history, Peacocke nonetheless contended that "Christian theology has been at its most creative and most vital when it has faced the challenges of engagement with new systems of thought encountered in new cultural contexts."[5] Hence, the paradigm shift brought about by scientific understandings of the cosmos, with its impact on understandings of the Triune God and of humanity, represents a *kairos* moment for Christian theology. Christian theology may choose to respond to the insights of science and maintain its relevance through transformation and development or it may distance itself from such understandings through retrenchment or regression and risk irrelevance to the faithful who have been and continue to be irreversibly formed by the contemporary scientific worldview.

Science in a Mechanistic Paradigm

NEWTON AND THE DETERMINISTIC MODEL OF THE UNIVERSE

Prior to the advent of twentieth-century scientific understandings of the cosmos, a mechanistic scientific model of the universe prevailed. Based on the work of seventeenth-century mathematician and physicist Isaac Newton, the mechanistic worldview reflected the epistemological priority of sensory experience and observation. As a result of experimentation with such sensory observations, Newton set forth the following "Rules for Reasoning in Philosophy" in his 1687 *Philosophiae Naturalis Principia Mathematica*, regarded as foundational in the so-called scientific revolution:

Rule I. We are to admit no more causes of natural things than such as are both true and sufficient to explain their appearances.

Rule II. Therefore to the same natural effects we must, as far as possible, assign the same causes.

Rule III. The qualities of bodies, which admit neither intension nor remission of degrees, and which are found to belong to all bodies within the reach of our experiments, are to be esteemed the universal qualities of all bodies whatsoever.

Rule IV. In experimental philosophy we are to look upon propositions collected by general induction from phenomena as accurately or very nearly true, notwithstanding any contrary hypotheses that may be imagined, till such time as other phenomena occur, by which they may either be made more accurate, or liable to exceptions.[6]

Hence, in the worldview that arises from such epistemology and philosophy, the universe operates according to repeatable and identifiable patterns of causes and effects, termed "natural laws." Objects within this system possess a determinate structure with independent existence, and the distribution of these objects changes according to immutable mechanistic "necessity," as if fixed in advance. According to the model typically associated with such a paradigm, the Newtonian worldview was that of a "clockwork universe," complete without intervening forces or laws and deterministic regarding prediction of future states. It was consistent in its conclusions based on particular circumstances regardless of time or place and independent of the observer's presence and expectations.[7]

THE CHALLENGE OF QUANTUM PHYSICS
TO THE MECHANISTIC MODEL

Within this Newtonian perspective, which dominated Western thought for more than two and half centuries, *matter*, the stuff of the world, possessed *energy*, with a location in *space* at a particular *time*. Although this understanding may have been applicable to overt sensory experiences, it tends to break down in the categories of the very small (subatomic), the very fast (speeds close to light), or the very large (cosmological).[8] Within these ranges, Newton's own touchstone of empirical evidence challenged his scientific worldview, as observations at these levels of the universe failed to agree with Newton's predictions or mechanics. Twentieth-century mathematician and physicist Albert Einstein, for example, demonstrated that relations among time, space, and the velocity of light relativized all temporal and spatial frames of reference regarding matter and energy, which undermined Newtonian absolutism regarding these essential aspects of the created order. Einstein's general theory of relativity demonstrated the inextricable meshing of space and time and contested the Euclidean notion of space as uniform, three-dimensional, infinite in extent, and continuously divisible, which grounded Newton's principles. Moreover, Einstein's special theory of relativity demonstrated that absolute simultaneity requires that events occur at the same location, whereas in the classical and Newtonian worldview, time was considered to be a single dimension that is homogeneous, continuous, infinite, and independent of objects and events.

The advent of quantum physics in the subatomic realm and the work of physicist Werner Heisenberg in the twentieth century further challenged Newton's principles concerning the physical structure of objects and the predictability of their attributes. With the establishment of the Heisenberg Uncertainty Principle, the concept that the act of observing alters the reality being observed, Newton's notion of the independence of physical structures became questionable. Furthermore, while Newtonian physics assumed a theoretically unlimited precision of measurability in the physical world, the findings of quantum physics concerning the "uncertainty relation" between the position and the momentum of a subatomic particle contradicted the determinacy of past and future events. In so doing, it reduced Newton's presumption of precise predictability to a range of probabilities. Hence, as Richard Schlegel notes, "We have learned that . . . on the level of individual atomic processes the scientist now finds that he in fact has a role in the creation of the world that he is describing,"[9] making scientists, in the words of Niels Bohr, "both onlookers and actors in the great drama of existence."[10]

Science in an Evolutionary Paradigm

DARWIN AND THE ORIGIN OF SPECIES THROUGH NATURAL SELECTION

With these and other twentieth-century discoveries in quantum physics and relativity theory, there occurred what Karl Heim called the "twilight of the gods" of absolute space, time, object, and determinism.[11] Nevertheless, before the demise of these gods of classical physics, the concept of the Creator God of classical theism faced its own challenges, when, in 1859, the work of British naturalist Charles Darwin was published under the title *On the Origin of Species by Means of Natural Selection, or the Preservation of Favoured Races in the Struggle for Life.*[12] In his own words, Darwin characterizes the theoretical context in which he wrote:

> Until recently the great majority of naturalists believed that species
> were immutable productions, and had been separately created.
> This view has been ably maintained by many authors. Some few
> naturalists, on the other hand, have believed that species undergo
> modification, and that the existing forms of life are the descendants by
> true generation of pre-existing forms.[13]

As a result of his studies in South America, the Galapagos Islands, and Pacific
coral reefs aboard the H.M.S. *Beagle* and influenced by the work of geologist
Charles Lyell, zoologist J. B. Lamarck, and the Reverend Thomas Malthus,
Darwin found himself in agreement with those "few naturalists." He therefore
concluded,

> I can entertain no doubt . . . that the view which most naturalists un-
> til recently entertained, and which I formerly entertained—namely,
> that each species has been independently created—is erroneous. I
> am fully convinced that species are not immutable; but that those
> belonging to what are called the same genera are lineal descendants
> of some other and generally extinct species, in the same manner as
> the acknowledged varieties of any one species are the descendants
> of that species. Furthermore, I am convinced that natural selec-
> tion has been the most important, but not the exclusive, means of
> modification.[14]

This Darwinian understanding of the evolution of species may be theoretically
summarized in two propositions. First, Darwin theorized that all organisms,
past, present, and future, descend from earlier living systems. Second, he proposed that species of organisms derive from prior varieties of species through
the process of natural selection of the best procreators. This process of selection, according to Darwin, follows from

> the struggle for life. . . . Owing to this struggle, variations, however
> slight and from whatever cause proceeding, if they be in any degree
> profitable to the individuals of a species . . . will tend to the preser-
> vation of such individuals, and will generally be inherited by the
> offspring. The offspring, also, will thus have a better chance of
> surviving.[15]

Having advanced these proposals on the *evolution* of life, however, Darwin does
not conjecture as to the process underlying the *origin* of life, nor does he identify what specific mechanisms are involved in the natural selection process that
Herbert Spencer called "the survival of the fittest." While recognizing that

"Naturalists continually refer to external conditions, such as climate, food, etc., as the only possible cause of variation," Darwin nonetheless maintained that it was "preposterous to attribute to mere external conditions, the structure, for instance, of the woodpecker, with its feet, tail, beak, and tongue, so admirably adapted to catch insects under the bark of trees."[16]

Confirming Darwin's contention regarding the mechanism of natural selection would be left to nineteenth-century biologist Gregor Mendel, who established the laws of heredity and the science of genetics. The dynamics of the process would be further clarified by twentieth-century molecular biologists James Watson and Francis Crick at the Cavendish Laboratory at the University of Cambridge and Maurice Wilkins and Rosalind Franklin at King's College, London, who discovered the helical structure of the DNA molecule, the carrier of genetic information. These amplifications in Darwin's theory of evolution through the findings of genetics and molecular biology would result in the "modern synthesis" termed neo-Darwinism. This synthesis, which takes into account the interplay of genetic constitution and the behavior of the organism with the environment the organism inhabits, concludes that natural selection occurs on the basis of genetic variations within individuals in populations. Mutations occurring randomly within the organism and within its population provide the main impetus for these genetic variations. However, because such mutations are both random and rare, neo-Darwinism also contends that evolution is a slow, gradual process, requiring great expanses of time.[17]

CHALLENGES TO DARWINIAN EVOLUTIONARY THEORY

Despite scientists' general acceptance of Darwin's proposals regarding the evolution of life in the universe, controversies concerning the theory of evolution persist. Some alternatives contradict the conclusions of Darwin and of neo-Darwinism; others remain within the evolutionary context but propose alternate processes, dynamics, and constraints on the evolutionary process. In the former category, the concept of *creationism* holds that species spontaneously come into existence, rather than evolve from other species through natural processes. Linked ideologically with ethical, political, and religious conservatism, creationism sets a theistic doctrine of creation in opposition to creativity through evolution, rather than incorporating elements of theistic and scientific understandings of the universe to form an integrated approach to comprehending reality. Also in direct conflict with evolutionary systematics is the phylogenetically based notion of *cladism*. Deriving its name from the word *clade*, which is the name for a branch of an evolutionary tree, cladism contends that "the amount of difference between forms is directly proportional to the age of their common ancestor." Hence, in opposition to the evolutionary principle that the earlier the common ancestor, the broader the range of affinities among organisms, cladism maintains that the earlier the ancestor, the further apart the genetic relationship between the resulting organisms. According to this perspective, only shared, derived homologies of the closest order indicate genetic relationship within any group of organisms.[18]

Representing those proposals that introduce alternative perspectives into the overarching construct of evolution, the concept of *punctuated equilibrium* concerns itself with the tempo and mode of the evolutionary process. Advanced by Niles Eldredge and Stephen J. Gould on the basis of changes in organisms evident in the fossil record, the concept of punctuated equilibrium indicates that, rather than involving great expanses of time in which minor variations accumulate within populations of organisms, evolution occurred relatively rapidly over short periods of time. Accordingly, Eldredge and Gould regard the process of evolution as consisting of long periods of biological equilibrium in a virtual stasis that is characterized by minor adaptations in a slowly changing environment. This stasis is then intermittently punctuated by relatively short bursts of rapid change, during which speciation occurs.[19] Akin to the pre-Darwinian proposal known as *Lamarckism*,[20] which held that traits acquired (or diminished) during the lifetime of an organism can be passed to its offspring, other contemporary scientific proposals concerning the effect of behavior on speciation deem increasingly inadequate the focus on the interplay between environmental pressures and genetic mutations as the sole mechanism of natural selection. One such proposal made by Richard Lewontin stresses that organisms are consequences of themselves and of the historical accidents present within their situation at any given moment, as well as of their genotypes or their environments.[21] Finally, the notion of *neutral mutation* suggests that certain genetic variations have no bearing on evolution in that such mutations offer no selective advantage or disadvantage to the organism. Because these neutral mutations produce no changes in the polypeptide chain of DNA, the survival of the mutation into the next generation depends solely on chance. Moreover, this chance itself varies, depending on the size of the population of the organism, with the passage of the mutation more probable in a smaller population.[22] The operation of chance within the process of natural selection and in biological evolution, however, is not limited to the probability of the survival of mutations from one generation to the next in populations of organisms. As scientific investigation and theory since the mid-1970s have shown, chance is operative within the very dynamic of natural selection and speciation through evolutionary processes.

Sciences in Synthesis: The Evolutionary
Approach of Arthur Peacocke

Against this variegated scientific backdrop, Arthur Peacocke traced the stages of the life process from its origins and discussed as he did so the duration, the mechanisms, and the characteristics of the evolutionary process as understood by scientists at the turn of the third millennium. He reminded the inquirer that scientific conclusions concerning evolutionary cosmology, biology, and physics are historical in nature. Because the original events are no longer observable or repeatable in their uniqueness, accounts of cosmological development result from extrapolations backward in time. These extrapolations are based on scientific knowledge accumulated and derived from astronomical observations of other planets and galaxies, geological observations of the constitution of Earth, and ongoing chemical, biochemical, and molecular experimentation and research. Within this framework, no inference from the past can be justified unless it accords with the laws, principles, or models verified by contemporary science.[23] However, "by inferring to the best explanation of the succession of states ... from the relevant data, we are now possessed with a remarkably coherent picture of the origin and development of the present state of the universe, of planet earth, and of life on earth."[24]

COSMIC ORIGINS THROUGH EVOLUTIONARY PROCESSES

The scientific description of evolution looks to a time in the order of 10 to 20 billion years ago. When no more than a fraction of a second old, the cosmos was in the form of a compressed fireball, a "primeval, unimaginably condensed mass of fundamental particles and energy," consisting of the most basic subatomic elements of matter-energy-space-time.[25] All elements of matter, energy, space, and time that would ever exist erupted as a single quantum gift of existence from what scientists ingloriously term the "the big bang" but which Brian Swimme and Thomas Berry characterize as "the primordial flaring forth."[26] From original unity came diversity. From primeval darkness came light. From conditions "scarcely present in the early stages of the universe's history" came "conditions of chemical composition and temperature and radiation, permitting, through the interplay of chance and necessity, the coming into being of replicating molecules and life. . . . Thus evolution began on planet Earth."[27]

There is, however, considerable debate as to the manner in which the earliest structures that could be called "living" came into existence with the capacity to self-replicate their complex structures. This uncertainty has led some in philosophy to postulate an extraphysical drive that brings emergent forms into existence, especially when such forms are living. Opposed to the concept of "mechanism," a scientific position that suggests that all biology is explicable in terms of physics and chemistry, this postulate of "vitalism" contends that the initial and ongoing emergence of novel forms of life on Earth cannot be explained in solely materialistic terms but must be attributable to a vital principle distinct from and irreducible to physics and chemistry. One principal proponent of such vitalism was French philosopher Henri Bergson, who, espousing a dualistic philosophy of opposition between the élan vital and the material world, hypothesized that this vital force was the source of efficient causation and of the evolution of emergent forms in nature. A second well-known advocate of the vitalist position was German philosopher Hans A. E. Driesch, who proposed the principle of entelechy as a vital force that directs an organism toward self-fulfillment.

Some Christian apologists also tended toward such a vitalist position because of its potential for interpretation in supernatural terms.[28] One such Christian apologist was Jesuit paleontologist Pierre Teilhard de Chardin. In his theory of orthogenesis, he hypothesized that a spark of divine life was present throughout the evolutionary process, forming and informing the process as much as were the material forces delineated by physical science. Characterizing these forces as types of energy, Teilhard proposed the existence of radial energy, which was mechanistic, causal, and quantifiable, and of tangential energy, the energy of the Divine within. Where radial energy predominates, the evolutionary process operates within the laws of chance and necessity; where tangential energy prevails, the forces of divine life and consciousness direct the course of evolution.[29]

CREATIVITY IN EVOLUTIONARY PROCESSES

While not suggesting a reductionism that claims that all emergent entities are ontologically or epistemologically reducible to their component parts, Peacocke contended that the continuity of evolutionary development and emergence can be inferred from or observed within the natural laws and regularities operating in the cosmos, rendering vitalist proposals superfluous. Augmenting this position is the scientific research of Ilya Prigogine and Gregoire Nicolis on the thermodynamics of irreversible processes in dissipative systems at the International Solvay Institute for Physics and Chemistry in Brussels, Belgium, and of Manfred Eigen on self-organizing systems and the evolution of biological macromolecules through time-dependent random processes at the Max Planck Institute for Physical Chemistry in Göttingen.[30] In their research on living systems, Prigogine and Nicolis investigated how living organisms could come into existence in a universe in which irreversible processes tend toward an increase in "entropy," the measure of the disorder or randomness in a system.

In their studies, they found a class of systems with "dissipative structures," that is, the capacity to maintain themselves in a state of order, although far from equilibrium. Their findings suggested that when fluctuations in a system are amplified to a particular frequency, the entire system undergoes structural change and thus becomes a newly ordered state with the capacity to take in energy and matter from the outside to maintain its novel form. Because of this capacity for order-through-fluctuations, Prigogine and Nicolis reasoned that such physicochemical findings made the initial and ongoing emergence of highly ordered living organisms highly probable. In their own words,

> We are led to a first parallelism between dissipative structure formation and certain features occurring in the early stages of biogenesis and the subsequent evolution to higher forms. The analogy would even become closer if the model we discussed had further critical points of unstable transitions. One would then obtain a hierarchy of dissipative structures each one enriched further by the information content of the previous ones through the "memory" of the initial fluctuations which created them successively.[31]

Further scientific support for the inherent creativity of the universe through evolutionary processes and for the redundancy of vitalist claims came from the research of Manfred Eigen and his colleagues at Göttingen. Through the use of the theory of games on the study of time-dependent random processes, Manfred Eigen and Ruthild Winkler researched the effect of the interplay of chance and law ("necessity") on the development of macromolecules.[32] Having established with some precision through ongoing research what combination of law and chance would permit a population of information-carrying macromolecules to develop into a dominant species with the capacity for further evolution, Eigen was led to conclude that

> the evolution of life, if it is based on a derivable physical principle, must be considered an *inevitable* process despite its indeterminate course . . . it is not only inevitable "in principle" but also sufficiently probable within a realistic span of time. It requires appropriate environmental conditions . . . and their maintenance. These conditions have existed on Earth.[33]

CHARACTERISTICS OF THE EVOLUTIONARY PROCESS

According to Peacocke, the process of the evolution of life that occurs "cosmologically, inorganically, geologically, [and] biologically" involves "a continuous, almost kaleidoscopic, recombination of the component units of the universe into an increasing diversity of forms."[34] Moreover, when considered from the perspective of the universe as ordered whole, this kaleidoscopic evolutionary process exhibits certain characteristics.

Continuity and Natural Law. Fundamentally, the universe displays a *continuity of development* from one organized form to another, from the inorganic sphere through the biological sphere to the ecological sphere and so on. Each level of the development of the cosmos manifests the potentialities of matter that have been implicit in it from its very beginning and that have gradually unfolded over expanses of time. This continuity, however, does not exist solely because of the course of time that marks the transition of novel forms from those forms that preceded them. Continuity also exists on the basis of *natural laws* that explain such transitions from one form to another. From hydrogen nuclei to heavier atoms to small molecules to macromolecules, through aggregates to primitive cells to living organisms and beyond, natural laws guide the rates and possibilities of cosmic change. The presence of such natural laws, however, need not imply the notion of a "Lawgiver" or the rigid determinism of mechanistic concepts of the laws of nature. Rather, "the relationships and metamorphoses between the various forms of matter which happened during the development of the cosmos are understandable instances of, extrapolations from, or inferences from relationships observed to be existing now between these various forms of matter."[35] Later experimentation, observation, and research, however, revealed that natural law was not the only dynamic operative in the evolutionary process.

Emergence and Creativity. As the universe continued to evolve, its natural processes produced organisms of increasing uniqueness and particularity, yielding a splendid diversity of forms appropriate to particular environments. In manifesting new forms that were not fully explicable in terms of the previous levels and components of matter of which they were constituted and from which they proceeded, the evolutionary process demonstrated its capacity not only for continuity and regularity but also for *emergence and creativity.* In evolutionary theory, the principle of emergence denotes novel forms that are not reducible or explicable entirely in terms of the form or elements that preceded them. Hence, emergence implies that "the whole is more than the sum of its parts," empirically, epistemologically, and, at certain stages of evolution, even ontologically. The phenomenon of emergence need not be attributed to some extraphysical drive or vital force, nor need it imply that new features of the emergent organism were necessarily present in rudimentary form in the organism that preceded it. However, the phenomenon of emergence does necessitate the development of new language and concepts with the capacity to describe and refer to emergent entities accurately and comprehensively in epistemologically irreducible ways. Based on this evidence of emergence, cosmic development at the biological level must be regarded as "creative" in ways analogous to creativity in humans. As human creativity produces sounds, words, objects, and events, for example, from constructions and integrations not predictable in advance, so, in biological evolution, the potentialities of one level of molecular or macromolecular organization become actualized in unforeseen new forms over great expanses of time.[36] As Kenneth Denbigh observes, "cosmic evolution has been attended by a great increase in the richness and diversity of forms ... [which] has made its appearance out of homogeneity. . . . [This] is an inventive process and is one that is still continuing."[37]

Chance and Causality. The unpredictability of outcome and form in the evolutionary process, associated with the phenomena of biogenesis, emergence, and creativity and with the dynamic of natural selection and speciation, led scientists to conjecture that this process unfolded not only through the guidance of natural laws but also through the impact of chance occurrence. In evolutionary biology, the attribution of chance is applicable in either of two scientific circumstances. On one hand, chance may be attributed to a situation in which there is scientific ignorance concerning the multiple parameters, conditions, and variables involved in the causality of a particular outcome. On the other hand, chance may be attributed as a result of the intersection of two otherwise unrelated causal chains that interact to influence an outcome. In this second case, although each causal chain may be explicable in itself, there is no explicit connection between these chains except at the point where they intersect. Hence, no particular cause or regularity applied that would have enabled scientists to predict the outcome of such a random crossing of causal chains.[38] Furthermore, recent scientific writings propose a third understanding of chance. These suggest that chance may be

> a non-technical way of describing the outcomes of events governed by quantum theory. Quantum mechanics, as usually understood, implies that these outcomes are *not* determinate until they occur—they can only be expressed in terms of probabilities. Not only is our knowledge of systems limited by the Heisenberg Uncertainty Principle, but there is an inalienable indeterminacy about the events themselves.[39]

Although some thinkers such as theologian and physicist Stanley Jaki would consider all chance to be essentially ignorance of actual causality,[40] the notion of chance in evolutionary science stresses the randomness of particular molecular events with respect to their biological consequences.[41]

In the process of evolution, all three understandings of chance apply. Ignorance of parameters and Heisenberg uncertainty are both operative in the first of two causal chains in evolutionary development, that of the mutation of the genetic material DNA. As Julian Huxley states,

> Mutation merely provides the raw material of evolution; it is a random affair, and takes place in all directions. Genes are giant molecules, and their mutations are the result of slight alterations in their structure. Some of these alterations are truly chance rearrangements, as uncaused or at least as unpredictable as the jumping of an electron from one orbit to another inside an atom; others are the result of the impact of some external agency, like X-rays, or ultra-violet radiations, or mustard gas. But in all cases they are random in relation to evolution. Their effects are not related to the needs of the organism, or to the conditions in which it is placed. They occur without reference to their possible consequences or biological uses.[42]

However, "the involvement of . . . 'chance' at the level of mutation in the DNA does not, of itself, preclude these events from displaying regular trends and manifesting inbuilt propensities at the higher levels of organisms, populations, and ecosystems."[43] Thus, the randomly altered genetic constitution of the organism is exposed to the second causal chain in evolutionary development, that of the environment to which the organism is exposed. This environment with its physical features, its predators, and its available food resources is governed by the regularities of the laws of nature—by the cycles of birth and death, by the network of neighboring organisms and their interrelations, by the irrevocable course of its natural history, and by the exclusion of certain biological potentialities because of the actualization of others. Hence, chance at microscopic biological levels of the organism operates within the lawlike framework that constitutes its macroscopic ecological levels. Hence, although chance introduces an element of unpredictability into the equation at the molecular level, the emergence of life clearly proceeds according to what Eigen and Winkler called "the rules of the game" at the statistical level of populations.

As a consequence of this interplay of chance and law, many scientists maintain that this interaction is the basis for the inherent creativity of the natural order, with its capacity to generate new forms, patterns, and organizations of living matter and energy. Although this creativity involves an inevitable element of contingency, the *tâtonnement* or groping suggested by Teilhard,[44] the interplay of chance and law ("necessity") provides a natural mechanism for the unfolding of wide-ranging potentialities within living matter through incessant randomization at the level of DNA. Because of this comprehensive generative capacity, some thinkers have elevated the operation of chance to the level of a metaphysical principle by which to interpret the universe. Representative of this position is biochemist Jacques Monod, who, in his book *Chance and Necessity*, asserted "chance alone is at the source of every innovation, of all creation in the biosphere. Pure chance, absolutely free but blind, [is] at the very root of the stupendous edifice of evolution."[45] In so stating, Monod sought to underscore the lack of foundation for any inference of direction or purpose in the development of the universe and thus to mount an assault on theism's claims to a teleological universe in which the existence of all creation, including human beings, revealed cosmic intent or meaning.

In disagreement with Monod, Henry Stapp remarks, "Chance is an idea useful for dealing with a world partly unknown to us. But it has no rational place among ultimate constituents of nature."[46] However, David J. Bartholomew, in his systematic analysis of the subject in *God of Chance*, contends that there are "positive reasons for supposing that an element of pure chance would play a constructive role in creating a richer environment than would otherwise be possible."[47] It is this position that finds support in the research of Prigogine, Eigen, and their colleagues as previously mentioned, as well as in the investigations of Richard Dawkins, using his "biomorph" computer program.[48] Using this program, Dawkins generated patterns of branching lines ("biomorphs") that he produced by randomly changing a defined number of features in combination with reproduction and selection processes. After but a few "generations," or repetitions of the procedures, varied and intricate patterns emerged, demonstrating how the diversity and complexity of biological organisms might arise through the operation of principles similar to those of natural selection. Hence, combined with the lawlike structures, processes, and systems at the macroscopic level of the universe, the operation of chance at the microscopic level has promoted not only the kaleidoscopic array of life forms in the universe of which Earth is a part but also the event of biogenesis itself. As a result, scientists insist that the interplay of chance and law in the cosmos is not merely functional but is, in fact, creative!

TRENDS IN THE EVOLUTIONARY PROCESS

The history of nature, therefore, is "a nexus of evolving forms," dynamic in character and always in process.[49] Because of this, scientists have long questioned whether discernible trends are evident in the evolutionary process.

Stephen J. Gould suggests that "life is a copiously branching bush, continually pruned by the grim reaper of extinction, not a ladder of predictable progress."[50] In contrast, Teilhard de Chardin maintained that evolution has a precise orientation toward cerebralization and a privileged axis in humanity. All of the eons of inorganic and organic development preceding the advent of humanity, according to Teilhard, were preparatory for human appearance, and all evolution proceeding from the appearance of humanity moves forward through the evolution of human thought, noogenesis, to the Omega Point, the incorporation of the world into the Divine.[51] While rejecting the notion of strict directionality and predictability, Karl Popper nonetheless contends that "there exist weighted possibilities which are *more than mere* possibilities, but tendencies or propensities to become real."[52] As Peacocke noted, there has been a proclivity to see all evolution as tending teleologically toward humanity, in that the emergence of new forms appears over time in a hierarchy of organization and complexity. Nevertheless, such teleology is anthropocentric and unscientific. Research must assess cosmic and biological development by means of nonanthropological criteria that do not assume that humanity is the climax or the culmination of the process.

It is in this spirit that George G. Simpson reviews a number of "trends in biological evolution" in *The Meaning of Evolution*.[53] Rejecting a vitalist stance in evolution and adopting a materialist position, Simpson suggests that there are not one but many different sorts of progress in the evolutionary process. Simpson cautions, however, that the search for signs of "progress" in evolution is impeded by a number of factors, including the diverse histories of species, the difficulty of devising an acceptable and inclusive definition of progress, and the contradiction of progress by evidence of degeneration. Nevertheless, Simpson proposes a number of criteria by which to assess evolutionary tendencies and estimates humanity's status within each criterion.[54] These criteria include the increasing tendencies of organisms toward specialization, efficiency, and adaptability; toward complexity; toward consciousness of and adjustment to the environment; and toward emergent subjectivity.[55] To these characteristics, Peacocke added the ubiquity of pain, suffering, and death in the cosmos, an evolutionary tendency in which humanity itself holds an unparalleled status.

Specialization, Complexity, and Consciousness. According to Simpson, *increased specialization* in a species sharpens its adaptation to a particular environment but reduces its adaptability in other directions. In comparison with other species, humanity ranks low on this criterion, because human persons characteristically expand the range of their adaptability in order to cope with a variety of environments rather than narrowly adapting to a particular environ. According to Simpson, this proclivity in the human species sets it apart from other forms of life and, thus, is not an inclusive category by which to judge evolutionary progress. Moreover, the human person not only continually adapts to various environments but also attempts to control them.

In contrast to the trend toward specialization, the criterion of *increased complexity*, particularly on a structural basis, is pervasive in the evolutionary process from its earliest stages. It is evident on the structural level in the progress from single-celled to multicellular organisms and in the spread of life to new spheres. Nevertheless, once the structural level of multicellular organisms has been reached, scientists once again have found it difficult to measure complexity objectively. This has led to the suggestion that complexity may be better assessed through information theory according to levels of functioning or through ethological studies of behavior. In his work, Peacocke assessed complexity by the number of different components in the organizational system under study. According to Peacocke, the tendency toward complexity stems from the process by which systems optimize their self-organization with respect to locally defined fitness requirements by admitting components more favorable to their increase.[56] Nevertheless, lacking objective criteria, many other writers on the subject deem the association of increased complexity with the process of evolution to be self-evident. This is a perspective that gained impetus based on the work of Teilhard de Chardin in his development of the law of complexity-consciousness.

By means of the law of complexity-consciousness, Teilhard proposed that evolution proceeded in the direction of consciousness from the "infinitesimal to the immense" and from the simple to the complex. Scientific observation, he maintained, revealed that as molecules increased in complexity, they showed evidence of life, and as living organisms increased in complexity, they displayed consciousness. Ultimately, in Teilhardian terminology, the biosphere inexorably evolved into the noosphere.[57]

According to Simpson, if the variables of function, behavior, and consciousness became factors in the assessment of evolutionary trends for other scientists as they did for Teilhard, then the human person would surely qualify as the most complex of all creatures. These factors, moreover, figure prominently in the trend toward *increasing consciousness of and adjustment to the environment*. This trend in evolution associates with the increased capacity in organisms for more and different types of information gathering in order to develop methods for adjusting to their environments. The greater the capacity for recording, analysis, and prediction based on information gathered from its environment, the greater the organism's capacity for survival.

The Ubiquity of Pain, Death, and Suffering. Associated with the development of sensory organs and nervous systems, increasing sensitivity to environmental stimuli enables acute awareness of the environment, an awareness that includes an increase in the organism's ability to experience pain, the warning signal of danger and disease. This leads to the conclusion that the greater the level of consciousness, the greater the capacity for pain. Hence, although increased sentience and sensitivity have the capacity to heighten and accentuate an organism's control over and experience of the life-enhancing elements of the environment, it comes with the price of expanding and intensifying the organism's experience of pain and its psychological concomitant, suffering, as consciousness increases. Thus, consciousness of pain and suffering, as well as of pleasure and well-being, seems to be emergent in the cosmos and possess some element of survival value for creatures when experienced as goads to action.

In view of this, Simpson's survey of evolutionary trends must be supplemented by suggesting, as Peacocke did, that pain and suffering are also trends in biological evolution and represent a mixed endowment, as it were, for sentient creatures of the world. From a biological perspective, the function of pain, suffering, and, ultimately, death in the universe is a necessary condition for both the maintenance of and the transition to novel and emergent forms in evolutionary selection. Pain and suffering—to whatever extent the latter occurs in creatures at various levels of consciousness—enhance the possibilities for the survival of creatures faced with threats to their existence. Moreover, the emergence of new forms and patterns within a finite universe can occur only when the death of old forms and patterns makes way for them. As Peacocke observed,

> There is a kind of *structural* logic about the inevitability of living organisms dying and of preying on each other for we cannot conceive, in a lawful nonmagical universe, of any way whereby immense variety of developing, biological, structural complexity might appear, except by utilizing structures already existing, either by way of modification (as in biological evolution) or of incorporation (as in feeding).[58]

From an anthropological perspective, however, the impact of physical pain and death present in the whole of the natural order is amplified in the human order by profound recognition of personal vulnerability and by acute experiences of emotional suffering as consciousness broadens, heightens, and deepens into self-consciousness. Although experiences of pain, vulnerability, and suffering continue to serve the survival function of goading the human creature toward self-preserving responses to danger and disease, such experiences beset the human being with a profound sense of tragedy and angst unparalleled in the experience of other creatures. Although human persons may acknowledge that pain and death in the universe function as a transformative principle in the cosmos, they nonetheless find themselves often burdened by an overwhelming sense of meaninglessness and powerlessness in the face of its immensity and inexorability. Furthermore, such a scientific understanding of the presence and function of pain, suffering, and death in the cosmos emphasizes that these experiences have existed as the condition for the survival of individuals and of species long eons before the appearance of the human species in the cosmos. Hence, from a theological perspective, "the presence of pain and suffering cannot be the result of any particular human failings, though undoubtedly human beings experience them with a heightened sensitivity and, more than any other creatures, inflict them on each other and on other living creatures."[59]

Emergent Subjectivity and the Anthropic Principle. Despite the mixed consequences of increased consciousness in human beings from scientific, psychological, and theological standpoints, there is no question that, on Simpson's criterion of awareness and sensitivity to the environment, human beings reach an evolutionary height unrivaled by other species. In view of humanity's perceptual and reactive capacities, which Simpson considers "incomparably the best ever evolved,"[60] the human species is undoubtedly one cosmic form that is uniquely evolved both in kind and in degree. Hence, the inevitable question of evolutionary teleology surfaces anew. Has all evolution tended toward the arrival of *Homo sapiens?* Scientist-turned-philosopher Michael Polanyi insists, "It is the height of intellectual perversity to renounce, in the name of scientific objectivity, our position as the highest form of life on earth, and our own advent by a process of evolution as the most important problem of evolution."[61] Moreover, as previously discussed, Teilhard envisions all of evolution as preparatory for humanity. However, Simpson more conservatively concludes, "Not all the chances favoured [humanity's] appearance, none *might* have, but enough did."[62]

Scientific observations along these lines, coupled with observations of coincidences in the physical constants of the universe that are conducive to the emergence of the human person, have led scientists to the proposal of what has been termed the "anthropic principle" in biological evolution. Originally proposed in 1974 by Brandon Carter in his article "Large Number Coincidences and the Anthropic Principle in Cosmology,"[63] the anthropic principle suggests that humanity lives in a universe in which its physical constants are "finely tuned" to the emergence and existence of intelligent life.[64] If the values of such constants had been even slightly different within the process of evolution, the principle suggests, life as it now exists would probably not have emerged. Carter articulated this principle in both weak and strong forms. According to the weak anthropic principle, "we must be prepared to take account of the fact that our location in the universe is necessarily privileged to the extent of being compatible with our existence as observers."[65] In the strong form of the principle, Carter states "that the Universe (and hence the fundamental parameters on which it depends) must be such as to admit the creation of observers within it at some stage."[66] In 1986, physicists John Barrow and Frank Tipler more fully articulated and critiqued the forms of this principle in *The Anthropic Cosmological Principle*.[67] Barrow and Tipler state that, according to the weak anthropic principle, "The observed values of all physical and cosmological quantities are not equally probable but they take on values restricted by the requirement that there exist sites where carbon-based life can evolve and by the requirements that the Universe be old enough for it to have already done so."[68] In contrast, the strong anthropic principle contends that "The Universe must have those properties which allow life to develop within it at some stage in its history."[69]

In its weak form, the anthropic principle simply states the obvious: that any theory of the universe must be consistent with the presence of the human observer in this time and place within the universe. In its strong form, however, it clearly fosters the notion of "intelligent design," the assumption that a particular being, principle, or mechanism exists that purposefully set the parameters of the universe for the emergence of intelligent life. This strong form of the principle has been characterized by some such as Anglican bishop Hugh Montefiore and physicist John Polkinghorne as supporting a theistic interpretation of creation and its processes.[70] However, some scientists like chemist Peter W. Atkins suggest that it renders the notion of a deity unnecessary because it implies that the universe itself possessed the requisite conditions for the advent of intelligent life.[71] In contrast, others such as mathematician David Bartholomew contend that the principle is irrelevant to any argument concerning a divinely determined universe.[72] Moreover, scientific speculation concerning multiple universes and "theories of everything" associated with the weak anthropic principle muddy any real clarity concerning the impact of the anthropic principle in either form for ultimate understanding of the emergence of the human person.[73]

Despite the ambiguity of the anthropic principle concerning the place of the *Divine* in the cosmos, this principle decidedly functions to support the integral place of the *personal* in the universe. First, it supports the contention that the universe, through its own inherent processes of law and chance and from its own intrinsic "stuff," has generated a distinctively new entity, a *personal* entity, characterized by cognition, consciousness, and self-consciousness that is inextricably interlocked with the universe itself. Hence, "Far from man's presence in the universe being a curious and inexplicable surd, we find we are remarkably and intimately related to it on the basis of this contemporary scientific evidence which is 'indicative of a far greater degree of man's total involvement with the universe' than ever before envisaged."[74] In addition, the anthropic principle supports the proposal that this qualitatively new entity introduces a qualitatively new mode of causality, that of *personal* causality, that has its ground and genesis within the very matter, structures, and processes of the cosmos itself. Hence, the anthropic principle suggests that the presence of human persons with their mode of personal causality results from the inherent inbuilt constitution and potentiality of the physical universe itself and, therefore, that the ultimate source of a universe that produces such a personal entity and causality must be at least personal or suprapersonal in and of itself.

The Limits of Science

Despite the anthropic principle and, in fact, all the scientific insight that comprises the magnificent saga of the evolution of the universe, there remain some questions of intelligibility and meaning that are not amenable to or resolvable by scientific research and speculation. These are the "why" questions that press science to its experimental and experiential limits. They ask: " 'Why is there a universe at all?' 'Why should it be of this particular kind?' 'Why is it open to rational inquiry?' "[75] These questions frame the search for intelligibility and for explanation of the universe from the scientific perspective of inquiry; further questions involve a search for meaning in a cosmic existence fraught with and framed by the coincidence of opposites such as fecundity and extinction, pleasure and pain, ecstasy and anguish, life and death that the epic of evolution has revealed.

According to Peacocke, the search for meaning in the midst of such paradoxes is most frequently pursued on religious and theological paths. However, in this contemporary age, these religious and theological paths toward meaning cannot circumvent the scientific sphere of inquiry. Although science alone cannot answer why the universe evolved toward sentience, how the experience of human subjectivity arose, or what processes influenced the emergence of human personality, those who quest for meaning in human existence cannot ignore the indissoluble bond between humanity and the rest of the cosmos made intelligible by the sciences. Moreover, one cannot disregard the fact that it is human persons themselves who quest for scientific intelligibility and personal meaning. Thus, the scientific search for intelligibility and the theological quest for meaning must inevitably merge through questions posed about the cosmos in forms that integrally include the questioners themselves.

Summary

Clearly the data, understandings, and proposals advanced throughout this chapter illuminate and affect much contemporary theological reflection and discourse, including reflection and discourse on the nature, attributes, and purposes of God, the doctrine of creation, and the understandings of theological anthropology. In the present chapter, this study has taken a stance beyond mechanistic understandings of the origin and structure of the cosmos and has engaged the evolutionary, relativity, and quantum theories that have presented a different picture of entities and processes of the cosmos. Within its multifaceted discussion of evolutionary cosmology and biology, it has described a cosmos in the process of ongoing transformation and emergence of life that suggests not only an original but also an ongoing activity of God as Creator of life, an activity that is immanent in the creativity of the cosmos itself. It has depicted a cosmic creativity that operates through the mutual interaction of both law and chance and that exhibits a freedom and autonomy that affects notions of divine omnipotence and omniscience in relation to cosmic events. This is a self-creativity that evidently produces fecundity, complexity, and ultimately human subjectivity in its free and autonomous unfolding. Nevertheless, it also features an intrinsic indeterminacy that puts the orderly unfolding of cosmic purposes at risk and that generates experiences of pain, suffering, and death in ordinary and extraordinary circumstances of its history that have both positive and negative functions. The reality of such risk and of such deleterious experiences leads to novel inferences concerning the nature and purposes of God revealed through such a cosmos.

However, before exploring the theological inferences that flow from the observations and insights of evolutionary science, we must first engage the final principle that undergirds Peacocke's evolutionary theology. This is the principle that suggests that the self-disclosure of God in the world must be articulated in appropriate metaphors and models in order that the ineffable and incomprehensible mystery of God might become intelligible, expressible, fruitful, and efficacious in the life of the cosmos and of its creatures. Peacocke brought this principle to fruition in the epistemology and methodology that supported his evolutionary theology, the epistemology of critical realism and the methodology of inference-to-the-best-explanation. The next chapter details the elements of these approaches that Peacocke used to construct his evolutionary theology of the Being and Becoming of the Divine, a theology that in turn led to the affirmation of the creative suffering of the Triune God in, with, and under the creative processes of an evolving universe.

3

Knowing and Naming
in Theology and Science

In the epic of evolution that unfolds the understandings of science
concerning the nature and attributes of an emergent cosmos, Arthur
Peacocke concretized three of the fundamental principles that un-
dergirded his evolutionary theology toward the suffering of God. He
characterized the entities, structures, and processes of the cosmos
as the manifold means by which the Creator God discloses Godself
through the works of God's creation. In doing so, Peacocke moved
toward merging the insights of two disciplines, science and theology,
that many have customarily considered incongruent. According to
many commentators on these disciplines, science deals with finite,
immanent, and measurable realities, whereas theology concerns itself
with infinite, transcendent, and ineffable Reality. However, science
and theology need not be characterized as dealing with two separate
and unrelated realities or with one reality in two separate and unrelated ways. Rather, science and theology may be conceived as interacting and mutually illuminating approaches to the same reality
that continually modify each other. On the basis of this insight,
therefore, the present chapter now investigates key elements of this
interactive and mutually illuminative relationship between science
and theology. It does so in terms of an epistemological approach and
a methodological process that exemplify and enhance the connection
between these two disciplines. These are the epistemological stance
of critical realism and the methodological process of inference-to-the-
best-explanation. In keeping with Peacocke's fourth fundamental

principle—the principle that contends that the self-revelation of God through the cosmos must be articulated in terms of appropriate models and metaphors that yield efficacious ways of articulating the God-world relationship—this chapter now analyzes Arthur Peacocke's approach of critical, skeptical, and qualified realism, with its essential dependence on the use of models and metaphors both in scientific theory and in theological doctrine. As a consequence, it examines the understanding of the nature and status of theological language that flows from such critical realism and compares it with a classical understanding of theological language set forth by Thomas Aquinas in the *Summa Theologiae* and *Summa Contra Gentiles*.

Because this investigation proceeds from scientific insights concerning the evolving, yet finite, cosmos toward theological affirmations concerning the infinite Creator of that cosmos, an exploration of the nature and status of language as used in the scientific and theological disciplines is crucial. One cannot speak naïvely as if a one-to-one correspondence existed between the meaning of one's words and the realities to which they refer in the realms of either science or theology. However, neither can one speak instrumentally as if one's words were simply useful fictions bearing no intrinsic connection to their referent. Concerning both finite reality in science and Infinite Reality in theology, therefore, one must speak critically and somewhat skeptically, to use Peacocke's terms. In so doing, the scientist or the theologian strives to indicate clearly that the reality to which one refers truly exists. Furthermore, in employing certain concepts or models, the scientist or the theologian strives to signify as accurately as possible something akin to the entity to which each refers. Beyond this, the scientist and the theologian must accept that finite speech will ultimately fail to adequately express the mysteries of creation and its Creator. Thus, both the scientist and the theologian must employ imagistic language—the language of analogy, of models, and of metaphors—to begin to fathom the incomprehensible and articulate the inexpressible. In employing such imagistic language, the affirmations of science and theology concerning the cosmos and its Creator are necessarily and unavoidably informed and constrained by the spatial, temporal, and material constructs of finite experience. And so it is with the affirmations to be set forth here. Nevertheless, the constraints of scientific and theological language do not call for apophatic silence. Rather, they call for kataphatic humility born from the realization that, although the finite reality and Infinite Reality of which science and theology speak are essentially mysteries, they are, nonetheless, continually self-communicating and infinitely knowable.

The epistemological stance of critical realism leads not only to a particular understanding of theological language but also to a distinctive methodology, that of inference-to-the-best-explanation (IBE). Unless the scientist ascribes to naïve realism or the theologian to literalism, each must acknowledge that no one-to-one correspondence exists between reality—either finite or Infinite—and human comprehension of it. Essentially, all is mystery. If this is so, then absolute certainty about causality, about purpose, and about meaning in the scientific and theological realms is impossible. A scholarly tentativeness must imbue interpretations, extrapolations, and implications drawn from the observed and applied to the unobservable in the cosmos or in its Creator. Thus, as the name "inference-to-the-best-explanation" suggests, the methodology of IBE aims not at certainty but at intelligibility, not at finality but at fecundity, not at immutability but at emergence, with regard to its proposals. It is this methodology that I appropriate from Peacocke in order to move from evolutionary insights about cosmic creativity to affirmations concerning the Creator of the cosmos. Thus, in this chapter, I analyze both the process of IBE as described by Peacocke and the criteria that he employed to evaluate his inferences. On the basis of such analysis, I will define the methodology I intend to use in affirming the concept of the creative suffering of the Triune God. In addition, I will establish and explain my own set of criteria, gleaned from those of Peacocke and of other scholars, by which I intend to assess my proposals.

As suggested at the conclusion of the last chapter, the paradigm of evolutionary cosmology and biology influences the model of God and God-world relationship from which one's theological affirmations derive. According to Peacocke, the epistemology of critical realism and the methodology of IBE lead to the inference that the existence of the world is grounded in a Reality other than itself as the source of its existence. Based on this inference, a Christian perspective would characterize the cosmos as creation and the Reality that grounds its existence as the Creator God, the self-existent, self-disclosive Source, Sustenance, and Goal of all natural and human being and becoming. Clearly, critical elements of these inferences are reminiscent of classical Thomism recast in contemporary terms. When set in an evolutionary context, however, these principles do not lead to a model of God consistent with that of Thomistic theism. Rather, the inferences that stem from an evolutionary paradigm result in a departure from such theism, because theism places undue emphasis on God as transcendent Creator of the cosmos and attends insufficiently to God's immanent creativity within the evolutionary processes of the universe. The inadequacies of the classical theistic model within an evolutionary paradigm, however, do not necessarily lead to the model traditionally contrasted to theism, namely, pantheism, because pantheism tends too far toward emphasizing the immanence of God to the exclusion of divine transcendence. As a result, this investigation proceeds with Peacocke along what many theologians consider the via media between the two. In so doing, it infers that the model that furnishes the best explanation of the God-world relationship within an evolutionary context is not theism or pantheism but rather pan*en*theism, which, in broad terms, denotes that the Being of God includes and penetrates the whole universe but is not exhausted by the universe.

Clearly, the panentheistic model of God and God-world relationship implies a wholly different relationship between God and the cosmos than that of theism or pantheism. Rather than imaging a God who exists above the existential fray of anguish and death in eternal bliss or a God essentially identified with the movements of cosmic travail, the panentheistic model of the Triune God suggests relationships of mutuality, of intimacy, of vulnerability, and of self-offering between the Creator and creation. In such a model, the finite being of the cosmos finds its place within the infinite Being of the Triune God who bears within the divine life itself the evolving life of the cosmos, with all of its cosmic unity and diversity, simplicity and complexity, pleasure and pain, joy and suffering, and birth and death. In such a relationship, the life and grace of the Triune God encompasses and permeates the cosmos in all its parts, vivifying, inspiring, healing, liberating, and transforming. Thus the Triune God continuously offers the cosmos the opportunity to experience, enjoy, and develop through the presence and action of the Divine. However, this relationship is not one-sided. The mutuality, intimacy, vulnerability, and self-offering implicit in the panentheistic model of God-world relationship suggest that cosmic existence is fully present, known, and experienced by the Divine. Indeed, the Divine has cause for delight in the kaleidoscopic diversity, fecundity, and creativity of the cosmos in all its life-giving processes and forms. However, the Divine also has cause for empathy, for compassion, for lament, and for anguish in response to the staggering atrocities, unmitigated violence, incalculable destruction, and inexpressible terror rampant in the cosmos through the centuries. Mass destruction, nationalistic genocide, and terroristic suicide; global, urban, and domestic violence; poverty, starvation, and AIDS; racism, sexism, and classism; exploitation, devastation, and pollution of earth's ecosphere and atmosphere rend the heart of the God who is Love. Accordingly, the panentheistic model of God cannot but entail the affirmation that God suffers in, with, and under the entities, structures, and processes of the evolving cosmos. However, while the Triune God is not spared the travail of the cosmos in this model, neither is the Divine inextricably mired within its pain, suffering, and death. For within an evolutionary paradigm, the Triune God in relation to the cosmos seeks to move creation and its creatures toward newness of life and full flourishing, a contention demonstrable through images and metaphors that arise from female experiences of procreation and mothering.

How does this panentheistic model, this symbol of God, function in Christian theology?[1] First, it functions to disabuse Christians of the notion that God or the will of God is the source of cosmic, systemic, or personal suffering. Rather, Christians are drawn to recognize that, in addition to the Incarnate One, God in divine Triunity is the companion-sufferer who intimately understands and deeply participates in the plight and the pain of the afflicted. However, in so doing, this model does not function to eternalize or glorify suffering, as its critics often suggest, but to reveal that suffering in the cosmos and in its inhabitants grieves the Creator as it grieves the created. By sharing the suffering of the beloved creation, the Triune God demonstrates that suffering itself is not redemptive and salvific. Rather, it is the love, the creativity, and the infinite possibility within the Divine that is redemptive through freely offered grace and unconditional presence. This affirmation is rooted in both Christian theology and evolutionary science. It arises from the theological understanding that the Creator God both is immanent within suffering creation and at the same time infinitely transcends it. Moreover, it arises from the evolutionary insight that the Creator and creation do not remain mired in pain, suffering, and death but, in infinite creativity, continuously move toward transformation, liberation, and new life. In addition, because it is the cosmos in its entirety and not simply humanity that participates in the being, life, and creativity of the Divine in the panentheistic model, this model functions to inspire an ethics of care that is not only personal and communal but also ecological. As Christians grow to comprehend that God embraces and permeates not just human being but all of cosmic being, action for justice and liberation extends beyond all manner of abused and violated persons to all levels of the abused and violated cosmos itself. Finally, as conceptualized in female images of procreation and mothering, the panentheistic model of the God-world relationship emphasizes and celebrates the sacredness of female embodiment and expands Christian consciousness with viable and intelligible female images of the Divine to balance the male images of the Divine that predominate in the Christian tradition.

Therefore, in its final section, this chapter explores the elements of the panentheistic model. It compares the panentheistic model with theistic and pantheistic models that are philosophically and ontologically opposed to it. It also sketches the common elements that characterize most panentheistic perspectives and points out those elements that this study rejects. Ultimately, this final section indicates the unique capacity that the panentheistic paradigm possesses to support a theology of divine suffering. In so doing, it sets the stage for the appropriation of this panentheistic paradigm in the theological affirmation of the creative suffering of the Triune God.

Epistemology of Critical Realism

Commenting on the human search for intelligibility, purpose, and meaning in existence, Sir Francis Bacon in 1605 counseled, "Let no man, upon a weak conceit of sobriety or an ill-applied moderation, think or maintain, that a man can search too far or be too well studied in the book of God's word or in the book of God's works . . . only let men beware . . . that they do not unwisely mingle or confound these learnings together."[2] The true advancement of learning, however, has demonstrated that Bacon's separatist stance toward science and theology has not been sustainable. The Copernican revolution altered humanity's understanding of its significance in the universe. The discovery of the historical character of the earth's processes affected humanity's sense of its own history. The Darwinian understanding of evolution informed humanity of its natural place in the scheme and history of organic life. Through these and other revisionings, the paths of science and theology have invariably intersected in their quests for intelligibility and meaning. This intersection, however, has not always facilitated interaction between the two disciplines, as both scientists and theologians have maintained diverse philosophies on the relationship between their areas of study and discourse.

In his critical appraisal of the interaction between the scientific and theological disciplines, Robert J. Russell discussed a variety of typologies through which the relation of science and theology might be understood. He identified four dimensions on which this relationship has been differentiated: approaches, languages, attitudes, and objects.[3] Based on these dimensions, Peacocke delineated eight relations between science and theology: four that allow some form of engagement and four that maintain theoretical separation. Of the former approaches, science and theology may engage the same reality (1) in two distinct and noninteracting ways, (2) in mutually illuminative and interactive ways, (3) in an integrated approach toward consonance, or (4) in terms of a scientific metaphysic through which theology is then formulated. Conversely, science and theology may remain separated because (1) each concerns its own distinct realm, (2) each is subservient to and exclusively defined by its objects of study, (3) each is generated by different attitudes in their practitioners, or (4) each employs its own Wittgensteinian language system, thus allowing no communication.[4]

Despite this variety of viewpoints, Peacocke insisted that the scientific and theological disciplines share several common elements. Each discipline purports to deal with reality. Each seeks to provide intelligibility and order based on empirical and experiential data concerning reality. However, in this attempt, both confront realities that can be referred to but cannot be literally described.

Thus, both describe reality in terms of models that employ metaphorical language. Finally, both science and theology combine such metaphorical models into conceptual schemes, yielding theories and doctrines, respectively.

Although science and theology share these commonalities, they tend toward different outcomes and, hence, pose distinctive questions.[5] The outcome of the scientific quest arises from questions concerning the causal nexus of the natural world and pertains to prediction and control. In comparison, the outcome of the theological quest arises from mystery-of-existence questions beyond the nexus of the natural order and bears instead on personal meaning and moral purpose. Holding in balance both the commonalities and the differences between them, science and theology can be viewed neither as totally distinct and noninteracting nor as fully integrated in a movement toward consonance. However, on the same basis, science and theology need not—and must not in the contemporary age—remain separated and incommunicado. Thus, the commonalities in the scientific and theological enterprises dictate an approach to reality that is interactive and mutually illuminative, whereas the distinctive aims of each dictate careful examination of their common elements and judicious application of their theoretical outcomes. Therefore, this chapter now examines these commonalities and differences in order to demonstrate the extent to which science and theology share epistemological and methodological approaches that are mutually illuminative and legitimately applicable to each respective discipline.

Critical Realism

CRITICAL REALISM IN SCIENCE

In her description of the standard account of the structure of scientific theory that dominated the discipline from the 1920s to the 1970s, Mary Hesse suggests that this structure, though continually refined and developed, was based on three assumptions: the presupposition of naïve realism, a universal scientific language, and the correspondence theory of truth. As Hesse explains,

> These three assumptions between them constitute a picture of science and the world somewhat as follows: there is an external world which can in principle be exhaustively described in scientific language. The scientist, as both observer and language-user, can capture the external facts of the world in propositions that are true if they correspond to the facts and false if they do not. Science is ideally a linguistic system in which true propositions are in one-to-one relation

to facts, including facts that are not directly observed because they involve hidden entities or properties, or past events or far distant events. These hidden events are described in theories, and theories can be inferred from observation, that is, the hidden explanatory mechanism of the world can be discovered from what is open to observations. Man as scientist is regarded as standing apart from the world and able to experiment and theorize about it objectively and dispassionately.[6]

The notions of objective experimentation and of dispassionate observation by scientists who stand apart from the world have clearly been challenged by discoveries in quantum physics and molecular biology. Moreover, the observational conditions on which scientific theories are based, such as the categories of time, space, and causality, have been subject to revision or even replacement in view of these recent discoveries. Hence, as Hesse asserts, in the latter part of the twentieth century, "almost every assumption underlying this account [of the standard view of the structure of scientific theory] has been subjected to damaging criticism."[7] This criticism of the structure of scientific theory received major impetus when, in 1962, Thomas S. Kuhn proposed that the history of science was characterized not by undisturbed consistency and continuity of ever more certain knowledge but by a series of iconoclastic paradigm shifts.[8] According to Kuhn, there have indeed been periods in the history of science in which widely accepted paradigms are employed, exemplified, and applied. However, revolutions in scientific discovery and thought—for example, those concerning microscopic levels of reality—have punctuated this history and have resulted in irreversible change to prevailing paradigms. Thus, under the influence of Kuhn's work, the last quarter of the twentieth century saw the demise of the standard view of scientific theory described by Hesse, as advances in quantum and molecular science effectively dismantled most of its underlying assumptions. In accord with this deconstruction, several alternative perspectives on scientific theory and language have developed.

The socially contextualized Weltanschauung (worldview) understanding of scientific theory characterized science as a continuous social enterprise in which the development, advancement, and replacement of scientific concepts and theories involved a complex of personal, social, intellectual, and cultural variables, influences, and interactions that determined the acceptability of a theory. This understanding suggested that scientists construct their theories according to their prevailing worldviews and, therefore, these theories are comprehensible only to those who understand the relevant worldview. Although the socially contextualized view of theory accounted for the influence of historical and sociological factors in scientific knowledge, it depended on a particularly complex and elusive entity—the worldview of the scientist—that becomes all the more complex when involving the scientific community as a whole. As a result of this complication, two other understandings emerged, the sociology of scientific knowledge and a form of scientific realism contoured by the critiques of naïve realism advanced over three decades.[9]

According to Michael Mulkay, a proponent of the sociology of scientific knowledge, one cannot assess claims of scientific knowledge according to any immutable or universal criteria. Rather, "it seems that scientific knowledge is not stable in meaning, not independent of social context and not certified by the application of generally agreed procedures of verification."[10] This perspective, of course, excludes any claim by science—or, for that matter, by theology—that it is a way to deal with and understand reality per se. Those who are critical of the sociological approach to science counter its conclusions by pointing to the fact that progressive testing and critique by the scientific community tend to filter out social or personal influences that might distort scientific claims. In addition, success in prediction and control arising from scientific outcomes suggests that experimental manipulation of the physical world yields rational and foreseeable results. Thus, in response to the antirealist and antirationalist position of the sociological understanding of scientific knowledge, the approach of scientific realism arose, claiming to ground its proposals in historical and contemporary scientific practice.[11]

The essential features of the scientific realist position relate closely to the philosophical problem of the nature of truth. According to Ian Barbour, Western thought identifies three main views of truth: the correspondence view, the coherence view, and the pragmatic view. The correspondence view, which Barbour correlates with naïve or classical realism, indicates that a proposition is true if it corresponds to reality. The coherence view, which Barbour associates with rationalists and philosophical idealists, indicates that a proposition is true if it is comprehensive and internally coherent. Finally, the pragmatic view of truth, which assesses a formulation by its consequences, indicates that a proposition is true if it works in practice. Concerning realism of any kind, Barbour simply notes that basic to any such position is the assumption that *existence* is prior to *theorizing*.[12] Peacocke considered the understanding of scientific realism articulated by Ernan McMullin to be the best expression of the essentials of his epistemological position. According to McMullin,

> The basic claim made by scientific realism ... is that the long-term
> success of a scientific theory gives reason to believe that something
> like the entities and structures postulated in the theory actually exist.

> There are four important qualifications built into this: (1) the theory
> must be a successful one over a significant period; (2) the explanatory
> success of the theory gives some reason, though not a conclusive
> warrant, to believe; (3) what is believed is that the theoretical struc-
> tures are *something like* the structures of the real; (4) no claim is made
> for a special, more basic privileged, form of existence for the postu-
> lated entities.[13]

Commenting on McMullin's rather tempered statement, Jarrett Leplin asserts
that, fundamentally, scientific realism is "a quite limited claim which purports
to explain why certain ways of proceeding in science have worked out as well as
they (contingently) did."[14] Although McMullin himself concedes that his statement is to some extent vague, he insists that such qualifications are essential to
a defensible realist position that acknowledges the discontinuities in the history
of science and opens itself to the emergence of new thought. Hence, as Joseph
Bracken summarizes,

> whereas classical realism assumes that models and theories are literal
> descriptions of extramental reality and whereas instrumentalism re-
> gards models as simply instruments for the correlation and predic-
> tion of observations within experience, critical realism claims "that
> there are entities in the world something like those postulated in the
> models."[15]

According to Peacocke, this "critical" (Ian Barbour and later Peacocke), "skeptical and qualified" (early Peacocke), or "conjectural" (Karl Popper) realism is a
defensible epistemological position for both science and theology. It is this
stance of critical realism, Peacocke argued, that working scientists adopt as they
propose and regard their scientific theories and models as "candidates for
reality."[16] In so doing, these scientists admit the limits of scientific and philosophical language to definitively or exhaustively describe the attributes of the
reality under their consideration. However, their models and hypotheses aim to
depict previously concealed or unknown structures and processes of the world
in terms and features genuinely intended to approximate and refer to reality
itself.[17]

Despite this intended aim, proponents of critical realism harbor no illu-
sions about the permanence of their proposals and wholly acknowledge the
range of conditions and qualifications that accompany any attribution of truth
to them. Rather than being concerned by the conditional status of their formulations or by the ongoing problem of translating scientific terms in the wake
of subsequent paradigm shifts (i.e., the problem of "incommensurability"),

critical realists maintain confidence in the capacity of their proposed scientific theories to reference reality validly. This conviction is based first on the continual historical reference of particular scientific terms and entities that are employed in a continuous linguistic community. Second, this continuity is augmented by the "experimental argument for realism," through which previously postulated entities are used successfully as tools for subsequent scientific experimentation and explanation.[18] This experimental argument for realism is not about theories but about "*entities*, whose existence is affirmed by discerning causal lines."[19] Third, the attributes of these entities are articulated in terms of models and metaphors that are more fluid and inclusive than strictly scientific or philosophical terminology. Thus, critical realists are able to refer imagistically to realities that cannot literally or definitively be described.[20]

Despite Peacocke's claims for its defensibility, critical realism is not without its critics. In response to Peacocke's presentation of critical realism in *Intimations of Reality*, Nancey Murphy suggests that, although critical realism may not be faulted if it is advanced solely to counter the errors of naïve realism or instrumentalism, because of its attempt to give a single account of the status of theoretical terms, it is nonetheless vulnerable to counterproposals concerning how language is tied to the world.[21] In later discussions about questions of epistemology, however, Murphy is more pointed in contending that critical realism continues to rely on and represent modernist thought processes when postmodernist categories are needed in contemporary science. According to Murphy, this modernist leaning is evident in the implicit influence that naïve realism continues to exert on a revised critical realism in its attempts to provide incontestable grounds for belief, in its tendency to utilize representational thinking and correspondence theory of truth, and in its inclination to foster an excessive individualism that inadequately considers the scientific community. In contrast, Murphy herself proposes a holistic, nonfoundational epistemology that is adequately attentive to the philosophical concept of language and that emphasizes the impact of context on the interpretation of meaning.[22] However, in her desire to remove any taint of naïve realism from its critical alternative, Murphy's postmodernist leaning tends toward an instrumentalist, socially constructed view of scientific knowledge, a view that rejects the possibility that scientific language has authentic reference in objective reality. Moreover, while the early Murphy questioned whether the qualified language of critical realism weakens its referential capacity to the point of vagueness or vacuity, her later socially contextualized proposal effectively does so itself, as it relegates scientific claims to the role of useful fictions about the indeterminately real.

Dealing explicitly with the ambiguities implied by Nancey Murphy, Philip Hefner pointedly suggests that claiming to be critical does not mean that one has "successfully avoided naiveté" and that asserting realism does not mean that the "relativity and the frustrations of ideological projection have been vanquished." Casting himself as "co-interrogator" with Peacocke on the issue of critical realism, Hefner contends that, although critical realism is often presented as an established theory of explanation, it is in fact no more than a "suggestive hypothesis that is struggling for credibility in the marketplace of ideas."[23] In point, Hefner remains unconvinced by McMullin's assertion that "something like" scientifically postulated entities and structures actually exist, as well as by Peacocke's proposal that such postulates may be considered as "candidates for reality." His particular argument questions the status of models and metaphorical language in the articulation of scientific knowledge and maintains that although such models may in fact contain an element of truth, they ought not contend for the classification of "real." Furthermore, Hefner, like Murphy, criticizes Peacocke's seeming disregard for the insights of the sociology of knowledge, while simultaneously asserting the influence of the continuous scientific community to address the problem of incommensurability.

At the heart of Hefner's critique, however, is his contention that "no amount of philosophical or linguistic sophistication will ever remove the need for that leap of faith" that is required for the assertion of reality in either science or theology. Citing Peacocke's assurance that "we can trust our minds and experience and we can intimate that something like what they tell us is a candidate for reality," Hefner contends that Peacocke's critical realism provides no real basis on which to ground such trust. Rather, Hefner claims, Peacocke actually provides "considerable evidence for discrepancy" instead of consonance. Hence, although "most human reflection, of all sorts, rests on the hope that Peacocke's confidence in realism is true . . . the adequate argument for that realism has not been made," according to Hefner, "and it is not at all clear that the current position that is named 'critical realism' will provide that argument."[24]

Hefner no doubt reads Peacocke correctly when he questions, "Hasn't Peacocke admitted as a premise that there is no way that we can confidently know or assert that either the entities referred to in scientific concepts or the God referred to by theologians really exists?" However, one suspects that even those who ascribe to naïve realism's correspondence theory of truth must ultimately acknowledge that their confidence finds itself supported more by hermeneutical preference than by invariant, demonstrable, and indisputable reality. In his proposal of critical realism, Peacocke simply exposed the foundation on which any true assertion of realism, naïve or critical, rests—the foundation of observation and experience, repeated over time, and subject to varied interpretations. As Peacocke suggested in his discussion of his experimental argument for realism, "Because of experimentation, the degree of attribution of reality to such postulated entities can change from doubt about their existence, through thinking that to postulate their existence affords successful explanation, to an assured confidence in their existence through knowing how to *use* them."[25] Thus, the critical realist understands that "there are surely innumerable entities and processes that humans will never know about. Perhaps there are many that in principle we can never know about. *Reality is bigger than us.* The best kinds of evidence for the reality of a postulated or inferred entity is that we can begin to...understand its causal powers,"[26] to engage its existence, to risk its appearance, to reverence its mystery, and then to articulate one's experience of it. Hence, the aim of reference in critical realism is not to describe "real" objects as much as it is to depict patterns of relationships that illuminate the attributes of the entities involved, even as the patterns themselves transcend those relationships. Furthermore, in addition to one's individual repeated experiences of engagement with reality, the critical realist understands that what further establishes reality of reference in science is "the social chain in a continuous linguistic community that could anchor our present usage . . . in the original introducing event."[27] Hence, the critical realist makes no claim to argue for realism per se—only for the way in which reality is to be approached and understood—critically, experientially, relationally, and reverently.

CRITICAL REALISM IN THEOLOGY

Despite the fact that critical realism has demonstrated its applicability for theological method and discourse to interdisciplinary thinkers such as Peacocke, Barbour, Bracken, and McFague, others like Vitor Westhelle question whether critical realism can bear the epistemological burden of theology. If theology is characterized by a sense of ultimacy, Westhelle asks, does it not have peculiar epistemological problems? According to Westhelle,

> The ultimate implies an epistemological break, a rupture with a given way to pursue an explanation. . . . A plausible case for an explanation other than the one provided by the sciences . . . is to recognize that the limits of the world as we know it to be are also the limits of the explanations that account for its being as science finds it to be.[28]

Nevertheless, Westhelle's critique seems to hinge on the Kantian notion of the great epistemological gulf fixed between the Creator and creation and between Divinity and humanity that precludes the possibility of knowledge and understanding. Peacocke's perspective, however, rests on the understanding that creation is revelatory of the Creator, that the observable and knowable are the disclosures of a self-communicating God. Although knowledge is never infallible and the inferences and postulates made concerning God are never considered to be other than partial and inadequate, they nevertheless provide humanity the means to say something about the Reality that is the ground and source of all other reality in the universe.

In view of this discussion, the epistemology of critical realism arguably provides a viable context not only for scientific discourse but also for theological discourse. It does so by addressing the difficulties identified both in alternative theories of scientific knowledge and in the status of theological doctrines. By acknowledging the necessity of employing metaphorical language to depict the nature of reality, critical realism rejects the stance of naïve realism and theological fundamentalism, which emphasize propositional language and a correspondence theory of truth. Moreover, by affirming that such language nonetheless intends to signify "something like" the entities and structures that actually exist, critical realism also counters the opposing stance of instrumentalism or ethical utilitarianism, in which models and metaphors are merely useful fictions and not signs of a deeper reality. Furthermore, by maintaining that its formulations have actual, albeit indefinable, reference, critical realism tempers extreme sociological or mythological interpretations of knowledge with their insistence on a socially constructed view of reality and their rejection of extramental reality.

Hence, by demonstrating its capacity to acknowledge and yet articulate the mystery inherent in the realm of nature with which *science* is concerned, critical realism has demonstrated its potential to approach and yet articulate the Ultimate Mystery at the source of the cosmos with which *theology* is concerned. Indeed, as Wentzel van Huyssteen points out in *Theology and the Justification of Faith*, a critical theological realism would recognize and acknowledge the relativistic, contextual, and metaphorical dimensions of human speech that permeate the discourse of theology and science alike.[29] This conditional status notwithstanding, like statements derived from critical scientific realism, assertions grounded in a critical theological realism purport to refer to the real, indeed, "to a Reality beyond and greater than ours."[30] Furthermore, like comparable scientific assertions, theological assertions refer to Ultimate Reality while maintaining the essential incomprehensibility and ineffability of the Goal of their references. Finally, by explicitly acknowledging the imagistic nature of its language and constructs, a critical theological realism, like its scientific counterpart, affirms that theological concepts and models are not only partial and inadequate but also necessary and indispensable as ways of referring to God and the God-world relationship. In so doing, a critical theological realism has the potential to foster an enterprise of constructive thought and an expansion of models and metaphors concerning the mystery of the Divine, an expansion clearly dictated by the critical realist position and by the demands of faith in a changing and challenging world.[31]

Of Models and Metaphors

MODELS IN SCIENCE

Throughout the discussion of critical realism in science and theology, I made frequent reference to the use of models and metaphors as the conceptual apparatus of scientific theory and theological doctrine. When used in theory and doctrine, a model is not to be regarded as "a literal picture of reality, yet neither should it be treated as a useful fiction. Models are partial and inadequate ways of imagining what is not observable. They are symbolic representations, for particular purposes, of aspects of reality which are not directly accessible to us."[32] They are, in the terminology of Harré suggested earlier, "candidates for reality," because "they make tentative ontological claims that there are entities in the world something like those postulated in the models."[33] Because of this, many scientists and theologians consider models—and the metaphors they generate—essential and permanent features of the discourse of their disciplines. As constructive and imaginative expressions of reality, models reflect networks of relationships, structures, and processes in the world, thus fostering discovery and opening the unintelligible to intelligibility. According to Janet Soskice, models and "metaphors are allowable, their vagueness valuable, and their relational structure useful to theoretical accounts . . . [since] one can refer to the little understood features of the natural world without laying claim to an unrevisable description of them."[34]

Focusing on the use of models in science, Ian Barbour defines a model as "a systematic analogy postulated between a phenomenon whose laws are already known and one under investigation."[35] This definition suggests that for a scientific model to be effective, there must exist an analogy or similarity between the source (the basis of the model) and the subject (the referent of the model), in order that characteristics may be "read off" from the source and predicated of the subject. The analogy between source and subject must be structural as well as systematic. It must pertain to the basic processes or laws of the source and the subject, and it must be suggestive of relationships or interactions intrinsic to the subject that are otherwise not readily apparent. In this way, the model may be used to explain existing laws and structures, as well as to uncover unknown relationships and processes.

According to Ernan McMullin, a good model serves as a fruitful and open-ended source of continuing ideas for expansion and adaptation and offers provisional indications toward the investigation of new domains.[36] Peacocke agreed:

> Not only does a good model allow logical inferences to be made about possible phenomena not already part of its original explanandum, but it functions rather like a metaphor does in language by throwing light forward . . . into new areas of investigation and raising previously unformulable questions about those new domains.[37]

In fact, metaphors invariably arise when one speaks on the basis of models, because the models themselves "generate metaphorical terms that suggest an explanatory network."[38] Peacocke himself pointed to the model of the "computer" as applied to the brain. Based on the model, metaphorical terms such as *input, output, information processing, feedback,* and even *wired* suggest themselves as ways of speaking about brain function that are consistent with the prevailing model. As noted by Barbour, however, models, although useful candidates for reality, are not literal. Because the realities they seek to illuminate often defy or transcend the explanatory capacity of even theoretical language, all models have a certain inadequacy. Nevertheless, their inadequacy serves both as an inherent safeguard against any interpretations derived from naïve realism and as an intrinsic and open invitation to expand existing models and devise alternative models.[39]

Despite the inherent conditionality of models, McMullin nonetheless insists that a model "gives insight into real structures."[40] In response, some scholars such as Philip Hefner question in what sense scientific theories based on analogy and expressed in models can provide such insight or be considered candidates for reality. Although Hefner acknowledges that the analogical statement may possibly be revelatory of truth, he wonders how scientists operating from anything other than a stance of naïve realism can speak in terms of reality. However, others such as N. R. Campbell and Janet Soskice contend that such analogies are not merely superfluous concepts that add style but no substance to theoretical constructs. Rather, analogies are integral to the scientific enterprise in their unique capacity to refer to, illustrate, and illuminate real relationships, processes, and entities otherwise indefinable. According to Campbell, "analogies . . . are utterly essential to theory,"[41] to which Soskice adds, "the model or analogue forms the living part of the theory, the cutting edge of its projective capacity and hence, for explanatory and predictive purposes, is indispensable."[42]

Hence, constructing a scientific theory is fundamentally a matter of conceiving a proper analogy, in terms of an adequate model, which is then the source of appropriate metaphors. In response to those like Hefner who call for grounds on which one might believe that referents of science are in fact real, one must acknowledge that scientists have made a variety of different judgments about the status of models in science. Peacocke characterized the range of these responses as extending from a "low" to a "high" view of models in terms of their usefulness and their ontological status. In the "low" view, the scientist understands models as useful, but of passing importance, and has no commitment concerning the model's relation to reality. For Peacocke, this understanding is associated with a positivist or instrumentalist "as if" view of scientific realism. At the "high" end of the range are those scientists like Campbell, Barbour, McFague, Soskice, and Peacocke himself who consider models to be essential and permanent features of science and who are committed to investing models with a genuine, albeit partial, ontological status. Such a status would suggest that the model discloses "the way things are" and does so to a greater or lesser degree, depending on its success in prediction and control and—one might add—contingent on its consistency with observation and experience. This understanding of models is in harmony with the critical realist epistemology and leads to Peacocke's assertion that, in view of "our experimental limitations and conceptual resources," we must be satisfied in science with candidates for reality that are "as close as we can approach to the reality."[43] Moreover, the condition for this satisfaction entails what Peacocke termed an "acceptance of revisability" in scientific models and metaphors, in that scientists go on "seeking to explore a world only partially and imperfectly understood—and whose ultimate reality is bound to be elusive since we ourselves are structures in the selfsame world we study."[44]

MODELS IN THEOLOGY

If, with all caution and restriction, models are nevertheless considered to be indispensable to the scientific quest for intelligibility concerning the realities of the natural world, how much more ought their use be so considered in the theological quest for intelligibility concerning transcendent Reality! According to Peacocke, while theological concepts and models must, like those of science, be regarded as partial and inadequate, they nonetheless represent the "necessary and, indeed, the only ways of referring to the reality that is named as 'God' and to God's relation with humanity" that are available to human persons.[45] As indicated by Ian Barbour in *Myths, Models and Paradigms*, by Sallie McFague in *Metaphorical Theology*, and even by Thomas Aquinas in *Summa Contra Gentiles*,[46] the theological enterprise makes wide use of the conceptual constructs of analogy, model, and metaphor to refer to the realities of God and of the God-world relationship that are beyond knowing *in se*. These constructs include various descriptions of God as father, creator, sovereign, or king; of Jesus as

Christ, messiah, second Adam, or redeemer; and of the Holy Spirit as ghost, comforter, advocate, or paraclete. They reference the God-world relationship as monarchical, organic, or emanationist, or as that of father to son, mother to child, lord to servant, hen to chick, or lover to beloved. They conceptualize notions such as transcendence and immanence or ransom, substitution, and redemption. In countless ways, all exemplify the dependence of theology on analogy, model, and metaphor in its attempt to articulate its understanding of Ultimate Reality *in se* and in relation to the cosmos. Moreover, from a critical realist stance, such analogies, models, and metaphors in theology, as in science, have ontological status, at least as candidates for reality. Thus, theologian Joseph Bracken, who identifies himself with critical realism, maintains that "without claiming to have a definition or exact description of the divine being, one should be entitled to say that with a given model of God one is making an ontological claim, however tentative, about the reality of God even apart from human experience."[47]

Therefore, from a critical realist viewpoint, models in theology share several conceptual similarities with models in science. Both scientific and theological models are analogical or metaphorical in nature and not explicitly descriptive. Models in each discipline are understood as candidates for reality with a degree of ontological status; however, these candidates are and must continue to be revisable. Moreover, models in both science and theology are less concerned with picturing objects than with depicting processes, relations, and structures, in that both matter in itself and God *in se* are essentially unknown and unknowable. Furthermore, both science and theology advance their models within the context of communities that possess living traditions of reference extending back to originating observations and experiences and forward into emergent and unpredictable futures. Within their respective communities, both scientific and theological traditions have developed and will continue to develop appropriate language and authentic symbols to maintain a continuity of intelligibility with each advancing era.[48]

Despite these similarities, significant differences exist between the function of models in theology and science. Models and metaphors in theology are more comprehensive in their scope and in their roles than are models and metaphors in science. As Sallie McFague observes, "the broadest type of theological model [the metaphysical model of the God-cosmos-human relationship] . . . is without limit and hence unfalsifiable. This is the root-metaphor or original model."[49] Other comparably foundational models, such as God as Trinity, generate similarly pervasive metaphors, such as Creator, Redeemer, and Sanctifier, that occupy a place at the summit of a hierarchy of models and metaphors that explicate the Christian experience. Moreover, models in religious traditions have a strong affective function that evokes emotion, inspires involvement, and stirs the will to commitment. Because of this, Thomas Fawcett suggests that models in science are "observer" models that explain, represent, and predict, in contrast to which models in theology are "participator" models that "enable us to think of the cosmos in such a way that man as a personal being is able to see himself as a fitting part of the whole . . . [and] that the cosmos is perceived as personal."[50] Although Fawcett's distinction tends to diminish the cognitive function of theological models, the religious culture itself invests theological models not only with evocative and illuminative value but also with explanatory power with regard to Ultimate Reality. Believers take such models to depict reality. As Janet Soskice indicates, "Typically Christians respond to models of their religious tradition not because they take them to be elegant and compelling . . . but because they believe them in some way to depict states and relations of a transcendent kind."[51] Nevertheless, the very reality believers seek to depict or to comprehend is, in *its* reality, incomprehensible, ineffable, and inexplicable *in se.* "*Ex hypothesi,*" Peacocke pointed out, "God as transcendent is beyond all explicit depiction whether by language or by visual image."[52]

If this is indeed the case, how can theologians respond to the necessity to show that theological propositions and models actually do refer to and, to some extent, depict reality? If such models are unable to demonstrate their referential capacity, then the use of models in theology "makes any assertion of the ultimate truth or falsehood of that belief logically impossible. Creation, incarnation, the Spirit all become mental notions to be accepted, rejected, or modified according simply to their usefulness."[53] To respond to this dilemma, one may return to Peacocke's criteria by which to judge the referential capacity of scientific models: the notion of contemporary causal experience and the linguistic social chain. The attribution of reality to an entity is supported and strengthened through experimentation in which that entity operates as a cause and its causal power is understood. Extending this argument to theology, Peacocke suggested that persons over time have continued to assert their experiences of God and to affirm that the one whom "men call God," to use the words of Thomas Aquinas, is that one who "causes" particular experiences to occur in oneself, in others, and in the universe.[54] In parallel to the scientific method, the more recurrent and widespread the experiences reported, the more secure the reference and the more assured the reality to which is referred. If one wishes to contest the validity of this array of individual experiences, then one still has recourse to more universal grounds for reference, such as the cosmological argument for the existence of God of Thomas Aquinas: motion, causality, contingency, degree, and design.[55]

Reservations exist, however, concerning this experimental approach to the reality of God and to language for God based on religious experience. These cautions arise from the theological insights of George Lindbeck and Edward Schillebeeckx among others. In his cultural-linguistic theological approach set forth in *The Nature of Doctrine*, Lindbeck contends that language and custom within a tradition tend to shape personal and communal reality and to evoke personal and communal experiences unlikely to arise gratuitously. Thus, Lindbeck regards religions as "comprehensive interpretive schemes . . . which structure human experience and understanding of life and world."[56] Although the experiential-expressivist approach that Lindbeck also describes would grant greater autonomy to unforeseen or unfathomable events, Edward Schillebeeckx in his turn maintains that the act of interpretation is intrinsic to one's very awareness of an event; hence, there is no such thing as uninterpreted experience.[57]

> Religious faith is human life in the world, but experienced as an encounter and in this respect as a disclosure of God . . . it is the *particular way* in which religious men in fact *experience* the events of their life. Here the experience influences the interpretation and calls it forth, but at the same time the interpretation influences the experience.[58]

Thus, to use terminology drawn from the scientific method, in the experimental argument for realism as applied to theology, one cannot determine or control all the variables that affect the outcome of the experiment. Both Lindbeck and Schillebeeckx, therefore, would caution that prior reference to God within a theological tradition clearly influences the likelihood that subsequent experiences would be causally referred to Divine Reality. While acknowledging the influence of society and culture, either civil or religious, on how one interprets one's experience of Reality, the critical realist approach that I have adopted here suggests that it is just such influences that have caused the rejection of a *naïve* realist approach, with its supposition of correspondence between reference and truth, in favor of a *critical* realist approach. The admitted influence of societal or cultural factors notwithstanding, critical realism continues to maintain that "something like" what one experiences and what one references does in fact exist.

In her contribution, Soskice references the Thomist designation of God as that Ultimate Reality who is the source and cause of all that is. This designation links God causally both to the world and to the human experience of it. According to Soskice, it is this referent that may claim primacy among others and that could well serve as the root metaphor that most closely depicts the reality of God. Having set forth this possibility, however, Soskice goes on to declare,

"To be a [critical] realist about the referent is to be a fallibilist about knowledge of the referent. . . . So the theist may be mistaken in his beliefs *about* the source and cause of all . . . for fixing a referent does not on this account guarantee that the referent meets a particular description."[59] This statement provokes Hefner to retort,

> Is it not utterly necessary that there be at least one statement about the nature of language and at least one statement about the referent that are *not* fallibilist, in order for the realist claims in any of its forms to make sense? . . . If the human mind can be said to have reliably ascertained that there is a God, then more than fallibilist knowledge about God is within that mind's grasp. Contrariwise, if the human mind can indeed gain only fallible knowledge about God (or about any other referent), then the claim, that God exists is also just as fallible as any other knowledge.[60]

From the critical realist stance, the human mind is finite; thus, the insights it grasps and the thoughts it formulates are fallible. Furthermore, there can be no doubt that a finite mind is incapable of infallible knowledge of the Infinite, though a critical realist would concede the possibility of fallible knowledge. Mystery—both immanent and transcendent—confronts the seeker of the essential and the real. Ultimately, if the Essential and the Real who is sought is God, then as Augustine himself cautioned, "If you think you have understood," that you have more than *fallibilist* knowledge, "then what you have understood is not God."[61]

Hence, it is wise for those who would speak of God to keep in mind the distinction between referring to God and describing God—a distinction that is crucial to the theological critical realist position. Aquinas emphasizes this distinction in the *Summa Theologiae*:

> [It] is evident that words relate to the meaning of things signified through the medium of the intellectual conception. It follows therefore that we can give a name to anything in as far as we can understand it. Now . . . we cannot see the essence of God; but we know God from creatures as their principle. . . . In this way therefore He can be named by us from creatures, yet not so that the name which signifies Him expresses the divine essence in itself.[62]

This distinction between referring to God and describing God is undeniably the meeting point of the apophatic and kataphatic traditions in their approach to the mystery of God, the intersection of the *via negativa* and the *via affirmativa* on the journey toward the *via eminentia* of what one may affirm about God. For, as Aquinas maintains,

> [No] name belongs to God in the same sense that it belongs to creatures; . . . no name is predicated univocally of God and creatures. Neither, on the other hand, are names applied to God and creatures in a purely equivocal sense. . . . Therefore it must be said that these names are said of God and creatures in an analogous sense, that is, according to proportion. For in analogies the idea is not, as it is in univocals, one and the same; yet it is not totally diverse as in equivocals; but the name which is thus used in a multiple sense signifies various proportions to some one thing.[63]

However, recognizing the analogous nature of language about God need not leave one speechless concerning the mystery "in whom we live and move and have our being."[64] Aquinas clearly maintains that one may predicate names substantially of God,[65] apply names to God in a literal sense,[66] and form affirmative propositions concerning God.[67] Moreover, such predications rate as candidates for reality in Aquinas's schema and possess varying degrees of ontological status, depending on whether they are attributed metaphorically or essentially to God.[68] Hence, mindful of the ever-present danger of creating God in humanity's image,[69] one may legitimately refer to God in models and metaphors drawn from cosmic events and human experiences. Though contingent and partial and dependent on the grace of divine self-disclosure, such affirmations nevertheless refer with varying degrees of ontological appropriateness. It is far more misleading for theologians to say nothing about God in the face of such Mystery than to modestly attempt to say something, however conditional and inadequate. Thus, those who would speak must do so judiciously, on the basis of authentic, repeated, and considered experiences, in an analogous way with the use of models and metaphors and with full awareness of their inadequacy and fallibility, in order that what is spoken may not be mistaken as naïvely or unrevisably conclusive.

Concerning the second basis on which to judge the referential capacity of theological language, the linguistic social chain, the existence of the continuous community represents an interpretive tradition that provides links to referential usage and experiences grounded in the "seminal initiating experiences of individuals and communities."[70] Awareness of these initiating experiences—with the models and metaphors they inspired—is preserved within the continuous community and affords a context in which additional or alternative experiences and references may find tests for assent and acceptance, such as ecumenicity, antiquity, and consent.[71] Although such experiences and references may commend revised models arising from reflection and reinterpretation, the community's assent and acceptance ensure that the revised models and metaphors cohere with and refer to the same reality to which earlier ones did. Thus, those individuals or communities who acquire authority by virtue of their presence at the initiating events, by their intellectual preeminence, or by their personal integrity become resources, "guides to bring harmony to the cacophony of voices that claim to speak of that reality which is God."[72]

A note of caution in conclusion: While one hopes for a complementarity between references of God mediated by the continuous community and those direct and no less real experiences occurring in the lives of particular individuals and groups, rigid structures, intransigent attitudes, and emotional resistance often confront paradigmatic shifts in theological and religious traditions. Although a critical realist reminder concerning the status of language in theology cautions that models and metaphors always imply simultaneously that "this is and is *not* like that," symbol systems in religious traditions, with their presumptive emotional, evocative, and explanatory power, prove to be highly resistant to revisions. Although the continuous religious and theological community can affirm the consistency of ongoing experiences within established paradigms of reference, the analogical and metaphorical nature of these very paradigms is often overlooked. This may prove to be the true challenge to the critical realist position in theology: the challenge of balancing the reformability, conditionality, and inclusivity of theological affirmations grounded in critical realism with the stability, indisputability, and uniqueness of theological references and affirmations characteristic of doctrinal and dogmatic religious traditions.

The Methodology of Inference to the Best Explanation

In response to critiques concerning the applicability and the explanatory potential of a critical realist epistemology for questions of God and of the God-world relationship, Peacocke, in *Theology for a Scientific Age*, laid out a methodology that he contends maintained the centrality both of religious tradition and of individual and communal religious experience. Peacocke's proposed methodology would allow for a hierarchy of truths, for gradations in levels of belief, and for the human incapacity to express in language the nature of that Ultimate Being called God.[73] However, because his critical realist epistemology can at best offer theology candidates for reality with greater or lesser ontological status, to what degree can any such formulation be considered explanatory for the purposes of theology? Moreover, in that Peacocke himself was wary of any explanatory approach that implied God is one causal entity within the causal nexus of natural events, then how was he to propose to make sense of the realities that both theology and science approach and to affirm that it is indeed God whom one encounters within the experiences of these realities? Without resorting to causal attribution, Peacocke suggested that identifying any experience within the natural order as an encounter with God is most credibly done through the process of "inference to the best explanation" (IBE) of an event or experience.[74] This process unfolds by applying "criteria of reasonableness" to affirmations disclosed through the cosmos as creation and through ongoing religious experiences. Might it not be more useful to theology, Peacocke questioned, to conceive not simply of "explanation" but also, more broadly, of "intelligibility," as "that which renders intelligible"? This concept, Peacocke insisted, is more amenable to the types of questions and answers with which theology deals, namely, the questions and answers of God and the God-world relationship that cannot be resolved by natural causal explanations.[75]

If it is God who has given the world the kind of being that it manifests, then, Peacocke contended, creation must be considered revelatory of God's nature and purpose. This presumption follows from the analogous application of a causal theory of reference to the relationship between God and the cosmos. In such a causal theory of reference, the referent of a term in a theory, in this case God, is that which causes particular effects or observable phenomena, in this case creation.[76] By observing and reflecting on a particular aspect of creation in dialogue with a theological tradition, one is able to refer, however partially and inadequately, to the reality of the Divine in nature, in attributes, and in purpose. Aquinas's own application of this analogy proceeds to a similar conclusion concerning the cause-and-effect relationship, that attributes of a cause, such as its nature or its purpose, can be discerned from its effects. As he writes in *Summa Contra Gentiles,*

> Effects that fall short of their causes do not agree with them in name
> and nature. Yet, some likeness must be found between them, since
> it belongs to the nature of an action that an agent produce its like,
> since each thing acts according as it is in act. The form of an effect,
> therefore, is certainly found in some measure in a transcending
> cause.[77]

Moreover, "When the existence of a cause is demonstrated from an effect, this effect takes the place of the definition of the cause in proof of the cause's existence. This is especially the case in regard to God."[78]

However, the quest for referents, especially in theology, has been hazardous.[79] Moreover, as Soskice indicated, "To be a realist about the referent is to be a fallibilist about knowledge of the referent . . . the theist may be mistaken in his beliefs *about* the source and cause of all."[80] Furthermore, the choice of the most appropriate model of reference often depends on the nature of the experiences to which it applies.[81] Hence, to be a critical realist about the reality of God is to acknowledge the fallibility of all language and claims concerning God. So, if one were to use the method of inference to the best explanation as Peacocke encouraged, how is one to test the validity of one's beliefs about the source and cause of all?

In response to such a question, Sallie McFague in *Models of God* insists "there is . . . no way behind our constructions to test them for their correspondence with the reality they presume to represent."[82] While affirming such a statement, one may still apply the IBE method of validation proposed by critical theological realism. In keeping with the reality of reference afforded by the linguistic social chain in critical realism, the IBE method always proceeds in dialogue with the traditions of a continuous community. Nevertheless, because of cultural-linguistic influence or its interpretive tradition, such a community may function to limit the range of models proposed of the referent. Therefore, if the process is to occur in a communal context per se, it must be a community that is open to the guidance of the *sensus fidelium* and willing to join in a movement toward collegiality. Rather than authority based on antiquity, authority "would have to be authenticated intersubjectively to the point of consensus by inference to the best explanation" while remaining open to the development of new ideas as human knowledge and experience expand and deepen.[83]

Thus, in response to Russell's question concerning the outcome that theology hopes to attain in its use of a critical realist or inferential approach—convergence, predictive success, or the like—the outcome of inference to the best explanation is neither that of total consistency with a linguistic chain, nor that of scientific control, but that of essential "reasonableness" within the context of the data obtained and the framework employed. Throughout the process of IBE, the individual or the community must continually apply particular criteria to proposals to test the reasonableness of their claims. Drawn from a variety of writers on the topic, Peacocke set forth several criteria of reasonableness appropriate for assessing proposals within the domain of theology. These include fit with data, internal coherence, general cogency, comprehensiveness, fruitfulness, simplicity, and meaningfulness.[84] In his work, Ian Barbour identifies four criteria based on scientific research: agreement with data, coherence, scope, and fertility.[85] These criteria suggested by Peacocke and Barbour also resonate with Sallie McFague's more poetically expressed claim that

> with any construction, the most one can do is to "live within" it,
> testing its disclosive power, its ability to address and cope with the

most pressing issues of one's day, its comprehensiveness and coherence, its potential for dealing with anomalies, and so forth. Theological constructions are "houses" to live in for a while, with windows partly open and doors ajar.[86]

When a proposal meets the particular criteria of reasonableness selected and set forth by a particular individual or community, when a proposal "houses" its community of origin hospitably and without constraint, it becomes an acceptable affirmation concerning God and the God-world relationship, though never finally beyond revision or revocation.

For this study, I have selected four criteria by which to evaluate its theoretical foundations and its theological proposals. These criteria are (1) fit with data, (2) simplicity, (3) fecundity, and (4) pastoral efficacy. The *data* with which its foundations and proposals must *fit* are threefold. The first are the broad features of the entities, structures, and processes characteristic of the evolving cosmos. Second, the proposal must resonate with the fundamental insights of the Christian theological tradition. Third, the insights must be consonant with the panentheistic paradigm of the God-world relationship. This study assesses the *simplicity* of a proposal by the directness and clarity of its expression, its freedom from circumlocution and convolution that serve to evade the logical consequence of an experience or of its inference. The *fecundity* of a proposal requires that it have generativity and a vitality about it that can foster new ideas and creative responses regarding God and the God-world relationship. Finally, its practical implications must extend beyond ethical praxis to possess *pastoral efficacy*. This study judges such pastoral effectiveness by a proposal's capacity to inspire, transform, revitalize, and liberate human persons and the universe as a whole in ways that promote the full flourishing of all manner of being in the midst of a suffering world.

Epistemology, Methodology, and Models of God

In view of the epistemology and methodology that this study employs and based on the evolutionary paradigm that it affirms, what theological models and metaphors might one propose that contribute to the aims of the investigation? While the case has been made throughout this chapter that a number of elements in the epistemology and methodology reviewed resonate with classical Thomism, the evolutionary lens through which this study views the created order suggests an alternative model to theism, that of panentheism, for imaging both the Creator of an evolving cosmos and the relationship of such a cosmos to its Creator. As an alternative to classical theism, the proposed model of panentheism is capable of provoking as iconoclastic a shift in theological paradigms of reference to God as that provoked in scientific paradigms of reference to the cosmos by the theory of evolution itself. This shift in paradigms prompted by an evolutionary approach to theology necessitates new criteria on which to judge the theological viability and pastoral efficacy of proposals based on its principles—criteria such as fit with data, simplicity, fecundity, and pastoral efficacy consistent with an evolutionary paradigm of God and the God-world relationship as previously proposed, rather than on centuries of religious and theological tradition established within a classical paradigm of God without real relation to the world. Consequently, the efficacy of theological proposals based on this relational and dynamic model may depend less on their capacity to elucidate truths that are irreformable and infallible than on their ability to foster relationships that energize, inspire, and transform, and less on their continuity with established explanations and conventional categories than on their capacity to propose new insights and to offer greater intelligibility concerning God and the God-world relationship to a world often numbed by suffering, confusion, and doubt.

The Panentheistic Model of the God-World Relationship

Based on biblical, philosophical, and theological insights, various scholars have explored the characteristics and implications of an array of images and models of God that have expressed Christian belief and experience throughout the centuries. Broadly conceived, these analyses reflect the philosophical paradigms of deism, theism, pantheism, and panentheism. *Deism* refers to the belief that God created a law-abiding universe that God then left to run on its own. This paradigm stresses the unequivocal transcendence of God and allows no interaction or involvement between God and the world. Its philosophical converse is *pantheism.* This paradigm identifies God with the totality of nature, with the laws of nature, or as the world soul inherent in nature. In contrast to deism, this paradigm stresses the immanence of God in the universe, a universe that God in no way transcends. *Theism* is the view that God is a personal and purposeful eternal being that both transcends the world and yet is immanent within it. Although this paradigm incorporates both the transcendent and immanent aspects of the divine nature, in its classical form it contends that while God causally affects and transforms the universe, the universe cannot affect God, who remains immutable and impassible. Moreover, although the universe relates to God, God bears no real relation to the world.[87] Finally, the paradigm of *panentheism* is defined as "the belief that the Being of God includes and penetrates the whole universe, so that every part of it exists in Him but (as against pantheism) that His Being is more than, and is not exhausted by, the universe."[88] This seeks to balance the aspects of divine transcendence and divine immanence and to maintain the ontological distinction between Creator and creature, while yet envisioning a God-world relationship in which God both affects and is affected by the world.[89]

Panentheism therefore represents a via media between classical theism, with its inordinate emphasis on the transcendence of God with regard to the cosmos, and pantheism, with its excessive identification of God with the cosmos. Thus, Curtis Thompson suggests that, as a middle way, panentheism

> affirms, on the one hand, with pantheism, that God is so immanent within the world that this divine interpenetration means that all things are within God, while, on the other hand, affirming, with traditional theism, that God transcends the realm of finite realities.[90]

Furthermore, as regards the ontological distinction between God and the universe insisted upon by Christian theology, panentheism maintains that "everything finite must somehow be contained within the infinite reality of God and be sustained by the divine power of being *even as it retains its own existence as a subsistent finite reality.*"[91]

For Peacocke, neither classical theism nor classical pantheism truly corresponded to the God of Christian belief revealed in the life, ministry, and paschal mystery of Jesus the Christ. According to Peacocke, "For Christians, Jesus the Christ constituted a radical revision, *the* most radical revision, of human ideas about God."[92] With the Doctrinal Commission of the Church of England, Peacocke maintained that Jesus the Christ, "by his suffering, death and resurrection . . . significantly enlarges the range of human experience which can be 'read' as testimony to the love and power of God; and in his teaching he offers new 'models' of understanding which go far beyond what was available before."[93] Hence, "panentheism is not a new position but a new appreciation of the proper conceptual structure of a dominant tradition of religious faith in God," a tradition that seeks to hold in balance both the transcendence and immanence of God in relation to the world.[94]

The frequent identification of panentheism with the metaphysical system of process thought has limited the consideration given to this paradigm by Christian scholars who do not espouse process theology. Nevertheless, one cannot legitimately discuss the paradigm of panentheism without due attention to this theological perspective because process theology has demonstrated its capacity to adequately address many of the critiques of classical deism, theism, and pantheism discussed previously. Its affirmation of human freedom, time, history, and nature calls human persons to be active participants in the continuing work of God in the universe. Its understanding of evil and sin as products of human freedom and insecurity and as distortions of divine purposes rejects the tendency of humanity to blame God for suffering and evil and allows God to be "the fellow-sufferer who understands" in Whitehead's oft-quoted phrase. Moreover, with regard to issues of inequity in imagery for God, process theology ascribes both masculine and feminine attributes to God and fosters relations of participation and cooperation rather than of hierarchical dualism. Anthropocentrism is mitigated as humanity takes its place within the community of life in which all creatures are intrinsically valuable and all creatures are respected. Finally, process theology is highly responsive to the insights of the evolutionary and quantum sciences in its recognition of both order and openness in nature and its affirmation of an unfinished and continually created universe. Despite its highly philosophical language, its inability to undergird the expectation for absolute victory of God over evil in history, and its reformulation of divine nature and power, process theology is consistent with the Christian God disclosed in Jesus the Christ, a God who is creative, redemptive, and pervasive in the cosmos, luring it toward harmony and enrichment.[95]

Although this study affirms and even demonstrates the validity of several of its conclusions, process theology's foundational proposition of dipolar theism restricts its applicability to the present study that desires to advance its claims within the tradition of Christian Trinitarian monotheism. In keeping with this tradition, this study maintains the ontological distinction between creation and its Creator. Furthermore, it contends that the Christian affirmation of God as Trinity is a fruitful and necessary foundation for any formulation of the capacity of the Divine to enter into, engage, and transform the suffering of the cosmos that has theological viability. Moreover, the concept of the Trinity enables this study to propose and discriminate among a variety of ways in which the God of Christianity involves Godself receptively and responsively in the events of the cosmos. In so doing, it hopes to enhance the pastoral efficacy of its proposals.

However, even as theologies that espouse the panentheistic paradigm differ in the interpretations of God and the God-world relationship that they draw from it, definitions and descriptions of the paradigm of panentheism itself differ among its proponents. In his ostensibly thick review of the "quiet revolution" of the turn to panentheism in modern theology, Michael Brierley lists more than seventy theologians, philosophers, and movements associated with panentheism. Because of this scope of adherents and because of the phenomenon among scholars of distinguishing different types of panentheism on the basis of what he calls "the ambiguity of 'in,'" Brierley suggests that eight different themes define the common ground on which those who identify themselves as panentheists take their stance. I will situate Peacocke's position within each of the eight themes to distill the similarities and differences between Brierley's and Peacocke's understandings of panentheism to better delineate the parameters of my project.[96]

Based on eight facets of language identified by Brierley that effectively explicate the "in" of panentheism, eight identifiable themes emerge: (1) the cosmos as God's body, (2) language of "in and through," (3) the cosmos as sacrament, (4) language of inextricable intertwining, (5) God's dependence on the cosmos, (6) the intrinsic, positive value of the cosmos, (7) divine passibility, and (8) degree Christology. The theme of the *cosmos as the body of God* in Brierley reflects the understanding of theologians such as Sallie McFague and Grace Jantzen.[97] The attraction of the concept, Brierley suggests, lies in its capacity to distinguish, yet not separate, God from the cosmos; to accommodate both the transcendence and immanence of God; and to express a relationship of asymmetrical interdependence. Its liabilities attend on the analogy of mind to body on which it is based. Peacocke rejected the concept of the cosmos as divine embodiment, because conceiving the cosmos as a "part" of God reduces God to the same ontological order as the cosmos. Although Peacocke held a model of personal agency for God's action in the world based on the same personhood/body analogy that grounds Brierley's theme, he qualified his conception by asserting, "We are not implying the 'world is God's body' nor that God is 'a person.'"[98] While panentheism conceives of the world "in" God, God is more than the world. Thus, fundamental ontological differences such as necessary and contingent, eternal and limited in duration, infinite and finite, and moral perfection and concupiscence remain.[99]

Concerning the *language "in and through,"* Brierley notes that this language implies both the immanence and the transcendence of the actor within the action. He further indicates that Peacocke is noteworthy in his use of such language. Peacocke used the triad "in, with, and under" to refer to the action of God in relation to the cosmos, a triad used by Luther to describe Christ's sacramental presence in the Eucharist. Brierley contends that this phrase is but a variation of "in and through" language and expresses the link between an agent and an instrument without identifying the two. Thus, Peacocke's sense of the sacramental quality of the universe makes him a prime exemplar of the third panentheistic theme, the *cosmos as sacrament.* As sacrament, the cosmos is that through, "in, with, and under" which God comes and discloses Godself.

For Peacocke, however, it was one notion to suggest that God is present through, "in, with, and under" the cosmos and its processes and quite another to affirm that God is *inextricably and interdependently intertwined* with the cosmos, such that there is distinction but no separation. The resonance of this theme with the prior theme of the cosmos as God's body and with the following theme of *God's dependence on the cosmos* marks further points of departure between Peacocke's understanding of the panentheistic relationship and that of Brierley. Because the three themes theoretically interrelate and mutually depend on one another, to dismiss any one is to substantially weaken the others. Peacocke understands the fundamental definition of panentheism as maintaining God's causal independence from the universe, such that God alone is necessary Being. In this, Peacocke found his common ground not with Brierley but with theologians like John Macquarrie who assert that "it is a misuse of language to say that it is necessary for [God] to create," in that such language implies coercion or limits on God's free and creative will. Peacocke and Macquarrie, like Augustine, contend that God freely creates, because to act freely is to act within the constraints of perfect love and within one's ultimate nature.[100]

Brierley's sixth theme suggests that as God is good, the cosmos through, "in, with, and under" which God continually creates and discloses Godself is good and has *intrinsic, positive value*. Although Brierley hinges this affirmation on the cosmos as the body of God, Peacocke affirmed the intrinsic value of the cosmos on the basis of the creative love and sheer delight with which God continuously creates, beholds, and sustains the cosmos. Furthermore, if the basis for the intrinsic value of the cosmos remains in the context of the cosmos as God's body, then the question of cosmic suffering and evil inevitably arise. This question moved Peacocke to contest the affirmation of process theology that all events find their place in the consequent nature of God, which persuades Philip Clayton to hold that the cosmos is not intrinsically valuable but is essentially neutral.[101] Unless one holds the Augustinian and Thomistic view that the nature of evil is the privation of good, the suffering and evil that exist in the cosmos as the body of God are inextricably part of the Being of God. However, holding this view, then one may suggest that God works through, "in, with, and under" the natural good in the universe to bring it to fullness of life.

In whatever way one conceives it, the presence of evil in the cosmos begs the question of how the God of panentheism responds to the presence of evil and to the suffering that attends it. According to Brierley, the nature of God as love and the fact of divine embodiment imply that God suffers through, "in, with, and under" the being of the cosmos. With many of the contemporary theologians who affirm *divine passibility*, Brierley supports this position by asserting that the nature of authentic love is to suffer with the beloved. Furthermore, divine embodiment implies that when one's "body" suffers, one's "person" suffers as well. Peacocke certainly accepted the former proposition, without, however, conceding the second. He instead maintained that if the body of the cosmos is within the Being of God, then God must surely know in a real and intimate way the suffering of the beings within, "including those events that constitute the evil intentions of human beings and their implementation." As Peacocke reasoned, "When the natural world, with all its suffering, is panentheistically conceived of as 'in God,' it follows that the evils of pain, suffering, and death in the world are internal to God's own self." This is so not because the cosmos is the embodiment of God, but because God envelops the cosmos as God's own, rather than relating to it from "outside."[102] Moreover, if God truly knows all that it is possible to know, as Peacocke defined omniscience, then this knowledge cannot be limited to merely intellectual knowledge but must include affective knowledge as well. Thus, on whatever basis panentheists espouse this theme, the passibility of God is one of the core affirmations resulting from this paradigm.

The final theme delineated in Brierley's common ground is the concept of *degree Christology*. According to Brierley, to hold a panentheistic model of God is to regard Christ as distinctive by *degree* from other persons, rather than by kind. Following the line of thought developed throughout this section that God is in the cosmos and the cosmos is in God, then consistency demands that God's embodiment in Christ be continuous with that cosmic activity. Peacocke wholeheartedly agreed.

> When we reflect on the significance of what the early witnesses re-
> ported as their experience of Jesus the Christ, we have found ourselves
> implicitly emphasizing both the *continuity* of Jesus with the rest of
> humanity, and so with the rest of nature with which *homo sapiens*
> evolved; and, at the same time, the *discontinuity* constituted by what is
> distinctive in his relation to God . . . in him there has appeared a new
> mode of human existence which, by virtue of its openness to God, is
> a new revelation of both God and humanity.[103]

Having figured Peacocke's panentheism against the ground provided by Brierley, how does the *gestalt* of Peacocke's position map out? Although spatial and locative models of the God-world relationship are inadequate by nature and by definition, Peacocke found it helpful to summarize his panentheistic system by concluding that "there is no 'place outside' the infinite God in which what is created could exist. God creates all-that-is *within* Godself."[104] According to Peacocke, a particularly fruitful model for communicating this reality stems from the way in which mammalian females bear and nurture new life within themselves. This insight will receive greater attention and expansion in the last chapter of this book, but it bears mention here that an imaginative shift from prevailing male images of divine creation to female images of procreation addresses many of the ontological critiques of panentheistic models of the

God-world relationship. Advanced by scientist-theologians such as John Polkinghorne and based on ontology of substance, these critiques find the panentheistic model suspect because of the possibility that it may compromise the substantial transcendence and distinction of God in relation to the cosmos. Nevertheless, based on an ontology of relationality and subjectivity, the female procreative model maintains distinctions on the basis of relation and of subject rather than of substance, the relation between the mother as transcendent subject and the autonomous subject within her.[105] Moreover, such reimagination may ameliorate many of the body-of-God panentheistic conceptualizations that come dangerously close to trading on classical mind-body and spirit-body dualisms in their analogies of the God-world relationship.

Elaborating the viability of the panentheistic model in terms of female procreativity, Elizabeth Johnson writes:

> To be so structured that you have room inside yourself for another
> to dwell is quintessentially a female experience. To have another ac-
> tually living and moving and having being in yourself is likewise the
> province of women. . . . This reality is the paradigm without equal
> for the panentheistic notion of the coinherence of God and the world.
> To see the world dwelling in God is to play variation on the theme
> of women's bodiliness and experience of pregnancy, labor and giving
> birth . . . as suitable metaphor for the divine.[106]

Only the female of the species can bear within herself "an other" with whom she is intimately and reciprocally related; "an other" who is essentially free, distinct, and autonomous subject; "an other" within whom her life and spirit are immanent, and yet beyond whom her life and being are transcendent; "an other" in whose struggle for life she passionately participates in anxious waiting, in anguished cries, and in exultation as a new creation bursts forth. As applied to the God-world relationship, in the divine womb, "God, according to panentheism, creates a world other than Godself and 'within herself.'"[107] Such is an insight worth exploring and nurturing to model panentheistically the creativity and suffering of the Triune God "in, with, and under" the dynamism of the evolving universe.

Summary

Guided by the four fundamental principles that undergird Arthur Peacocke's evolutionary theology, we have explored the scientific understandings of creation that Peacocke conceived as the self-revelation of the nature, attributes, and purposes of its Creator and the epistemology and methodology through which this self-revelation may be articulated in theologically viable and efficacious language. Having done so, we are now primed to engage the implications of these elements for the nature, attributes, and purposes of the Triune God, especially as they relate to the ubiquity of suffering in the cosmos. The epistemology of critical realism and the methodology of inference-to-the-best-explanation discussed in this chapter contribute in three ways. First, they set forth the understanding of the nature of and the connection between the finite reality of creation and the Infinite Reality of its Creator. Second, they set the parameters concerning the capacity of language to make affirmations about God and suffering on the basis of evolutionary insights. Third, they discuss the criteria under which the proposals of this book may be evaluated and appropriated within a tradition such as that of Christianity.

In addition to their theoretical contribution to this undertaking, critical realism and IBE lead to a critical and integral theological shift. This is the shift from the classical theistic model of God to a panentheistic model of God in which God and the cosmos are ontologically distinguished on the basis of subjectivity and relation, rather than substance. This shift is made necessary by the interaction and mutual illumination of both Christian theology and evolutionary science. Hence, if the interaction and mutual illumination of Christian theology and evolutionary science demand that the Triune God be conceived as simultaneously transcendent and immanent in relation to the cosmos, then the viability of any model of God and God-world relationship depends on its capacity to express this balance with imagistic clarity and consistency. As classically conceived in model and metaphor, neither theism nor pantheism has proven to maintain this balance. Hence, in terms of the God-world relationship affirmed by this investigation, only the panentheistic model adequately represents the transcendence-in-immanence and the immanence-in-transcendence characteristic of the Creator God of the evolving cosmos. Based on these understandings, this study now moves to an examination of Peacocke's proposals concerning the transcendent, incarnate, and immanent God in panentheistic relation to the cosmos.

4

Divine Being and Becoming

Informed by the insights of evolutionary science, by the epistemology of critical realism, and by the method of inference to the best-explanation, we reach a decisive moment in our theological enterprise. We now begin investigating the extent to which the perspective on the world given by evolutionary cosmology and biology might, from a critical realist standpoint, affect the concepts, models, and images of the Christian theological tradition as regards the creative suffering of the Triune God. In his own quest to explore the influence of evolutionary science on Christian theology, Arthur Peacocke began by dividing his evolutionary insights concerning the cosmos into "what is there," that is, the "being" of the cosmos, and "what is going on," that is, the "becoming" of the cosmos. According to Peacocke, this distinction between the being and becoming of the cosmos, arising as it does from the scientific perspective, impels philosophers of religion, as well as the religious believer, "to reckon with their one God's relation to a continuously developing world," which implies, in turn, "a continuously changing relation of God to the world, including persons, and to the further possibility that God is not unchanging in certain respects."[1] Hence, two things are clear from Peacocke's perspective. The first is that one cannot separate one's understandings of the nature and attributes of Godself from the way in which God interacts with the world as conceived by the natural sciences. The second is that the influence of the natural sciences inevitably leads to a change in the classical understanding of the attributes of the Divine, especially as concerns the attribute of immutability and, as a consequence, impassibility.

Peacocke expanded his understanding of the distinction between the being and becoming of the cosmos by proposing an analogous distinction in the nature, attributes, and purposes of God. He suggested that one consider God not solely in terms of Divine Being, who God is in Godself, but also in terms of Divine Becoming, how God acts and expresses the divine purposes in the cosmos.[2] In this affirmation of Divine Being and Divine Becoming, the evidence and insights from evolutionary cosmology and biology come to theological fruition to support an understanding of a transcendent Ground of Being who immanently participates in the becoming of the cosmos. In so doing, God in Divine Being and Becoming embraces and pervades both the multiformity and the cruciformity of the cosmos, the abundant diversity and the ubiquity of pain, suffering, and death. Nevertheless, as the cosmos itself reveals, in the movement toward the multiformity that takes place through cruciformity, unity in diversity endures, new life emerges, and vitality prevails. These insights of evolutionary theology within the context of the panentheistic paradigm of God-world relationship support the affirmation of the concept of the creative suffering of the Triune God in the midst of the travail of the cosmos.

This chapter traces Peacocke's understanding of Divine Being and Becoming in dialogue with the distinction between the being and the becoming of the cosmos. The first stage of this unfolding considers God in Divine Being and explores the attributes and purposes of God inferable from "what is there" in the cosmos. These inferences suggest that the essential nature and attributes of God include God as Ground of all being and as Sustainer of the cosmos; as unity-in-diversity and as supreme rationality; as Continuous Creator and as personal and purposive. The second stage explores Peacocke's proposals concerning the Divine Becoming of God inferable from "what is going on" in the cosmos. These inferences reveal an understanding of God's immanent participation in the world: as taking joy and delight in creation and as source of chance within law; as self-limited in omnipotence and omniscience and as temporally related to the cosmos; and as vulnerable in self-emptying love and as suffering in, with, and under the creative processes of the cosmos. Ultimately, through our examination of the Divine Being and Becoming of God, this chapter approaches the threshold of affirming the theoretical, theological, and pastoral validity of the notion of the creative suffering of the Triune God in, with, and under this suffering world.

The Divine Being of God

Introduction

Focused on "what is there" in the being of the cosmos, Arthur Peacocke unfolded his understanding of the nature and attributes of the Divine Being of God. According to Peacocke, "what is there" in cosmic "being" concerns the entities and structures of the cosmos that are largely observable, generally unchangeable, and highly lawlike. Based on scientific observations of such cosmic "being," which is contingent and owes its existence to a Being beyond its own finitude, Peacocke inferred that the Divine Being of God is the transcendent Ground of the entities, structures, and processes intrinsic to the universe. These contingent entities, structures, and processes display both a remarkable unity and a fecund diversity, suggesting that the source of such unity and diversity must be both essentially one and yet unfathomably rich in Being. The inherent order and regularity of these structures demonstrate the supreme rationality that underlies such cosmic properties, the rationality of the God who is the Creative Ground of an orderly universe. The persistence of such order in the midst of a constantly changing universe moreover implies that God acts not only as Creator but also as Sustainer and Faithful Preserver of the cosmos throughout the passage of time. Nevertheless, within this order and regularity, scientists have observed a remarkable dynamism through which new entities and structures appear in the course of time. Because of this phenomenon, God must be conceived not only as original Creator, Faithful Preserver, and Sustainer but also as Continuous Creator of the cosmos. Such continuous creativity in the cosmos leads to the most remarkable observation that science makes concerning the being of the cosmos, namely, that from the very stuff and the very processes of the cosmos has emerged the human person, an entity of unparalleled complexity, reflective consciousness, irreducible subjectivity, and unfettered freedom. Hence, God, the continuously creative Source of such a personal being, must be at least personal or suprapersonal in nature and, on analogy with created personal beings, must have and express divine purposes through self-revelatory creative acts.

God as Ground of Being

Peacocke began unfolding his consideration of Divine Being with the overarching notion of God as the Ground of all Being.[3] He contended that the human person is engaged in two types of searches in relation to the cosmos of which humanity is an integral part. The first search is the quest for intelligibility concerning the cosmos, phrased in terms of the questions, "Why is there anything at all?" or "Why does the world exist?" or, further, "Is there a reason for the existence of the world?" This quest for intelligibility leads in turn to the quest for meaning in personal and in cosmic existence. This is a quest that has been intensified by the revelations of twentieth-century science, which indicate that the universe is of such a type that it has the capacity to generate from its cosmic stuff and from its innate processes the selfsame persons who seek its meaning. This intensification leads to a merging of the quests for intelligibility and meaning, which produces more complex questions. These questions include "What is the intelligible meaning of a cosmos in which the primeval assembly of fundamental particles has eventually manifested the potentiality of becoming organized in forms which are conscious and self-conscious . . . human and personal and in their very thinking transcend that out of which they emerged?" Or, pushing it further, "If we continue to press for 'explanation' and to search for 'meaning,' does not the very continuity of the universe, with its gradual elaboration of its potentialities . . . to the emergence of human persons . . . imply that any categories of 'explanation' and 'meaning' must at least *include* the personal?" For Peacocke, the nature of these questions implies that a response about the source of explanation and meaning in the universe could be adequate only if that source both subsumed and transcended the physical and personal categories for which it gives explanation and meaning. Hence, "This is nothing else than to assert that the source and meaning of all-that-is is other than the world, transcends the world and is least misleadingly described in supra-personal terms. In English, the concept of 'God' has served to name this transcendent source and meaning—that is, the doctrine of creation is a response to both searches."[4]

It is this concept of God that Peacocke considered an indispensable response to the mystery-of-existence question from a theological perspective and a respectable response to the mystery-of-existence question in the face of the limits of scientific research and explanation. Despite its vast accomplishments, science inevitably encounters limits in its quest for an ultimate explanation for particular aspects of cosmic existence. These ineffable aspects include the contingency of the cosmos and its entities; the lawfulness of its processes from the macrolevel to the quantum level; the presence of the quantum field that underwent fluctuation and set off the expansion of the universe; and the ongoing evolution of the entities, structures, and processes from the primordial event and the relationships that govern their unfolding. In light of what one might term this "boundary experience" of scientific insight, a sense of mystery pervades the very question of the nature of physical existence, a sense that deepens and expands when the properties of consciousness, self-consciousness, and personhood consistently exceed the capacity of reductionism or scientism to define these experiences by means of biochemistry and physiology. In view of these barriers to comprehension and verifiability, the affirmation of God as the transcendent Ground of being becomes all the more acceptable a response. It is this response that is articulated theologically in the doctrine of God as Creator and of the cosmos as creation.[5]

Traditionally, the notion of God as Creator tended toward an understanding of creation as a singular event, effected by a sole Creator, through which the cosmos came into being from nothing (*creatio ex nihilo*) at a moment long past. However, the postulate of God as Creator is less a statement about what happened at one point of time than about a perennial relation of God to the world. According to Peacocke, this relation involves both differentiation and interaction.[6] The relation of differentiation preserves a twofold understanding concerning God and the cosmos. With regard to God, differentiation preserves the understanding that God is totally other than the cosmos.[7] It therefore further affirms that God is not one ordinary cause among others in the physical nexus of the cosmos. With regard to the cosmos, differentiation preserves the notion of the dependence and contingency of all entities, structures, processes, and events in the universe on the creative, sustaining, and preserving will of God.[8] It is this relation of God to the world, God as Ground of Being, which Peacocke suggests is rightfully termed divine transcendence. The relation of interaction that Peacocke terms divine immanence presents itself through the notion of God as Continuous Creator, a notion that will be examined in the course of Peacocke's thought.

God as Source of Unity in Diversity

Although evolutionary cosmology and biology have encountered mysteries of existence that transcend the limits of theoretical explanation, science has nonetheless been successful in extrapolating theories concerning the beginning of the cosmos and of cosmic life from the entities, structures, and processes observed in the present. Based on the theory of the origin of the universe that he himself finds most plausible, namely, the cosmological theory of the hot, big bang, Peacocke pointed out that, from a scientific perspective, all the diversity, fecundity, and pluriformity that have manifested themselves with greater and greater complexity throughout cosmic history have their origin in an original unity. This original unity was the initial singularity of the compressed fireball, a "primeval, unimaginably condensed mass of fundamental particles and energy," indisputably physical, consisting of the most basic subatomic elements of matter-energy-space-time.[9] Throughout the unfolding of cosmic history, this initial unity has continued to reveal itself to scientists through the "intricate interconnectedness of the natural world at many levels," as well as in "the ultimate and beautiful, though abstract, unity of at least some of the fundamental forces and principles."[10] Nonetheless, this original and pervasive unity has for billions of years demonstrated its capacity to produce kaleidoscopic diversity in creation and in its creatures, as well as in the unfathomable range and richness of human experiences, societies, and cultures.

This interplay of unity and diversity in the cosmos suggests a Source of Being that is both one in essence and diverse in creativity. Thus, the scientific perspective on the cosmos points to the Christian theological insight that God's Being is characterized by both unity and differentiation.[11] From this perspective, God is not only the ground of cosmic being but also the source of its unity and interconnectedness. Moreover, this unifying ground of all-that-is does not express itself solely in terms of the profound singularity of origins and unity of processes but in the magnificent diversity of hierarchies of complexity, of emergent properties, and of modes of existence as well. Therefore, Peacocke infers, as this unifying ground of being, God not only must be *One* but also "*must be a Being of unfathomable richness* to be able to conceive of and to bring into existence a cosmos with such fecund potentialities."[12]

God as Supremely Rational

Pointing to the insights on the cosmos that the sciences provide, Peacocke suggested that the scope and scale of these revelations could cause one to miss two of the most significant insights that concern the cosmos and that serve as the presuppositions of all the rest.

> These are, firstly, that the things and events of the cosmos are amenable to that rational ordering of which human minds are capable; and secondly, that the minds which effect this ordering are themselves the product of the cosmic process itself, which is thereby engendering that which reflects upon it.[13]

This remark is reminiscent of an observation by Albert Einstein concerning the intelligibility of the universe. Reflecting for his own part on the mystery of the existence of the universe, Einstein mused, "The eternal mystery of the world is its comprehensibility. . . . The fact that it is comprehensible is a miracle."[14] This intelligibility and comprehensibility of the cosmos generates for scientists in particular and for human persons in general a sense of well-being and order and of predictability and control. However, although there has been an incredible expansion in human comprehension and prediction of cosmic events, this expansion has been attended by recognition of the fragility and tentativeness of human knowledge. This fragility stems in part from the loss of the objective observer associated with quantum physics and theories of relativity and also from the limit situations beyond which science is unable to advance in its exploration of the universe. Hence, the comprehensibility of the cosmos inspires a sense of awe and wonder when scientific inquiry reaches a point of impasse because of the profounder rationality it encounters in quantum theory, in random events, and in emergent entities and processes.[15] According to Peacocke, however, these limitations on what humans are capable of fathoming ought to come as no surprise to science, since "the human brain ... is itself made up of the same matter-energy in space-time as the world it is investigating."[16]

For Peacocke, the intrinsic reasonableness of the cosmos, coupled with the inability of science to resolve all mysteries concerning the origin of existence, implies the existence of a suprarational Creator, the essential "profounder rationality," who provides the best explanation of the inherent intelligibility of the entities, structures, and processes of the cosmos.[17] Based on similar insights, some scientists, like Gunther S. Stent, equate God with the rationality of the universe and with its openness to understanding and explanation. For Stent, " 'God' is the single principle that regulates everything and makes science possible."[18] In recent years, however, the juxtaposition of the intelligibility and the ineffability of the cosmos, combined with evidence of the irreducible complexity of certain biochemical structures, has led other scientists to suggest that this complexity requires the concept of intelligent design in the universe and, for some, of an Intelligent Designer. However, thinking on this point is by no means conclusive. Some theorists do suggest that the intrinsic rationality of the cosmos supports a deistic or theistic interpretation of creation by an Intelligent Designer. Others propose that it renders the notion of a deity unnecessary because it implies that the universe itself possessed the requisite conditions for the advent and emergence of the myriad forms of cosmic life. Finally, others contend that the principle is irrelevant to any argument concerning either the divinely designed universe or the existence of a Designer.[19] For Peacocke, the suprarationality that underlies the cosmos is not linked theologically to an interventionist or vitalist notion of intelligent design or an Intelligent Designer. It links to the notion of God immanent in creation, "which makes intelligible that striking rationality of the created order"[20] and which enables humanity to discern from creation God's " 'meanings' (his intentions, proposals, and purposes) *within* the world of which we are a part."[21]

God as Sustainer and Faithful Preserver of the Cosmos

Scientific research, in its observations of the order and regularity of the cosmos, in recent years has focused less on the search for causes and effects and more on the network of relationships that exist in the universe.[22] Because of this scientific de-emphasis on sequences of cause and effect, ways of speaking about God that accentuate Thomistic notions of causality have had reduced theoretical and theological impact.[23] As a result, Peacocke maintained, arguments such as the Thomistic Second Way of demonstrating the existence of God lose their theoretical cogency and impact. If divine immanence is to be held in balance with divine transcendence, God must not be regarded solely as a First Cause in the sequence of natural events, that is, as a spatial, temporal, or existential limit to the infinite regress of efficient causes. Rather, God must be regarded as intrinsically causative in, with, under, and through the creative processes of the cosmos itself.

In this regard, Peacocke's interpretation of God as First Cause may not necessarily reflect a generally accepted perspective. In his writing, Frederick Copleston offers the following exposition:

> When Aquinas talks about an "order" of efficient causes he is not talking of a series stretching back into the past, but of a hierarchy of causes, in which a subordinate member is here and now dependent on the causal activity of a higher member. . . . We have to imagine, not a lineal or horizontal series, so to speak, but a vertical hierarchy, in which a lower member depends here and now on the present causal activity of the member above it. It is the latter type of series, if prolonged to infinity, which Aquinas rejects. And he rejects it on the ground that unless there is a "first" member . . . a cause which does not depend on the causal activity of a higher cause, it is not possible to explain the . . . causal activity of the lowest member. His point of view is this. . . . Suppress the first efficient cause and there is no causal activity here and now. If therefore we find that . . . there are efficient causes in the world there must be a first efficient and completely nondependent cause. The word "first" does not mean first in the temporal order but supreme or first in the ontological order.[24]

Operating within his own understanding of God as First Cause, however, Peacocke contended that, in view of theories such as that of general relativity, scientific research demands a revision in the very notion of temporality in relation to God. Although Peacocke's proposals concerning the relationship between God and time unfold more fully in his discussion of Divine Becoming, at this stage of his thought Peacocke indicated that this revision needs to be twofold. First, if time is considered to be an integral aspect of the created order—inextricably entwined with space, matter, and energy—*and* the created order is conceived as within God and God is conceived as within the created order, then time must be regarded as a real relation both within the created order and between the created order and its Creator. This is, of course, a contention that pointedly counters the Thomistic notion that "there is no real relation in God to the creature" because God and the creature are not of the same ontological order. According to Aquinas,

> As the creature proceeds from God in diversity of nature, God is outside the order of the whole creation, nor does any relation to the creature arise from His nature; for He does not produce the creature by necessity of His nature, but by His intellect and will, as is above explained (14, 3 and 4; 19, 8). Therefore there is no real relation in God to the creature; whereas in creatures there is a real relation to God; because creatures are contained under the divine order, and their very nature entails dependence on God.[25]

Peacocke's second foundation for calling for a revision of the notion of God's relation to time is based on the scientific realization of the directionality of time. If this is so, then the laws and regularities that produce the temporal emergence of all-that-is must be understood not only as inbuilt by God as Creator but also as sustained by God throughout changing creation. Hence, God is not only the Ground of all-that-is but also its *Sustainer and Faithful Preserver* through time. This understanding of God as Sustainer and Faithful Preserver resonates with the biblical notion of *hesed*, the steadfast love of God proclaimed in the Hebrew Scriptures. Furthermore, it implies an immutable moral quality in the Being of the Divine. However, while such moral immutability is altogether desirable in God, the concepts of sustaining and preserving tend toward static conceptions of the God-world relationship and of the Creator as "a somewhat Atlas-like figure holding up the world."[26]

God as Continuous Creator

In contrast to the stasis implied in the notion of God's sustaining and preserving the cosmos, evolutionary cosmology and biology have continued to discover evidence of dynamism in the cosmos. Research has indicated that cosmic creativity has been ongoing since the origin of the universe and has exercised such creativity in and through the very stuff of the material world. Because of these scientific understandings, the theological notion of *creatio ex nihilo* as traditionally interpreted is an inadequate representation of the creative relation of God to the cosmos. Although *creatio ex nihilo* could preserve the transcendent differentiation of God from the universe and the dependence and contingency of the universe on God, it could not accommodate the scientific understanding of the ongoing creativity of the cosmos in new and emergent forms. Hence, static conceptions of God's differentiated relation to the cosmos, such as those of origination and preservation, have to be augmented and nuanced by a notion of dynamic interaction between God and world. Theologically, this dynamic interaction between God as Creator and the cosmos as creation has been termed *creatio continua.* This notion arises from the understanding that the cosmos possesses a continuous, inbuilt creativity. Therefore, if God is understood as Creator and the process of creation has been ongoing throughout cosmic history and into the cosmic future, then the ceaseless creative processes revealed by the physical and biological sciences must be identified with the creative activity of God's very self. If this conclusion is valid, then this identification necessitates a radical stress on the understanding of God as continuous and immanent Creator in relation to the cosmos, exercising divine creativity "in, with, and under the very processes of the natural world from the 'hot, big, bang' to humanity."[27] However, Peacocke maintained, this immanent creativity of God in the cosmos is not to be conceived as an instance of primary and secondary causality "but rather that the natural, causal, creative nexus of events *is* itself God's creative action . . . manifest in his mode as continuous Creator."[28]

In this radical emphasis on divine immanence, God is understood as *semper Creator*, in and through the inbuilt creativity of the universe. Hence, God is not perceived as a separate being dwelling in serene detachment from the cosmos but as One who is directly involved in the continuing processes of the cosmos. The model that Peacocke used to image the continuous creativity of God within the cosmos has usually been termed "top-down" or "downward" causation, although Peacocke interchanged this terminology with "whole-part influence" in his own work. It derives from the insights of Donald Campbell and Roger Sperry in their work with dissipative systems in which the state of a system as a whole influences the behavior of its component parts.[29] In many of the systems they had considered, scientists theorized that the direction of causality proceeds from the "bottom up"; that is, the properties and behaviors of a system's constituent parts influenced the properties and behavior of the system as a whole. However, in dissipative systems that demonstrate order through fluctuation such as those studied by Ilya Prigogine, scientists have detected the influence of the system as a whole on the behavior of its component parts.[30] Thus, according to Campbell and Sperry, changes in the behavior of constituent units occur because of their incorporation into the system as a whole. The constraints that the whole exerts on them cause these units to behave differently than if they were in isolation. However, both directions of causality are operative and interactive in such systems; therefore, realities at higher levels ("the whole") not only affect the realities at lower levels ("the parts") but also are affected by them.[31]

As applied to the God-world relationship, the notion of whole-part influence demonstrates a means by which one could conceive of God's interaction with the world without violating the laws and regularities operative in the cosmos, that is, in a way that would not be deemed interventionist. Peacocke applied this notion to the God-world relationship through two models. The first is the panentheistic model. In this model, God is the "circumambient Reality in which the world persists and exists."[32] The world-as-a-whole is thus conceived as within God, who is present to the world both in its totality and to its component parts. In this model, God is seen as always and everywhere freely and autonomously interacting with the world through an input of information. God communicates Godself and God's purposes to the world-as-a-whole through an all-embracing and all-pervasive presence that is essentially self-communicating.[33] In the panentheistic whole-part model, this self-communication upon the world-as-a-whole trickles through the levels of its parts to those capable of receiving this communication, namely, human persons. Although some, like Ian Barbour, question how such a model can be efficacious in producing effects in inanimate objects other than through the mediation of human persons,[34] Peacocke insisted that the relationship between the levels of creation and the human person is interactive and mutually transformative. Divine self-communication engages human persons as collaborators in the ongoing creativity of the Divine in relation to both animate and inanimate entities, structures, and processes of the cosmos. At the same time, however, these animate and inanimate entities, structures, and processes of the universe efficaciously mediate divine self-communication to humanity.[35] According to Peacocke, "God is then to be conceived of as communicating meaning and significance to constituents or patterns of events . . . [through which] insights into God's character and purposes for individuals or for groups of individuals can be generated."[36]

A second model Peacocke used for the notion of God's whole-part influence on the cosmos is that of the analogy of the mind:body relation in the human person. Peacocke unfolded this model through the concept of personal agency and extrapolates from his observations toward a notion of divine agency. "In this model, God would be regarded as exerting continuously top-down causative influences on the world-as-a-whole in a way analogous to that whereby we in our thinking can exert effects on our bodies in a top-down manner."[37] Although perhaps conceptually clearer than Peacocke's panentheistic model of whole-part influence, the analogy of mind:body :: God:universe is not without problems. John Polkinghorne notes the all-too-well-understood difficulty of extrapolating from human reality to the reality of the Divine. Furthermore, he points out that although human beings may directly experience themselves as agents, their knowledge of their personal potency remains a mystery to them.[38] In addition to these difficulties, Peacocke recognized that, despite his emphasis on the psychosomatic unity of the human person as a "mind-in-a-body," this model applied to God as "mind" who transcends the cosmos as "body" could reinforce the very dualism his anthropology tries to avoid. Moreover, despite his characterization of this model of the God-world relation in panentheistic terms in which God as "mind" still transcends the universe as "body," the threat of pantheistic identification of God and the cosmos still lurks behind this proposal.

In spite of the challenges of imaging the relationship of God to the cosmos in terms of whole-part influence, the insights of this model of God-world interaction are theologically significant. First, this model balances the notions of divine transcendence and immanence. It does so by imaging the possibility of God's "top-down" or "whole-part" influence on the cosmic system-as-a-whole (transcendence), which nonetheless efficaciously permeates the cosmos in the very depths of its constituent parts (immanence), an imaging wholly consistent with the panentheistic paradigm of the God-world relationship. In the top-down or whole-part model, God is the transcendent overarching context of reality, the "System of systems,"[39] so to speak, in which the cosmos lives, moves, and has its being. At the same time, however, God in this model permeates the system to all levels of its constituent parts and, thus, influences events and behaviors at all levels in a whole-part fashion. Hence, there is no aspect of space, time, matter, or energy to which God is not present. Second, this whole-part model also suggests that the behavior and intentionality of the constituent parts of the cosmos are capable of exerting a "bottom-up" or "part-whole" influence on the activities and potentialities of the system-as-a-whole. In a panentheistic framework, this means that creation has the capacity to affect and even constrain the intentions and activities of its personal Creator in a part-whole fashion. Third, whether in whole-part or in part-whole influence, the Creator and the created retain their inherent capacities to act, to receive, and to respond without coercion, and thus no violence is done to the essential freedom and autonomy of either the Creator or creation.

Hence, coupling the theological concept of God as immanent Continuous Creator with the earlier understanding of God as Ground of cosmic being suggests that the creative relationship of God to the world must always be expressed as a twofold understanding. First, God's relationship to the cosmos must be understood both in terms of initial creativity (*creatio ex nihilo*) and in terms of ongoing cosmic creativity (*creatio continua*). Through the theological claim of *creatio ex nihilo*, one affirms that all of creation has its common source in God. Through the claim of *creatio continua*, one also acknowledges that the creative intentions and activities of God perpetually permeate the evolutionary unfolding of the cosmos through all eons of cosmic history. As *creatio ex nihilo* suggests that God alone directly produced the conditions for the entire physical universe out of Godself with no mediation or dependence on other entities or forces, *creatio continua* supplements this understanding by affirming that the ongoing creativity of God is also indirect and mediated through the entities, structures, and processes of the cosmos itself.[40] These insights concerning God as transcendent and immanent Creator find their utmost expression in the panentheistic model of the God-world relationship in which God circumambiently, intimately, enduringly, and unboundedly maintains divine presence to creation. As Peacocke concluded, "God in his being transcends, goes beyond, both man and nature, yet God is either in everything created from the beginning to the end, at all times and in all places, or he is not there at all."[41]

God as Personal Creator of an Anthropic Universe

The understanding that, as Continuous Creator, God continually communicates divine meaning and purpose through the constituents of the cosmos suggests attributes of a personal nature in God, because it is the nature of the personal to be purposive and to communicate those purposes through actions.[42] However, Peacocke's development of his concept of the personal or suprapersonal nature of the Creator of the cosmos has more complex roots than this and stems from the convergence of three lines of thought. The first line of thought is that of the Christian tradition in which Peacocke emphasized the covenantal nature of God's interaction with the Jewish ancestors of the Christian community, the Incarnation of God in Christ, and the Christian experience of God in terms of Trinity. Peacocke's second line of thought derived from a philosophical consideration of what it means to be a "person" in human experience—an experience that encompasses consciousness, self-consciousness, agency, and communication. Peacocke also pursued a third line of thought through science toward the personal nature of God, a line of thought that understands the creative movement of evolution toward the human person as the ultimate substantiation for the inference of personal attributes in God.

GOD AS PERSONAL IN CHRISTIANITY: GOD IN SCRIPTURE AND TRADITION

As Christians in every age have experienced the embrace and the activity of Divine Being in their human becoming, they have, for the most part, employed images, models, and metaphors of a *personal* nature to speak of God and the God-world relationship. Such imagistic language has found its way into traditional discourse in a variety of ways. In the biblical account of the genesis of the universe, the Cosmic Creator spoke, and the chaos responded to the divine command. The God of Israel revealed Godself to the chosen people in relational metaphors such as Lord, father, and husband, as well as in agential metaphors such as Creator, vineyard owner, and potter. Moreover, Yahweh—"I Am Who Am," the eminently personal One—continuously shared an intimate and affective relationship with the Jews, disclosing the Divine Self in anthropomorphic and anthropopathic terms. With the Incarnation of God in the person of Jesus of Nazareth, the sense of the personal nature of God deepened and the terms of personal relationship with God intensified. For those who were disciples of Jesus of Nazareth, the relationship with the God of Jesus Christ was to be modeled on the familial intimacy of father and son, the intimacy that Jesus shared with his *Abba*. Based on this revelation of God in Christ, the Christian tradition grew in its renewed and deepened understanding of God as personal.

As the doctrine of the Trinity developed, various terms attempted to describe the personal nature of this triune experience of God. Although theologians throughout the centuries have bemoaned the inadequacy of the traditional terminology of "person," contemporary theologians have turned their emphasis from the discrete persons of the Trinity to the relations among them. Nevertheless, "because God was experienced as transcendent ground of all being . . . as incarnate in Jesus . . . and as possessing the disciples of Jesus . . . a threefold diversity within the never-doubted unity of the divine life was inferred."[43] In this experience of diversity-in-unity, one glimpses "the beginnings of the one God as triune in his character, as personally transcendent, personally incarnate, and personally immanent" in relation to the cosmos and its creatures.[44]

GOD AS PERSONAL IN A PHILOSOPHICAL PERSPECTIVE: GOD AS AGENT

In addition to the revelation concerning the Jewish and Christian experience of God's presence and action in the world, Peacocke also attended to the philosophical debate concerning human personhood and its impact on the relation of God to the world. Peacocke approached this question through the notion of "agency," which he explored in relation to humanity and then extrapolated in relation to God. In considering "man as agent," at one level, the human being is describable in reductionist physical terms as "a brain in a body." However, at a higher level, that of consciousness, self-consciousness, and sociality, the human being must be described in "the non-reducible language of persons (of selfhood, self-conscious agency) . . . to explicate the mental activity he manifests, experiences, and communicates." Consequently, Peacocke engaged the problem of how human mental events that are identifiable with neurophysical events can be expressed in terms that include selfhood, agency, and physicality. In other words, how can one best express the activities of the human person in terms that express immanent action in a causal nexus that results from mental activity that transcends that causal nexus? When expressed in these terms, it becomes evident that "this problem of the human sense of being an agent, of being a self, an 'I,' acting in this physical causal nexus, is of the same ilk as the relation of God to the world." Unfolding this insight in terms of human activity, Peacocke explained,

> *I* am the agent of this action . . . *I* am not external to the process. . . .
> Nevertheless, in my experience as agent, I transcend any particular
> action or intended group of actions. . . . Moreover . . . I am rarely fully
> expressed in my actions . . . and this, too, is an aspect of my transcendence over my actions. Thus in my mental experience I am
> a transcendent causal agent expressing myself in and through the
> physical structure of my body.[45]

When applied analogously to God, this model of personal agency provides a means by which one could conceive of God as the transcendent agent who is immanently active in physical processes. Of course, one must not conceive of God as strictly "personal" but, more accurately, as "at least personal" or "suprapersonal," for God's transcendence is of a higher order with regard to the world process. This caution notwithstanding, Peacocke asserted an analogous relationship between human agency and divine agency. Placing this analogy within a panentheistic context, Peacocke explained, "In other words, the world is to God, rather as our bodies are to us as personal agents, with the necessary caveat that the ultimate ontology of God as Creator is distinct from that of the world (pan*en*theism, not pantheism)."[46]

In later writings, Peacocke amplified this position through the work of Richard Swinburne.[47] According to Swinburne's description, to say "God exists" is to affirm that "there exists a person without a body (i.e. a spirit) who is eternal, is perfectly free, omnipotent, omniscient, perfectly good, and the creator of all things."[48] Swinburne goes on to explain that the attribution of "person" is appropriate to God "because a person is a being with power (to do intentional actions), knowledge, and freedom (to choose, uncaused, which actions to do)."[49] Peacocke qualified the analogy between the God-world and the person-body relationship. He distinguished God from humanity as that personal agent who creates, gives existence, and infinitely transcends the world in ways that the human person does not in relation to the human body. Moreover, although referring to the Divine in terms of personal agency, he is clear to emphasize that God is not "a person" but rather is conceivable as "at least personal," "supra-personal," or "transpersonal" in order to affirm that there are facets of the divine nature that are inexpressible in terms of human categories.[50] Recognizing further that the analogy at the human level seems to support a mind-body dualism, Peacocke invoked recent neurological and psychological evidence that views the activities of the brain and nervous system and the events of human consciousness as two facets or functions of one psycho-somatic unity.[51] Nevertheless, with regard to God and the cosmos, Peacocke continued to maintain an ontological dualism between the Creator and creation and rejects the concept of the world as God's body to avoid any implications of pantheism in his theology of a God-world relation modeled on the personal.

GOD AS PERSONAL FROM A SCIENTIFIC PERSPECTIVE: GOD AS CREATOR OF AN ANTHROPIC UNIVERSE

These biblical, theological, and philosophical precedents for conceiving of God in terms of the personal serve as reinforcements for Peacocke's contention that the least misleading way to speak of the best explanation for the existence of all-that-is is in terms of the personal. The particular insight of evolutionary science that Peacocke pointed to as support for this inference is the so-called anthropic principle, which refers to scientists' recognition that if a variety of physical constants that characterize the cosmos had differed only slightly in value, then the development of the universe as it is now known would have been drastically different and the possibility of carbon-based life developing in this universe significantly decreased. This anthropic principle was discussed in a lecture by Brandon Carter, whose study of the universe led him to believe that "large number coincidences" had led to the development of carbon-based and, therefore, human life in the cosmos and that this development was "crucially and sensitively dependent" on these precise physical values.[52]

Carter's insights first reinforced Peacocke's understanding of biological and human life as contingent and dependent. Furthermore, they demonstrated with new emphasis the inextricable link between human existence and the physical nature of the universe: "we are stardust, for every carbon atom of our bodies, every iron atom in our blood's haemoglobin was made in stars and scattered by supernovae explosions before the Earth existed as a planet." For other scientists, the revelation of the anthropic principle suggested the viability of the argument from design and for an Intelligent Designer who alone could have set these relations in such a way as to produce human life. Wary of such apologetic use of scientific data, Peacocke concluded: "What *can* be said on the basis of the anthropic principle is that our emergence in this universe is at least consonant with the postulate of a Creator God who has the purpose of bringing into existence living and eventually self-conscious persons."[53]

In his Bampton Lectures, Peacocke further appraised the anthropic principle as consistent with the evolution of life in this particular universe through the interplay of law and chance in the cosmos. As Peacocke maintained,

> [If] we are to look upon the role of "chance" as the means by which all the potentialities of the universe are explored . . . the existence of life and, indeed, of our actual universe, is the result of its operation. . . . [The] fact is that matter-energy has in space-time, in *this* universe, acquired the ability to adopt self-replicating living structures which have acquired self-consciousness and the ability to know that they exist and have even now found ways of discovering how they have come to be.[54]

Over time, however, Peacocke's reflections turned to the impact of the anthropic principle on inferences about God. As he reflected on the emergence of human subjectivity and personhood, Peacocke found himself face-to-face once again with the concept of human agency, that "distinctively new kind of causality" which the universe introduced into itself and which presented "the possibility of a new kind of explanation" for events in the universe, "namely *personal* explanation." Now, if the fundamental constituents of the universe produced over time a quality of existence characterized by consciousness, self-consciousness, subjectivity, and personal agency, do they not "point us in the direction of the 'best explanation' of all-that-is . . . in terms of some kind of causality that could *include* the personal in its consequences?" Furthermore, if the best explanation of all-that-is is the *transcendent* Ground of the existence of all-that-is, must not this best explanation be of a "quite different essence, over and beyond the order of created beings"? And further still, if this explanatory Ground for the existence of creation must itself be "over and beyond" the created order of being, does it not follow that this best explanation, this "X" as Peacocke named it, "must transcend the personal in such a way that 'X' could be the ground of that distinctive mode of actual being we call personal, as well as the non-personal being we have already considered"? And finally, if the personal is the highest mode of being included within the hierarchy of created being, then must one not move to the inevitable assertion that "God is the name that we give to this 'X'" and that theologians "have good reason for saying that *God is (at least) personal* or 'supra-personal' and for predicating personal qualities of God as less misleading and more appropriate than impersonal ones— even while recognizing, as always, that such predications must remain ultimately inadequate to that to which they refer, namely, God"?[55]

God as Purposive

Following his inference that God is truly to be regarded in personal terms, Peacocke proceeded to propose "it is of the nature of human persons to have purposes . . . [and] goal-seeking patterns of behavior." If, therefore, human persons are such carriers of values in their biological, intellectual, and social existence, then the God who created the human person must be the ultimate source of such values, because "by their very nature values transcend the physical and biological and partake of the nature of the personally purposive."[56] Because of this connection between the personal and the purposive, Peacocke maintained that a God who is considered at least personal or suprapersonal must also, of necessity, be conceived as purposeful. Moreover, these divine purposes must be conceived as manifesting themselves not only in cosmic order and regularity but also in the existence and destiny of human persons who embody values in themselves.

However, arriving at this affirmation of the Divine as suprapersonal and purposive, Peacocke recognized with particular clarity "the inadequacy of our talk only of the 'being' of God, of God as the one Ground of being." This is so because "It is of the nature of the personal not only to be capable of bearing static predicates . . . but also of predicates of a dynamic kind." It is of the nature of the personal to possess not only "stabler settled characteristics" but also those characteristics of a dynamic nature that belong to the "flow of experience . . . quintessential to being a person." Hence, on one hand, in affirming the nature of the Divine as Ground of cosmic being, as Source of the unity and supreme rationality of the cosmos, Peacocke affirmed predicates for the Divine Being of God that reflect the static classical attributes of God as simple, rational, omniscient, omnipotent, and immutable. However, on the other hand, in attending to the nature of the Divine as Continuous Creator within the processes of the cosmos, as Source of diversity, and as suprapersonal and purposeful Creator of an anthropic universe, Peacocke concluded that such static predicates need enhancement, revision, and even replacement by more dynamic predicates for

God. It is these dynamic predicates that Peacocke derived from the panentheistic paradigm of God-world relationship, from the immanence of God in the continuous creativity of the cosmos, and from the phenomenon of personal subjectivity. Therefore, Peacocke understood that it becomes more appropriate to move forward from his consideration of the Divine Being of God to a consideration of a more dynamic understanding of the creative nature and activity of a personal God, an understanding subsumed under the notion of Divine Becoming.[57]

The Divine Becoming of God

Introduction

Shifting his scientific focus to "what is going on" in the becoming of the cosmos, Arthur Peacocke entered into his discussion of God in Divine Becoming. At this stage, scientific insights caused Peacocke to part ways with the classical tradition concerning the seemingly immutable, impassible, omnipotent, and omniscient God of Divine Being. Rather, they led him to affirm a God who is neither an omnipotent deity who overrides cosmic autonomy and freedom nor an omniscient deity who foreknows all things before they occur. Scientific observations concerning the kaleidoscopic fecundity of the cosmos suggest that God in Divine Becoming is a God who takes joy and delight in the pluriformity of creation. However, according to evolutionary science, this pluriformity results not only from the order and regularity considered earlier but also from the operation of chance occurrences within such lawlike regularity. Because Peacocke already suggested that God is Continuous Creator within the self-creativity of the cosmos, his recognition of the operation of chance within law led to the inference that God is not only the Source of the regularity of law but also the Source of the operation of chance in the cosmos. However, both evolutionary and quantum science insist that the operation of chance within law is in principle unpredictable and uncontrollable. Therefore, God cannot be considered unconditionally omnipotent and omniscient; rather, God must be conceived as self-limited in knowledge and power. Following from this self-limitation, God-in-Becoming must be also be a vulnerable God who is self-emptying and self-giving in love, a God who is familiar with suffering and who bears cosmic grief. This God of Divine Becoming is that one who attentively and lovingly participates in the cosmic unfolding of the universe through its own inherent creativity and power. In this cosmic unfolding, God in Divine Becoming relates and responds intimately, affectively, and temporally to creation and its creatures, penetrating its very being, becoming, and history. This is not a God who dwells in undisturbed eternal bliss but a God who embraces and permeates the cosmos, suffering its pain and death in, with, and under its costly unfolding in time.

God's Joy and Delight in Creation

In his consideration of "what is going on" in the cosmos, Peacocke suggested that the most obvious aspect of the universe that captures human attention is the cornucopian fecundity of the natural world with its various levels of complexity in the hierarchy of created being. These observations earlier led to the inference that the nature of Divine Being is unity-in-diversity, an unfathomable richness springing from an essential oneness. However, if the Continuous Creator of such diversity is essentially personal and those who are personal are also purposive, then the fecundity and heterogeneity of creation must reveal the Creator's purposes for the unfolding of the cosmos.[58]

Consequently, if such fecund diversity is indeed God's purpose for the cosmos, if "the *whole* tapestry of the created order in its warp and woof" is intended by its Creator and "not simply as stages on the way to *homo sapiens*," then, Peacocke inferred, the Creator must take joy and delight in the fulfillment of such divine purposes.[59] This signals an affective response in the Divine to the multiformity of creation, one that Peacocke suggested is intimated in the Genesis account, in which God, embracing all that had transpired from divine creativity, "saw everything that he had made, and, behold, it was very good."[60] Moreover, this notion of divine joy and delight suggests other images of divine delight and the notion of divine play in creation.[61] This scenario resonates with the Indian concept of *lílá*, "the creative urge of . . . God [which] is really his/her play."[62] It also echoes through the Wisdom literature of the Hebrew Scriptures in which Divine Wisdom exults, "Then was I beside him as his craftsman, and I was his delight day by day, playing before him all the while, playing on the surface of his earth; and I found delight in the sons of men."[63] Further, it appears in the writings of the Greek patristics[64] and in the theology of Jürgen Moltmann.[65]

From a scientific standpoint, moreover, the notion of God's play in creation suggests another notion of play, the interplay between chance and law that is creative in the cosmos. According to the insights of neo-Darwinian science, the remarkable diversity in the cosmos derives from this creative interplay of random occurrences at the multiple levels of the universe ("chance"), which produce effects at the macrolevel of the universe that operate within the lawlike framework of natural systems ("necessity"). This interplay supports Peacocke's intuition that the character of God's play in creation is "akin to a game of chance."[66] The play of chance operates unpredictably yet purposively within the framework of law to elicit the potentialities that the cosmos has possessed from its beginning. If, however, the operations of both chance and law are inherent capacities of the cosmos and the cosmos is truly the result of divine creation by a personal Creator, then these operations must be regarded as God-endowed features of the cosmos and as consistent with God's purposes for the cosmos. This realization leads to the affirmation that God not only is the ultimate and necessary Ground of the cosmos in Divine Being but also is, in Divine Becoming, the ultimate and necessary Source of the creative and unpredictable interplay of chance and law that effects the becoming of the cosmos.

God as Ground and Source of Law and Chance

The scientific evidence concerning the creativity of chance and law in the "life-game" provokes new possibilities for additional dimensions, models, and images for divine creativity in the cosmos.[67] Although Peacocke underplayed the role of chance in biological development in his early work,[68] he later asserts, "This role of chance is ... simply what is required if all the potentialities of the universe, especially for life, were going to be elicited effectively."[69] In response to this suggestion, critics objected that if the cosmos were constituted with these properties and behaviors at its genesis, then God's activity is fundamentally restricted to the first moments of the cosmic epoch, with no room for the personal and intentional agency of God through history.[70] However, in the light of God as immanent and continuous Creator in, with, and under the creative properties of the cosmos, the continuous constitution of the cosmos through the operation of chance and law is indicative of personal and intentional divine agency. The inbuilt creativity of the cosmos is conceived as the modality through which God-*qua*-Creator empowers the actualization of cosmic matter-energy throughout the expanse of space-time. Thus, Peacocke maintained, these potentialities "are unveiled by chance exploring their gamut, a musical term which has come to mean 'the whole scale, range or compass of a thing' (O.E.D.)."[71] Through this interpretation, Peacocke not only rejected the notion of God as a deistic onlooker in the evolutionary process but also contradicted the concept that the operation of chance is a manifestation of irrationality in the cosmos. Although

> this unfolding of the hidden potentialities of the world is not a predetermined path ... the creativity of God is to be seen as genuinely innovative and adaptive, but not inchoate and without purpose. In other words, we have to conceive of God as involved in explorations of the many kinds of unfulfilled potentialities of the universe he has

created. . . . For there are, as we saw, inbuilt propensities—a theist
would say "built in by God"—in the natural creating processes which,
as it were, "load the dice" in favour of life, and once living organisms
have appeared, also of increased complexity, awareness, consciousness and sensitivity, with all their consequences.[72]

This interpretation of God's exploratory activity in, with, and under the creative
processes of chance within law inspired in Peacocke several highly "evocative
images"[73] through which chance is understood as a creative agent in the cosmos
and as an instrument of divine creativity itself.[74] Regarding these and other
images, Nancey Murphy has remarked that there is "no one who refurbishes
our images of God in the light of contemporary science as beautifully as Peacocke does."[75] One enduring example of these evocative images, which have
become like refrains that echo down the years and throughout Peacocke's
writings, is the understanding of chance as "the search radar of God, sweeping
through all the possible targets available to its probing."[76] Although some would
have liked to see this image of God as explorer further developed,[77] Peacocke
quickly showed a decided preference for musical models to express the interplay of chance and law in cosmic and divine creativity. Pressing the musical
analogy introduced in his notion of the "gamut" of potentialities written into
the cosmos by its Creator, Peacocke initially conceived of God's role in "the
music of creation" as "a bell-ringer, ringing all the possible changes, all the
possible permutations and combinations he can out of a given set of harmo-
nious bells—though it is God who creates the 'bells' too."[78] However, Peacocke
almost immediately supplanted this imagery with his most robust and elaborate musical model for divine creativity through the interplay of chance and law,
that of God as the composer of the cosmic fugue. Peacocke noted that other
theorists such as Karl Popper and Manfred Eigen have also proposed this analogy and found it useful for its connotation of music as "a flexible form moving
within time."[79] According to Peacocke's own expansion of the insight,

> [In] music there is an elaboration of simpler units according to, often
> conventional, rules intermingled with much spontaneity, surprise
> even. . . . Thus does a J. S. Bach create a complex and interlocking
> harmonious fusion of his seminal material, both through time and at
> any particular instant. . . . Thus might the Creator be imagined to
> enable to be unfolded the potentialities of the universe which he
> himself has given it . . . [as] an Improvisor of unsurpassed ingenuity.
> He appears to do so by a process in which the creative possibili-
> ties, inherent (by his own intention) within the fundamental entities
> of that universe and their inter-relations, become actualized within

a temporal development shaped and determined by those selfsame potentialities.[80]

In his evaluation of this model, Hugh Montefiore pointedly criticizes it as leading to the God of the deists, to "a remote, unmoved, unloving" absentee landlord who sets the universe with its inherent processes and potentialities in motion and then leaves it to spin out on its own.[81] Although Ian Barbour acknowledges the possibility of a deistic interpretation, he nonetheless counters Montefiore's objection by pointing to Peacocke's clear interpretation of the cosmic causal nexus as divine creative action.[82] For his own part, Peacocke reiterated that the enduring emphasis that he places on the immanence of God in the processes and potentialities of the cosmos leads not to deism but to an integration of divine transcendence and immanence in this model of creativity. As Peacocke himself explained,

> There is no doubt of the "transcendence" of the composer in relation to the music he creates—he gives it existence and without the composer it would not be.... Yet, when we are actually listening to a musical work, say, a Beethoven sonata, then there are times when we are so deeply absorbed in it that for a moment we are thinking Beethoven's musical thoughts with him.... [If] anyone were to ask at that moment, "*Where* is Beethoven now?" we could only reply that Beethoven-*qua*-composer was to be found in the music itself.... This very closely models ... God's immanence in creation and God's self-communication in and through what he is creating.[83]

Putting it another way, Peacocke suggested, in listening to a piece of music by Mozart, if one asks where Mozart is, one must admit that he is nowhere but in the music. "If you listen to that music and really absorb it so you are reliving the music deep within you, then you are meeting Mozart as composer. God's creation is that kind of activity, where that which is created is the very vehicle of the One who does the creating."[84]

Peacocke's musical model has also been challenged as overemphasizing the "harmony of creation" and, strangely enough in view of earlier deistic critiques, as attributing too much control over creation to God.[85] However, although Peacocke contended that God did indeed fashion and determine the capacity and potentiality of cosmic creativity through chance and law as part of the God-givenness of creation, the unfolding and outcome of these potentialities through the operation of chance and law remains indeterminate. This is so both because of the autonomy and freedom implied in the notion of the God-given self-creativity of the cosmos and because of the unpredictability inherent in the operation of chance within law itself.[86] The interaction of the autonomy, freedom, and unpredictability of creation through the interplay of chance and law does not preclude the activity of the Divine, because these creative processes are understood as the immanent creativity of God as continuous Creator. However, the indeterminacy of creativity through chance and law does suggest that there is a risk incurred by God in the divine decision to create such a self-creative cosmos.[87] Although the inbuilt creativity of the cosmos is indeed God at work, creating in and through the stuff of the world, the emergent forms of the cosmos, nonetheless, are the lawful consequence of a "concatenation of random events ... arrived by means of an open-ended trial-and-error exploration of possibilities, an exploration that is [not] devoid of either false trails or dead ends." Hence, if God is involved in creation in this way, as exploring in and through the cosmos, then it is an involvement that inevitably places the divine purposes at risk, opens the Divine to the creative vagaries of the interplay of chance and law, and entails the limitation of divine omnipotence and omniscience by the processes of the cosmos constituted by divine intent. Furthermore, it is undoubtedly the kind of involvement that implies the possibility and ultimately entails the reality of divine suffering in, with, and under these self-same cosmic processes.[88]

God as Self-Limited in Omnipotence and Omniscience

Based on his inference concerning God as the Source of chance and law, on the scientific evidence of the creative and unpredictable role of chance in the evolution of the cosmos, and on the model of whole-part interaction between the cosmos and its Creator, Peacocke proceeded to infer that one must "recognize more emphatically than ever before the constraints which we must regard God as imposing upon himself in creation." Giving existence to the cosmos implies the omnipotence of God in Divine Being, in that omnipotence is God's ability "to do whatever it is *logically possible* to do."[89] However, "in order to achieve his purposes, [God in Divine Becoming] has allowed his inherent omnipotence and omniscience to be modified, restricted, and curtailed by the very open-endedness that he has bestowed upon creation," particularly as this open-endedness relates to the exercise of human freedom.[90] Yet, these modifications, restrictions, and curtailments of divine power and knowledge must, in Peacocke's estimation, be self-imposed limitations, in that it is God who has freely chosen to make the cosmos in such a way that there are particular areas over which God freely has not chosen to exercise divine power. Thus, as elaborated by Lucien Richard, "In creating, God limits self and allows a cosmos to emerge with its own autonomy. God, in God's creative causality, makes room for human freedom and autonomy to emerge and for a natural order to be characterized by open-endedness and flexibility."[91]

GOD IN SELF-LIMITED OMNIPOTENCE

In the natural order, biological parameters act as "inherent restraints on how even an omnipotent Creator could bring about the existence of . . . a cosmos not a chaos, and thus an arena for the free action of self-conscious, reproducing entities and for the coming to be of the fecund variety of living organisms whose existence the Creator delights in."[92] Thus, by divine intent, the universe is an "arena of improvisation" of chance within law, a creation made to make itself and to realize its potentialities through processes of self-exploration in autonomy and freedom. However, neither the divine intent nor the process itself is without cost because, for the Divine and for the cosmos, there are both grace and freedom in an exploratory universe. As "evolution unavoidably makes 'mistakes,' enters blind alleys, and produces much suffering,"[93] both fruitfulness and frustration result. In such a universe, God acts transcendently and immanently but is not coercive and does not overrule. In such a universe, God guides purposefully and lovingly but respects the integrity of creation and preserves its autonomy.[94] In asserting the concept of God's self-limitation of omnipotence, therefore, Peacocke struck a characteristic balance between the freedom and autonomy of the Creator and that of the created. Commenting on this balance, Ron Highfield asserts that Peacocke "protects God's deity while giving . . . freedom to the world and autonomy to science. God . . . allows an evolving universe to explore its own possibilities through indeterminate quantum events and random mutation and natural selection."[95]

Although this balance undoubtedly provides for the inherent creativity and fecundity of the universe from a scientific perspective, it nonetheless does so at the risk of outcomes deleterious to the life and well-being of nonhuman and human creation alike. Hence, from a theological standpoint, the notion of the self-limitation of God's omnipotence clearly requires a modification of the classical understanding of the nature and attributes of God in relation to the cosmos. As regards such a modification, Peacocke, with other Christian theologians, suggested that such divine self-limitation is actually the definitive demonstration of the nature and attributes of the God of Jesus Christ, to whom Christians "have come to ascribe . . . so far as human speech can indicate, self-offering 'love' as his most distinctive attribute." According to Peacocke,

> They have affirmed that God has to be described as "love" because,
> in creation, he deliberately limits himself, by allowing a cosmos to

remain in being which is other than himself, which is given its own autonomy and so limits his freedom, and which in man can consciously repudiate his creaturehood; they have affirmed that God was revealed as self-offering love in the self-limitation which was his incarnation in Jesus Christ and in the self-offering of Jesus's human life for men.[96]

In Peacocke's Christian interpretation of God as Love, therefore, such self-limitation is not only the "precondition for the coming into existence of free, self-conscious human beings, that is of human experience as such" but also the prerequisite for the event of the Incarnation and of the affirmation of the suffering of God.[97] From another vantage point, Peacocke in his later works retrieved the notion that Christian theology has always maintained that God can act only in accord with God's nature. Hence, if the nature of God is Love, then "God can only do what is consistent with God's nature as Love." If, in God's nature as Love, God created both the cosmos and humanity as free and autonomous, then God has chosen not to exercise coercive power over the cosmos and its creatures. Hence, Peacocke contended, in Christian understanding, "divine omnipotence has always been regarded as limited by the very nature of God." In this way, Peacocke found he was able to assert with theological integrity both the omnipotence and the self-limitation of God in relation to the cosmos: *"God is omnipotent, but self-limited by God's nature as Love."*[98]

This line of thought by Peacocke is characteristic of his inclination to do "traditional Christian apologetics in a modern mode,"[99] an inclination that ordinarily results in insightful, creative, and logical reinterpretations of Christian theology in dialogue with evolutionary science. In this case, however, some confusion results. As Highfield describes the underlying issue,

> mindful of the dangers posed by theories that limit God eternally, many contemporary theologians and philosophers of religion employ the concept of self-limitation to ward off those threats. God limits his power and knowledge . . . freely rather than of necessity. The notion of self-limitation thus secures the advantages of a limited God without jeopardizing God's deity.[100]

Hence, to fit with both his scientific and his theological "theories" (to use Highfield's category), Peacocke needed to advance a plausible explanation that could preserve his affirmation both of the God-given freedom, autonomy, and self-creativity of the cosmos from the perspective of evolutionary science and of the freedom, autonomy, and omnipotent creativity of the Divine espoused by his Christian tradition. As a result, Peacocke inferred from the evolutionary evidence that the self-limitation of divine omnipotence is not necessary, but contingent, with its contingency based on God's original intentions for the cosmos. But herein lies the rub.

If God-*qua*-Creator has made the eternal decision to create this particular cosmos in freedom, autonomy, and self-creativity, and *if* the notion of an interventionist, God-of-the-gaps is scientifically inconsistent with Peacocke's evolutionary worldview, *then* is not the unlimited omnipotence of God precluded *by logical necessity*, rather than by divine choice? Throughout his works, Peacocke rejected the notion of God's intervention at the level of quantum indeterminacy[101] and maintained that "God as the faithful source of rationality and regularity in the created order appears to be undermined if one simultaneously wishes to depict his action as *both* sustaining the 'laws of nature' that express his divine will for creation *and* at the same time intervening to act in ways abrogating these very laws." Moreover, Peacocke indicated that the concept of the self-limitation of divine omnipotence is particularly crucial with regard to evil in the cosmos, questioning, "if God *can* intervene consistently with his own being and purposes, why did he not do so to avert disasters in the world or human history, floods in Bangladesh or concentration camps in Auschwitz?"[102]

There are, moreover, other theological, scientific, and moral considerations that exacerbate Peacocke's theoretical bind. The Christian tradition of biblical revelation and special providence remains difficult to reconcile with the notion of a God who is *necessarily* limited in power by the cosmos that God's own will created. Hence, Peacocke was forced to consider whether God might not subordinate the divine will expressed in natural law to "higher levels" of God's volition.[103] In response to this question from his *Christian* perspective, Peacocke was inclined to suggest that "we cannot but allow the possibility that God, being the Creator of the world, might be free to set aside any limitations by which God has allowed his interaction with that created order to be restricted." From his *scientific* perspective, however, Peacocke reminded that "we also have to recognise that those very self-limitations that God is regarded as having self-imposed are postulated precisely because they rendered coherent the whole notion of God as Creator with purposes that are being implemented in the natural and human world and unveiled by the sciences."[104] Furthermore, from his *moral* perspective, Peacocke recognized that to allow for the possibility of God's breach of self-imposed limitation in the face of the ubiquity of pain, suffering, and death in the cosmos provokes the question of theodicy with even greater intensity. Confronted with these conflicting perspectives, Highfield asks, "Does invoking the concept of self-limitation, however, solve the problem . . . effectively? Is the hyphen powerful enough to reconcile heaven and earth? Or, is this an example of theology-by-punctuation?"[105] For Peacocke, the conflict remained unresolved.

GOD IN SELF-LIMITED OMNISCIENCE

Moving to Peacocke's notion of God's self-limited omniscience, we must begin by distinguishing between knowledge and *fore*knowledge with regard to divine omniscience, that is, between the knowledge of cosmic entities, structures, processes, or events that have been actualized and belong to present and past existence, and the knowledge of cosmic realities that have not yet been actualized and belong to an unformed and undisclosed future existence. Like Peacocke's definition of omnipotence, omniscience is defined as "the ability to know all that it is *logically possible* to know."[106] This definition of divine omniscience excludes, therefore, knowledge of those things that are not *logically* coherent. However, it also excludes precise knowledge of future events, including those that human beings might freely choose, that is, *fore*knowledge. This is so because "it would be logically incoherent if God did know this *and* human beings were genuinely free."[107] Although this conclusion conflicts with assumptions of Christian theism,[108] Peacocke supported this position by asserting that, from an evolutionary viewpoint, the future has no ontological status; it does not yet exist in any sense and thus has no content for God to know.[109]

In addition to the exclusion of divine foreknowledge of future human actions, Peacocke also suggested that certain events cannot be known in advance by God because they are in principle not foreknowable. These conditions that limit divine omniscience once again stem from the way in which God has created the cosmos and concern random events precipitated by the operation of chance and quantum events within the Heisenberg range of uncertainty. According to Peacocke, "God has so made the natural order that it is, in principle, impossible even for God, as it is for us, to predict the precise, future values of certain variables."[110] Hence, contingency and unpredictability are ontological features of the cosmos and not simply epistemological deficiencies in human knowledge. While affirming this to be the case, Peacocke again asserted that this limitation on divine omniscience must be considered self-imposed because the conditions that produce the operation of chance and the Heisenberg range of uncertainty are contingent on the way in which God created the universe. Self-limitation of divine omniscience, like self-limitation of divine omnipotence, is not necessary, but contingent, with its contingency once again based on the divine intention for the cosmos.[111] Nevertheless, although divine omniscience is limited with regard to the precise outcomes of conditions, events, and choices within the cosmos, Peacocke maintained that God still possesses "probabilistic knowledge" of outcomes in any situation and in every system.[112] Therefore, God's self-limitation does not preclude divine influence on the general direction of human and nonhuman events, namely, through top-down influence on the cosmos as a whole.[113]

Theological response to the notion of self-limited divine omniscience is basically divided along two theoretical lines. The first line of thought, which supports Peacocke's inferences, bases its rationale on the scientific notion of the intrinsic freedom, autonomy, and unpredictability of the cosmos and its creatures. The second line of thought, which disputes Peacocke's inferences, bases its logic on classically conceived notions of God's eternity and relation to time. Scientist-theologians such as John Polkinghorne and Keith Ward are among those who agree with Peacocke on the basis of cosmic freedom, autonomy, and unpredictability. Polkinghorne suggests that one aspect of what he terms the "kenosis of creation," God's loving letting-be of the inherent creativity of the cosmos, is that even God "does not know the unformed future.... [However, this] is no imperfection in the divine nature, for the future is not yet there to be known." Furthermore, Polkinghorne maintains that God's self-limitation of omniscience, like God's self-limitation of omnipotence, "arises from the logic of love, which requires the freedom of the beloved."[114] For his part, theologian Keith Ward affirms the contentions of both Peacocke and Polkinghorne concerning the self-limited omniscience of the Divine, considering God's omniscience as "the capacity to know everything that becomes actual, whenever it does so."[115]

Despite the support that Peacocke enjoyed from these colleagues based on God's relation to a self-creating cosmos, his theology of self-limited divine omniscience was criticized on the basis of the classical notion of the relation of God to time. This tradition holds that the relation of God to time follows from divine immutability. Because time is "nothing but the numbering of movement by *before* and *after*" and by beginning and end, God, who is wholly immutable, has no movement of before and after and no beginning or end.[116] Hence, on the basis of divine immutability, two implications flow concerning the relation of God to time. First, the immutability of God implies a lack of succession in time, because the notion of time derives from the notion of mutability or change. Second, the immutability of God implies unending duration; thus God has no beginning or end. Furthermore, because of the lack of succession in God, created time exists as an instantaneous whole before God, as "the simultaneously-whole and perfect possession of interminable life."[117] Thus, God does not have knowledge of future events successively, as creatures do, but apprehends all creatures and events in the simultaneous present of divine eternity. According to Aquinas, "The reason is because His knowledge is measured by eternity, as is also His being; and eternity being simultaneously whole comprises all time."[118] Accordingly, God not only knows those things that exist in actuality but also knows those things that are in potency. God therefore knows those particular events and actions of creatures that will be actualized in the future. However, such divine knowing is not *fore*knowledge of cosmic events and actions, which militates against the real exercise of creaturely freedom, but is *simultaneous* or *contemporaneous* knowledge of cosmic history. Therefore, cosmic freedom is preserved in Aquinas's formulation because the acts of created agents are not *fore*known in advance and thus remain truly free.[119]

Connecting this line of thought with the insights of evolutionary science, Denis Edwards first expresses partial agreement with Peacocke and Polkinghorne in their affirmation of God's respect for and responsiveness to "the freedom of human persons and the contingency of natural processes," as well as the divine self-limitation of omnipotence that it entails. Nevertheless, on Thomistic grounds, he parts ways with these thinkers concerning divine knowledge of the future. Citing Peacocke and Polkinghorne's argument concerning the intrinsic unpredictability of natural processes, he considers it an "unwarranted logical leap" to go from God's respect for such intrinsically unpredictable processes to the proposition that God cannot foresee future outcomes. Appropriating the classical position concerning the eternality of God, Edwards maintains that God's knowledge of future events is not based on the divine capacity for prediction but on the divine embrace of all time by the eternity of God. Because of this divine eternality, God's knowledge of the whole of time does not conflict with the inherent unpredictability of the cosmos. Thus, while the future remains radically open and undetermined by the present, God's omniscience remains unlimited because of God's particular relationship to time.[120]

God in Relation to Time

While affirming Peacocke's inference concerning God's self-limitation of omniscience based on the evolutionary understandings of the freedom, autonomy, and unpredictability of the cosmos, I consider the underlying rationale for maintaining or disputing divine omniscience more significant for this project. This underlying rationale has two points: the freedom and autonomy of the cosmos and its creatures and the classical understanding of the relationship of God and time. These concepts are significant because, along with the other aspects of Divine Becoming, they exert a critical impact on whether God may be conceived as suffering creatively in, with, and under the creative processes of the cosmos with their costly unfolding *in time.* If God is conceived as totally transcending time and temporal events, as suggested by the classical understanding of God's relation to time, this conception would prove a liability not only to my present argument but also to the biblical tradition and to religious experience that witness to the passibility and responsiveness of God to cosmic and human events. Hence, as John J. Davis maintains, "A God whose emotional states never change is not the God of the Bible." Rather, "the *personal* and *living God* of biblical theism," of evolutionary theology and of this thesis "is a God who changes not in his essential nature, character, or purposes, but who does change in the way he responds to his covenant people."[121] This is especially so in response to the ubiquity of pain, suffering, and death endemic in the cosmos and in human experience.

For his part, Peacocke had an evolving notion of God's relation to time. In *Science and the Christian Experiment*, Peacocke conceived of God as "outside" time, such that "time itself is other than God and part of the created cosmos." However, because God's creative activity in the cosmos is, from the evolutionary standpoint, perennial and not completed, "there is no more difficulty in regarding God as having a creative relationship with the cosmos at all times . . . if he himself is not in time at all, that is, if his mode of being is not within the temporal process." Peacocke suggested that a "conceptual impasse" exists in trying to understanding how God as transcendent Other can be related to time at all, an impasse stemming from the fact that humans can never truly assert who or what God is in Godself.[122] Despite this apophatic demurral, Peacocke discussed at some length the notion of God as Holy Spirit, immanent in the cosmos and working through the laws and regularities of nature. In conclusion, he contended, "If God is in the world-process of matter at all, he is in it all through, in all its potentialities, whether actualized or not, and he continues to hold it in being by his will with these potentialities and not otherwise." Rather than conceiving of God as deus ex machina, intervening from time to time to transition from one stage of the cosmic hierarchy to another, "it now seems more consistent to urge that God has been creating all the time through matter and the 'laws' governing its transformation"—yet presumably all the while "outside" time.[123]

In *Creation and the World of Science*, however, similar thoughts by Peacocke concerning God's mode of being and the temporal process provoke a rather extended footnote that effectively reveals the intellectual struggle to reconcile the notions of God's activity in time and God's creation of time. This excursus to his Bampton Lecture, "Cosmos, Man and Creation," features several pervasive themes in his theology and bears quoting at length.

> But if God's mode of being is not within the temporal process, does this not mean that God is "timeless"? This is a particular form of the problem between transcendence and immanence that always arises in any discussion of the various models of the activity and nature of God as Creator. How can God be thought to act *in* time and yet be

the creator *of* time? Recent analyses of this question show that a number of important traditional attributes of God (e.g. his person-hood, his ability to act in the cosmos, his ability to know the world as temporal and changing) lose coherence and meaning if God is re-garded as "timeless" in the sense of being "outside" time altogether in a way which means time cannot be said to enter his nature at all, so that he can have no temporal succession in his experience. But sim-ilar remarks pertain to space in relation to God: how can God be thought to act *in* space, and to be the creator *of* space, and yet to be non-spatial, to have no spatial location? . . . We must therefore posit *both* that God transcends space and time, for they owe their being to him, he is their Creator; *and* that space and time can exist "within" God in such a way that he is not precluded from being present at all points in space and time, a way of speaking of the world's relation to God we shall have cause to employ again.[124]

One can clearly see in this reflection the emergence of Peacocke's thinking on the panentheistic paradigm of the God-world relationship. Through this par-adigm, he envisions a means by which to integrate, reconcile, and reflect on the nature and attributes of God in response to his cognitive dissonance. In these reflections, it is clear that Peacocke moved from his prior notion of God as absolutely timeless to a more nuanced notion of the relation of God and time.

In his lecture on "Creation and Hope," Peacocke reflected on the issue further through the theology of Wolfhart Pannenberg concerning the futurity of God. Peacocke agreed with Pannenberg's notion of time as "the locus and occasion of divine free creativity," as well as his understanding that "all times are present to God." According to Peacocke, the notion of time at issue here is that of "physicists' time" or that time which is intertwined with the matter-energy-space continuum as part of the natural order. In this sense of time, God is "timeless" or beyond the created order of which time is a part. However, in another sense of time, the sense of time that is conceived as a succession of events or successive consciousness, Peacocke agreed with Pannenberg that such succession must exist within God if God is to have a self-disclosive rela-tionship to the cosmos within historical time. Within this approach to time, human persons have a sense of the succession of their conscious states that is bound up with and yet transcends physical created time. Similarly, if one is to conceive of God as personal or suprapersonal, then one must postulate an in-herent self-awareness of successive states of consciousness within Godself that, though linked to physical time, is nonetheless distinct from time itself.[125] Such a postulate is necessary, in the words of J. R. Lucas, because "to deny that God is temporal is to deny that he is personal in any sense in which we understand personality."[126] Furthermore, Lucas suggests that to be a person is to be capable of consciousness and to be conscious is to be aware of the passage of time. In addition, Lucas links temporality to another of Peacocke's core concepts concerning the personal nature of God, that of personal agency. As regards personal agency, Lucas contends that to act as agent is to bring about change, and change results in things being different than they would have been otherwise.[127] Hence, whether one focuses on the notion of successive consciousness in God, on the concept of God as personal or suprapersonal, or on the understanding of God as agent, one is led to Peacocke's conclusion that God must be regarded as not only beyond time but also in some way temporal.

Peacocke's reference to the scientific understanding of time introduced a second avenue through which Peacocke reflected on God's relation to time. As suggested in this discussion, "physicists' time" is a fundamental and integral aspect of the matter-energy-space-time matrix that constitutes the created order. As an aspect of the created order, time owes its existence to God and is essentially "other" than God. Thus, on this basis, God transcends the temporal order. However, the scientific understanding of the cosmos as continuously productive of emergent and irreducibly complex forms as *creatio continua* in theological terms—introduced into the concept of God's relation to the world a temporal dynamism that had always been implicit in the Hebrew notion of the living God. Confronted once again with the understanding of God as both transcendent over and immanent in creation, Peacocke combines his psychological and scientific insights concerning time with the theological notions of God as transcendent Creator *of* and immanent Creator *in* time. In so doing, Peacocke conceives of God as transcendently creating each instant of physical time within the time-space-matter-energy complex of the cosmos, within which God then immanently and continually participates. God creates each moment of time with its open, undetermined outcomes and its possibilities not yet realized and, at the same time, is present and active in every moment of it. Hence, "God [may be] conceived as holding in being in physical time all-that-is at each instant and relating his own succession of divine states (the divine 'temporality') to the succession of created instants without himself being subject to created physical time." As a result, Peacocke affirms that

> *God is not "timeless"; God is temporal in the sense that the Divine life*
> *is successive in its relation to us—God is temporally related to us;*
> *God creates and is present to each instant of the (physical and, deriva-*
> *tively, psychological) time of the created world; God transcends past and*
> *present created time: God is eternal, in the sense that there is no time*

at which he did not exist nor will there be a future time at which he does not exist.[128]

Consequently, God cannot be considered immutable or impassible in the strong classical sense of the term, that is, as not subject to change in any way. John Polkinghorne concurs, contending, "It is clear that the God of the temporal process is more vulnerable in relation to creation than is the atemporal God of classical theism."[129] While David Pailin suggests that such a position is controversial, he nonetheless agrees with Peacocke that divine actuality must be conceived as having temporal dimension if human beings are to make any sense of their relation to God within temporality and of the nature of God as intentional and personal.[130] In response to such critiques, Peacocke acknowledged that a "weaker, though more intelligible and relevant, sense" of immutability of divine character, purpose, intent, and disposition may be held in tandem with a notion of God who is conceived as passable in time.[131] Nevertheless, "such a God, by virtue of creating in Space and Time a universe with some degree of inbuilt freedom, exposes himself to being acted upon and, in that sense, being compelled to change."[132]

When considering the ultimate implications of God's decision to limit Godself in power and knowledge and to expose Godself to effect and to change, Peacocke pointed out that these divine choices are immensely costly to God. Such divine choices entail the cost of continually placing the divine purposes for the cosmos at risk, a risk that entails the pain, suffering, and death that are ubiquitous in the cosmos. Undeniably, these are costs and risks borne inherently by the cosmos in its costly unfolding in time. However, these are also costs and risks borne by God "in the act of self-limitation, of *kenosis*, which constitutes God's creative actions—a self-inflicted vulnerability to the very processes God had himself created."[133] In this vulnerability, God opens Godself to and involves Godself in the panoply of pleasures and pains, joys and sufferings, life and death inherent in all levels of the cosmos. Moreover, this vulnerability is borne by God in a triune manner. God as Transcendent encompasses and embraces the cosmos within the Divine Being itself; God as Incarnate enfleshes divine love, life, and purpose by becoming one with the cosmos in its costly being and becoming; and God as Immanent labors, creates, and transforms the cosmos from within.

God as Vulnerable, Self-Emptying, and Self-Giving Love

Recognizing that "in creating the world continuously God has allowed himself not to have overriding power over all that happens in it nor complete knowledge of the directions events will take" and maintaining that such "self-limitation is the precondition for the coming into existence of free self-conscious human beings," Peacocke suggested that these divine self-limitations "render it meaningful to speak of the *vulnerability of God*, indeed of the *self-emptying* (kenosis) *and self-giving of God* in creation."[134] According to Peacocke, in biological evolution, the self-creative processes of the cosmos, which include the interplay of chance and law, have elaborated over time complex self-reproducing systems capable of receiving and reacting to stimuli from the environment, that is, systems capable of consciousness and, in the human person, systems capable of self-consciousness. This evolutionary movement toward self-consciousness is associated with increasing independence and freedom that, in humanity, is exercised not only in and through the created order but also over and against this order and not only in and through the intentions of the Creator's own self but also over and against these intentions. Based on these observations, Peacocke concluded,

> God intended that out of matter persons should evolve who had freedom, and thereby allowed the possibility that they might challenge his purposes and depart from his intentions. To be consistent, we must go on to assume that God had some overarching intention which made this risk worth taking, that there was and is some fundamental way of God being God which allows God's relationship with freely responding persons to be valued by God over that of other forms of matter, which have no option but to be what they are created to be in their relation to God.[135]

Peacocke noted that his postulate of God's overarching purpose for and value of humanity over other forms of matter "is not meant to be at all dismissive of the significance of non-human creation" because at each level of creation "something is reflected in its own measure of the divine purpose." Nevertheless, because humanity has been given "this hazardous yet potentially creative ability to be free," Peacocke inferred that God has "higher purposes" for humanity that warrant a gift of such great cost to God. For, through this gift of freedom, God risks that "God's own ability to effect his purposes would be frustrated by the actions of another personal existence, namely man." Thus, in creating humanity with such freedom, God acted with "supreme magnanimity on behalf of the good of another existent," a magnanimity that must be conceived as an expression of God as Love. Therefore, creation, for Peacocke, must be regarded as "a self-emptying by God, a risk he incurs lovingly and willingly for the opportunity of the greater good of freely responsive man coming to be within the created world." Moreover, because, in persons, the creation of an "other" with independent existence suggests the presence of *pathos* in such persons, then, for a personal God, "love and self-sacrifice are, from this perspective, seen as inherent to the divine nature."[136]

It is curious that Peacocke found it necessary to postulate the "overarching purpose" of human emergence for the self-limitation, vulnerability, and self-emptying love of God when the inbuilt propensities of the cosmos as freely and autonomously self-creative with the interplay of chance within law seem to disclose the self-limitation, vulnerability, and self-emptying of its Creator far before the emergence of humanity in the universe. Although Peacocke contended that he did not intend to be dismissive of nonhuman creation, his inference in this case did not seem to bear him out. If, as James Huchingson suggests, God appreciates and delights in the natural world, why is greater attention given to the *theosis* of humankind as the aim of creation, rather than to the inherent worth of creation as a whole?[137] Clearly, the postulate of an overarching intention is anthropocentric rather than cosmocentric in nature. Consequently, it implicitly depreciates the intrinsic value of the cosmos *in se* and suggests that the cosmos and its processes as inbuilt by God possess only instrumental value as the conduit for the emergence of the human person. Furthermore, such a postulate makes a teleological claim that suggests, in a Teilhardian fashion, an ultimate directionality to the evolutionary process that, although consistent with the anthropic principle, does not allow for the de facto fits and starts, the wrong turns and dead ends, the trials and errors characteristic of the evolutionary process.[138] In view of these realities, it may have been more consistent with Peacocke's overall approach to assert with D. G. Trickett, "There can be no creature which does not somehow display within itself the being of the creator; it is not only human beings but also all other creatures who bear God's image and are God's fellow creators."[139]

In his later writings, Peacocke associated the creative self-emptying and self-offering of God with Isaac Luria's Jewish kabbalist notion of *zimzum*, which suggests that "God withdrew his omnipresence in order to concede space for the presence of creation . . . 'Where God withdraws himself from himself to himself, he can call something forth which is not of divine essence or divine being.'"[140] However, in addition to this notion of the self-emptying of God as withdrawal to make space for creation within Godself, a notion that is clearly panentheistic in nature, Peacocke pointed out that this creative self-emptying is also revealed in God's entry into the evolutionary processes of creation themselves. Because Peacocke had always regarded these processes as God-*qua*-Creator immanently active in the evolution of the cosmos, then the pain, suffering, and death that affect the cosmos in these processes of creation must be conceived as also affecting God as Creator. Unfolding this understanding as "the costliness of creativity," Peacocke further explained,

In other words the processes of creation are immensely costly to God in a way dimly shadowed by and reflected in the ordinary experience of the costliness of creativity in multiple aspects of human creativity—whether it be in giving birth, in artistic creation, or in creating and maintaining human social structures. . . . Now, as we reflect on the processes of creation through biological evolution, we can begin to understand that this . . . involved God's costly, suffering involvement in them on behalf of their ultimate fruition in the divine purpose and in their ultimate consummation.[141]

Clearly, if God is immanently present and active in creative processes of the cosmos that are pervaded by pain, suffering, and death, then this inevitably implies God's own costly suffering within these processes themselves. According to Peacocke, "we can perhaps dare to say that there is a creative self-emptying and self-offering (a *kenosis*) *of God*, a sharing in the suffering of God's creatures, in the very creative, evolutionary processes of the world."[142] However, the creative processes of the cosmos in which God is immanently present and active also *produce* pain, suffering, and death for the cosmos and its creatures. This is especially so in the presence and action of that unique emergent of the cosmos, humanity. Hence, in view of the pain, suffering, and death that both pervades and results from the "uncertain clashes of the contingent process"[143] of cosmic creation, Peacocke arrived at a theological conclusion: "for any concept of God to be morally acceptable and coherent . . . we can not but tentatively propose that *God* suffers in, with, and under the creative processes of the world with their costly unfolding in time."[144]

The Creative Suffering of God

As the scientific evidence from evolutionary cosmology and biology has repeatedly demonstrated, "creation is not . . . something done once for all." Hence, God's activity as Creator is ongoing in, with, and under the entire cosmic process. Such processes include several dynamics:

> the operation of chance in a law-like framework as the origin of life; the emergence of new forms of life only through the costly processes of natural selection with the death of the old forms; and the emergence of sensitive, free, intelligent persons through a development that inevitably involves increasing sensitivity to pain and the concomitant experience of suffering.[145]

This convergence of cosmic dynamics, what Polkinghorne calls the elements of "free process,"[146] frequently results in what humans term "natural evil," that is, "those events, involving apparently pointless suffering and tragedy, which are inimical to human health, welfare and happiness, and indeed life."[147] These are events that proceed from the nonhuman world—earthquakes, floods, hurricanes, tsunamis, and the like, as well as the natural biological breakdown of living organisms in diminishment and death. However, although the operation of law and chance, of natural selection, and of the emergence of human persons produce situations of sometimes immeasurable tragedy, it is ironic to acknowledge that these eventualities, according to Peacocke, are also "the fundamental basis for there being any life at all and any particular form of biological life, especially free-willing, self-conscious life such as our own."[148]

Hence, because of the divine choice to create the cosmos in the way in which science describes it—in autonomy and freedom, through chance within law, and unpredictable in principle—the conditions do exist within the cosmos itself for the existence of pain, suffering, and death. In the self-creativity of the cosmos through the interplay of chance and law, the continuing creation of the cosmos exhibits not only the emergence of new life forms but also the inevitably costly process of natural selection. It produces not only the kaleidoscopic fecundity that delights both creatures and Creator but also the calamitous events of pain and suffering in the natural world. It creates not only serendipitous moments of joy and well-being but also events that cause the destruction and extinction of certain forms of cosmic life.

Ultimately, this self-creativity through chance and law results in the emergence of sensitive and free persons with not only increased consciousness and self-consciousness but also increasingly acute sensitivity to pain and suffering. It brings forth beings who "are *not* the mere 'plaything of the gods,' or of God" but who are sharers "as co-creating creatures in the suffering of God engaged in the self-offered, costly process of bringing forth the new."[149] However, in bringing forth such beings, a new dimension of suffering appears, a suffering that is not a necessary concomitant of evolution through free process but is a contingent consequence of the exercise of human free will in ways inimical to the life and well-being of others and to the creative intentions of God. "For humanity is free to go against the grain of creative processes, to reject God's creative intentions, to mar God's creation, and to bring into existence disharmonies uniquely of its own . . . humanity has the ability to cause God to suffer in an especially distinctive way."[150] Hence, in risking both the means and the results of cosmic instantiation of *Homo sapiens*, God—and in fact creation and its creatures—risks and suffers effects that are unfavorable to the living organisms of the cosmos. However, Peacocke contended, it is unavoidable. If it is God who "wills into existence the kinds of living creatures that depend on the operation of the same factors that produce those particular 'natural' evils," then, Peacocke inferred, "even God cannot have one without the other."[151]

Recognition of the risk, however, suggests a new richness and dimension in the Christian affirmation of God as Love. Divine love is manifest in the creative self-emptying and self-offering of God in creation, a sharing in the sufferings of God's creatures in the evolutionary processes of the world. Not only does God self-offer and self-empty in love for the created "other" but also God "suffers the natural evils of the world along with ourselves because . . . God purposes to bring about a greater good thereby, that is, the kaleidoscope of living creatures, delighting their Creator, and eventually free-willing, loving persons who also have the possibility of communion with God and with each other."[152] The inevitable conclusion of such observations, Peacocke suggested, is that "love and self-sacrifice are . . . seen as inherent in the divine nature and expressed in the whole process of creation. Perhaps this is what the author of the Revelation was hinting at when he described Christ, whom he saw as now present within God, as 'The Lamb slain *from the foundation of the world.*'"[153]

Moreover, according to Peacocke, Christians have experienced this richness and dimension of God as suffering love preeminently communicated and incarnated in and through the life, suffering, death, and resurrection of Jesus the Christ. Those who believe in Jesus the Christ "as the self-expression of God in the confines of a human person" find the conception of suffering in God as "entirely consonant with those conceptions of God . . . derived tentatively from reflection on natural being and becoming, which affirm that God, in exercising divine creativity, is self-limiting, vulnerable, self-emptying, and self-giving— that is, supremely Love in creative action."[154] Elaborating this insight, Peacocke contended,

> If God was present in and one with Jesus the Christ, then we have to conclude that *God* suffered in and with him in his passion and death. The God whom Jesus obeyed and expressed in his life and death is indeed, therefore, a "crucified God," and the cry of dereliction can be seen as an expression of the anguish of God in creation. . . . The suffering of God, which we could infer only tentatively in the processes of creation, is in Jesus the Christ concentrated into a point of intensity and transparency that reveals it as expressive of the perennial relation of God to the creation.[155]

It is significant to understand, however, that the love of God revealed in the Christ event discloses more than the self-limiting, vulnerable, self-giving, and suffering love of God revealed in the evolutionary processes of the cosmos.

Divine love further disclosed itself in an all-the-more striking way through the "action and expression of Love . . . that eventually overcomes evil in humanity" through raising Christ from the dead.[156] The Christ event dramatically discloses the creativity of divine suffering love that ultimately overcomes the pain, suffering, and death endured by Jesus the Christ in the power of the resurrection, a creativity disclosed as well in creation. Although God does not prevent the occurrence of either the inherent pain, suffering, and death that result from the free and autonomous evolutionary self-creativity of the cosmos or the inflicted pain, suffering, and death that result from the free and autonomous abuse of volition in its human creatures, neither does God's creativity intend that pain, suffering, and death endure or triumph. Dimly reflecting the creative Love that raised Jesus from the death inflicted by aberrant exercise of human freedom, the evolutionary process has demonstrated that there is a potential for new life that proceeds in some way from the death or transformation of entities and structures that already exist in the cosmos. Hence, the resurrection of Jesus the Christ and the evolutionary process of the cosmos reveal that pain, suffering, and death are within the liberating and transforming embrace of the creative Love of God whether such pain, suffering, and death result from the dysteleological designs of human sinfulness or from the evolutionary processes of cosmic self-creativity. The God who suffered in Jesus the Christ is ceaselessly active in continuous and loving creativity in the vagaries of the creative processes of the cosmos, even as God was definitively active in raising Jesus the Christ from the dead—acting to renew and transform all entities and structures that suffer pain and death, to reveal that life is changed and not ended, and to bring forth from the events and entities of cosmic history new and emergent modes of enduring life.

The understanding of the suffering of God as "an identification with, and participation in, the suffering of the world" as it struggles to push beyond suffering to new and transformed life further clarifies that creativity is an essential aspect of the suffering of God in Peacocke's evolutionary theology.[157] The creativity that is an intrinsic aspect of divine suffering—an aspect that does not allow it to become mired in futility but dynamically moves toward new and abundant life—not only serves to distinguish it from the dysteleological and meaningless suffering endured by countless victims of inflicted violence throughout history but also gives further support to the panentheistic understanding of the God-world relationship. It suggests with "new and poignant pertinence" the Pauline vision of creation in the pangs of giving birth, a "creation that waits with eager longing . . . groaning in labour pains until now."[158] Moreover, it leads to the suggestion that the most appropriate expression of suffering toward new life is found in the travail of female procreativity.

The panentheistic model also serves to refute the classical theistic conception of God's existence as "spatially" separate from the world. In this conception, "there is an implied detachment from the world in its suffering." Hence, if God is to respond in some way to the evil and suffering of the cosmos, God must do so "from outside" in an interventionist manner. Aside from the scientific problem this poses, the theological dilemma is all the more acute. As Peacocke summarized this dilemma, "Either God can [intervene] and will not, or would but cannot: God is either not good or not omnipotent. The God of classical theism witnesses, but is not involved in, the sufferings of the world— even when closely 'present to' and 'alongside' them." However, when the relationship between God and the cosmos is conceived panentheistically, there is no such detachment. The sufferings of the world become internal to Godself in an intimate and actual way. Hence, the link between evolutionary science and the suffering of God forged by Jesus the Christ is all the more fortified through the panentheistic model. Thus, Peacocke translated the good news of his Christian theology of the suffering of God into authentically panentheistic terms:

> God in taking the suffering into God's own self can thereby transform it into what is whole and healthy—that is, be the means of "salvation" when this is given its root etymological meaning. God heals and transforms from within, as a healthy body might be regarded as doing. The redemption and transformation of human beings by God through suffering is, in this perspective, a general manifestation of what is, for Christians, explicitly manifest in the life, death, and resurrection of Jesus the Christ.[159]

Clearly, in an evolutionary understanding of the creative suffering of the Triune God, divine suffering cannot be construed as passive but, rather, "as active with creative intention...[through which] God brings about new creation through suffering."[160] This does not valorize or glorify suffering in itself but acknowledges that, in a cosmos that evolves through free process and free will, suffering is an inevitable concomitant. Surely, "Nothing," not even understanding the genesis and inevitability of pain, suffering, and death in a free cosmos, "can diminish our sense of loss and tragedy as we experience or witness particular... evils, especially in individuals known to us."[161] However, when considered within the context of cosmic creativity, this evolutionary understanding of suffering resonates with the suffering of God in Jesus the Christ. His was a suffering brought about through the aberrant exercise of free will, but his also was a suffering transformed by the creative impetus of the immanent Spirit of God, bringing life and liberation out of death and destruction. Hence, at the end of its exploring of Divine Being and Becoming, this chapter has arrived at where it started, at the revelation of the suffering God of the cosmos in the life, death, and resurrection of Jesus the Christ.[162]

There is a certain propriety to this, in that the realization of the active, creative, and salvific suffering of the Triune God emerged for Arthur Peacocke at this very same place. For Peacocke, "what were glimmers of light on a distant horizon," the horizon of the natural being and becoming of an evolutionary cosmos, became in Christ "shafts of the uncreated light of the Creator's own self." What were "hints and faint echoes of the divine in nature" became in Jesus the Christ "a resonating word to humanity from God's own self"—a word of self-offering, self-emptying, and creative Love, capable of bringing newness of life from suffering and death for the transformation and liberation of the world.[163]

Summary

Along the journey through this chapter toward his affirmation of the suffering of God, Arthur Peacocke provided guidance with both scientific research and theological inferences and laid the groundwork for the affirmation of the creative suffering of the Triune God. This groundwork began with Peacocke's fundamental understanding of the relationship between the cosmos itself and the source of its existence, a relationship that, within his Christian tradition, Peacocke understood as that of creation to its transcendent Creator. As transcendent Creator of an ordered cosmos and the ground and source of its very being and regularity, God shares a unique and inextricable relationship with the cosmos, in which the cosmos is fully dependent for its very being on the Being of the Divine who faithfully, intentionally, and purposefully sustains and preserves the life of the cosmos.

However, illumination of science upon this groundwork demonstrates that the evolving life of the cosmos neither reflects the seemingly static condition of sustenance and preservation nor suggests a condition in which creativity is intermittent or episodic. Within the vivified, dynamic, and emergent self-creativity of the cosmos, God is revealed as the continuously creative and immanent Source of cosmic creativity in, with, and under the self-creativity of the cosmos itself. Moreover, this cosmic self-creativity is not to be understood as a separate movement or energy apart from or alongside the creativity of God as immanent and continuous Creator but truly as Godself immanently present and active in and through the self-creativity of the cosmos. This God-world relationship of both transcendent and immanent creativity is most fruitfully imaged in a panentheistic model, a model that conceives the cosmos within God as its transcendent Ground of Being, and God within the cosmos as its immanent Source of creativity, without identifying the cosmos with its creative Ground and Source.

The groundwork laid through the interactive and illuminative approach to reality through science and theology reveals not only the creative *activity* of God but also the creative *essence* of God, disclosed as Divine Being. The order and regularity of the cosmos disclosed divine rationality, and the kaleidoscopic and fecund variety of the cosmos revealed divine unity-in-diversity. The cosmological conditions that resulted in the emergence of *Homo sapiens* disclose the personal nature of the Divine, because only a God conceived as personal could be considered the ultimate source of a cosmos that includes human personhood at the summit of its hierarchy of created being. Furthermore, only a God who is conceived in truly personal terms can be considered relational and participative vis-à-vis the entities, structures, and processes of the cosmos. Finally, only a God such as this can be the God of Christianity, the God of Triune personhood, the God Who is Love.

This acknowledgment of God as immanently and continuously creative and as eminently personal suggested that the underpinnings of this theology must also include elements that are dynamic and vibrant and images that befit the receptivity and responsiveness of personal and relational beings. Hence, the theological groundwork of this exploration expanded to include not only concepts of God as Divine Being but also concepts of God as Divine Becoming. God is affirmed as more than the transcendent ground and sustenance of the original being of the cosmos. God is also the immanent source of its continuous, open, free, and autonomous becoming. Therefore, God as Creator is conceived not only as the source of order and regularity in the cosmos but also as the cause and catalyst of the creative interplay of chance.

However, if such chance occurrences contributed to an essential indeterminacy and unpredictability in the evolving cosmos, it is apparent that God does not avail Godself of the unlimited power and knowledge that initially brought the cosmos into being. Rather, in creating a cosmos in love—and thus in freedom and autonomy—God chose to limit Godself in divine omnipotence and omniscience. In so doing, God chose to become vulnerable to the openness, freedom, and autonomy of the cosmos and, ultimately, to risk the divine purposes in order to safeguard cosmic integrity with its self-creative unfolding in time. Hence, in a cosmos beset by the suffering that attends inherent and inflicted pain and death, God's self-limitation, vulnerability, and risk strongly suggest that God, too, suffers in, with, and under the entities, structures, and processes of the cosmos, with their costly, open-ended unfolding in time. If this inference holds true, then the nature of this divine suffering must be consistent with the nature of Divine Being and Becoming. It must be a suffering that is both transcendent and immanent, that is suprapersonal and relational, that is self-limited and vulnerable, and that is creative and transformative.

In the next chapter, I examine these underpinnings afforded by the dialogue between theology and science and test whether this groundwork is able to bear the weight of the affirmation of the creative suffering of God. In so doing, many of the insights are assessed for their fit with the data of evolutionary science, of the Christian tradition, and of the panentheistic model of God-world relationship. I examine their simplicity and fecundity in providing images and metaphors for right speech about God in the midst of suffering and experientially assess the pastoral efficacy of such speech. On the basis of this assessment, I elaborate three areas of an evolutionary theology of the creative suffering of the Triune God in theological, ethical, and pastoral directions. Theologically, I advance a panentheistic-procreative model of the creative suffering of God based on female images of the Divine drawn from the Jewish and Christian religious traditions. Ethically, I propose an ecological ethics for an evolving cosmos based on the model of midwifery derived from a female panentheistic-procreative paradigm. Pastorally, I explore a triune understanding of the suffering of God in terms of divine sympathy, empathy, and protopathy for the life of the world.

5

Evolution and Divine Suffering

In my opening chapter, I joined my voice with a chorus of twentieth- and twenty-first-century theologians, including Jürgen Moltmann, Jon Sobrino, and Sallie McFague, to maintain that one cannot "do theology as usual" after the Holocaust, or after Hiroshima, Nagasaki, September 11, and Iraq, or in the specter of Ethiopia and Darfur, or in the aftermath of Hurricanes Katrina and Wilma and the tsunami of Southeast Asia, or against the backdrop of global oppression and violence and ecological despoliation. In my own voice, I articulated my conviction that the affirmation of the concept of the creative suffering of the Triune God in, with, and under the sufferings of the cosmos is a theoretically defensible, theologically viable, and pastorally crucial response to such existential realities. In the chapters that followed, I joined another chorus of theologians, including Arthur Peacocke, John Polkinghorne, and Ian Barbour, who further contend that one cannot "do theology as usual" after the disclosures of evolutionary cosmology and biology and quantum physics concerning the cosmos and its creatures. In this present chapter, I test the validity of this contention by analyzing and evaluating key concepts in evolutionary theology as they relate to the concept of the creative suffering of the Triune God.

Key Confluences toward the Suffering of God

In any constructive enterprise, the groundwork on which one seeks to build must be robust enough to support the structure. Such strength comes not only from the individual elements of the groundwork but also from the fusion of these elements into an integrated whole. Such is the groundwork that Arthur Peacocke provided in his evolutionary theology of Divine Being and Becoming toward the creative suffering of the Triune God. Each constituent part of his evolutionary theology supports the others in so integral a fashion that none is dispensable to his ultimate task. Because I am focusing on that particular aspect of his evolutionary theology that concerns the creative suffering of the Triune God, however, I find that certain elements of his evolutionary groundwork are especially salient to a proposal of divine suffering: the costliness of the evolutionary process, the existential reality of cosmic indeterminacy, the whole-part interaction of God and the world, the anthropic principle of cosmic development, the transcendent and immanent creativity of God, and the panentheistic paradigm of God-world relationship. The sections that follow reprise critical aspects of each of these key concepts. Furthermore, they analyze and assess how each specifically contributes to the affirmation of the creative suffering of the Triune God in, with, and under the creative processes of the cosmos in its costly unfolding in time.[1]

The Costliness of Evolution

Evolutionary theology's proposals concerning divine suffering in relation to the cosmos find their frame of reference in an understanding of creation as "a costly process."[2] Although many scientists dismiss the common notion of the process of natural selection as principally the struggle for survival, a notion caricatured in Tennyson's poem "In Memoriam" as "nature red in tooth and claw,"[3] Peacocke acknowledged "the structural necessity" that "new life can only emerge if other forms of life are, as it were, incorporated into, or sacrificed on behalf of, the higher forms." Consequently, in the process of emergence through which novel forms and patterns arise from forms preceding them in evolutionary complexity, Peacocke also recognized that "there is a cost when new forms of life emerge which are dependent on simpler forms for their continued existence."[4]

Those like Peacocke immersed in the Christian tradition inevitably correlate this scientific insight with the theological insight of God as vulnerable, self-emptying, and suffering love disclosed through creation and Incarnation.

Peacocke did so in a Trinitarian way. First, "God has to be described as 'love' because, in creation, he deliberately limits himself, by allowing a cosmos to remain in being which is other than himself, which is given its own autonomy and so limits his freedom, and which in man can consciously repudiate his creaturehood." Second, God is affirmed "as self-offering love in the self-limitation which was his incarnation in Jesus Christ and in the self-offering of Jesus's human life for men," in which Jesus as "God-made-man" reveals "the true character of God." Third, "God the Holy Spirit is characterized especially by his communicating to those who follow Christ the ability to love."[5]

In later works, Peacocke expanded these earlier inferences concerning the vulnerable love of God for the cosmos by means of scientific insights concerning the inherent open-endedness of creative processes through law and chance. For Peacocke, elements of this loving vulnerability to the random forces of the cosmos and its creatures were also disclosed in the life of Jesus the Christ. According to Peacocke, "[Jesus'] path through life was pre-eminently one of vulnerability to the forces that swirled around him, to which he eventually innocently succumbed in acute suffering and, from his human perception, in a tragic, abandoned death."[6] Nevertheless, through evolutionary science and through the Christ event, Peacocke understood that death need not have the last word. As evolutionary science demonstrated, life is sustained by and is emergent from the death or transformation of entities and structures that already exist in the cosmos. In this insight, Peacocke saw a dim reflection of the divine creativity that transforms suffering and death to new life and understood it as the divine creativity that raised Jesus from the dead. Therefore, the evolutionary process, like the paschal mystery, reveals that pain, suffering, and death, though ubiquitous in a cosmos of free process and free will, are within the liberating and transforming embrace of the creative Love of God. Hence, God both suffers and saves in the costly evolution of the cosmos, even as God suffered and saved in Jesus the Christ.

The Existential Reality of Cosmic Indeterminacy

A critical advance occurs in an evolutionary theology of the suffering of God with scientific developments in biology, cosmology, and quantum physics as they related to the inherent unpredictability of the cosmos. Despite the virtual demise of the Newtonian mechanistic model of the universe, science still assumed and depended on a level of predictability in its discipline.[7] Such predictability seemed to be obvious at the macrolevel of cosmic events, that is, at the level of the operation of necessity or natural law. However, biological observation of the emergence and evolution of life in the cosmos and quantum experiments with subatomic particles revealed that there seemed to be an intrinsic indeterminacy and unpredictability at the microlevel of the cosmos. This is the level associated with the operation of chance in cosmic creativity and with the apparent unpredictability in measurement of particle position and movement.[8] Throughout his writings, Peacocke continually confronted the theological challenges posed by such manifestations of cosmic indeterminacy in relation to the classical postulates of divine omnipotence, omniscience, immutability, and impassibility in relation to the cosmos. If the operation of chance and the phenomenon of quantum indeterminacy are intrinsic elements of the cosmos—a cosmos deemed the creation and self-communication of a rational and purposeful Creator—then in what way and to what extent can Christians affirm the power and knowledge of God as regards the cosmos?

Following Peacocke's reasoning, if there is irreducible autonomy, freedom, and unpredictability evident in the cosmos from its micro- to its macrolevels; if such autonomy and freedom express themselves in the God-given self-creativity of the cosmos through the interplay of chance within law and the indeterminate events of quantum physics; and if such autonomy and freedom are intended by and disclosive of a rational, purposeful, and loving Creator, then God as omnipotent and omniscient Creator must have imposed limitations on God's creative Self in order that the cosmos might unfold its potentialities in the open-ended and free self-creativity intended and inbuilt by God's own Self. Peacocke's unwavering affirmation of the self-limitation of God that results from the randomness of cosmic creativity and from quantum indeterminacy, however, has drawn criticism for offering what one writer terms a "weakened and vitiated" theism.[9] However, according to Nicholas Saunders, Peacocke denies that God can switch cosmic propensities on and off. "Indeed," as regards quantum indeterminacy and divine omniscience, Saunders argues, "God in [Peacocke's] view is so coherent that he cannot both support a truly indeterministic scheme and have knowledge of it at the same time."[10] Despite his affirmation of Peacocke's theological coherence, however, even Saunders questions whether "the need to allow God to act in history and revelation . . . means that any autonomy in the God-cosmos relationship must be qualified by God's providential sovereignty over his creation."[11]

Peacocke's refusal to equivocate on the integrity and autonomy of the cosmos also led to criticism that he has allowed the idea of divine self-limitation and suffering to dominate his concept of the Christian God to the exclusion of redemption and transformation.[12] This in turn suggests more poignant questions of the pastoral efficacy of the notion of the self-limitation of God. Does the attribution of self-limitation and suffering in God solve the problem of suffering? Does the "hyphen" have the power to reconcile Creator and created, or is it, in Highfield's term, simply "theology-by-punctuation"?[13] Can one build trust in a Creator in the face of divine self-limitation, suffering, and risk?[14] In the effort to redress past theological imbalances, has the pendulum swung too far?[15] Is it enough to claim that suffering is natural and that God suffers with human beings? Although I address these vital questions in greater depth later in this chapter, I must note at this point that such critiques and questions reflect an inadequate understanding of Peacocke's evolutionary theology as a whole. While plainly affirming the self-limitation and suffering of God, Peacocke's theology also strongly asserts the omnipotence and omniscience of the Divine Being of God as transcendent Creator. While clearly acknowledging the pervasiveness of divine and cosmic suffering, Peacocke emphatically maintains that suffering in God and in the cosmos is not static but inexorably moves toward new or transformed life. While the freedom and autonomy of creation in general and of humanity in particular sometimes hampers God's insistent urging toward life in cosmic history, the dynamism of redemption, liberation, and transformation toward new and abundant life is nonetheless the essential and indisputable dynamic of the Christian God. Thus, in unequivocally maintaining both the transcendence and immanence of God in relation to an evolving and indeterminate cosmos, Peacocke avoids the situation posed by John J. Davis in which the Christian is forced logically and theologically to choose between a God conceived as timeless, omniscient, impersonal, and unresponsive and a God conceived as temporal, personal, responsive, and self-limited.[16]

Whole-Part Interaction of God and the Cosmos

In his understanding of God as Creator of the universe within a noninterventionist scientific model, Peacocke proposes that God's interaction with the cosmos comes through whole-part influence, a proposal that clearly and directly addresses the means by which the Creator can influence the creation. However, if one follows Peacocke's own fuller understanding of his whole-part model, one finds that he understood the movement of influence in this model not solely as "top-down" but as bidirectional. Despite this understanding on Peacocke's part, theologians such as James Wiseman have criticized him for lacking a bidirectional component and, therefore, for de-emphasizing the immanent relationship between God and the cosmos.[17] However, this is clearly not the case, as one can see in Peacocke's explanation in *Theology for a Scientific Age*:

> It is important to emphasize again that recognition of the role of such "top-down" causation in no way derogates from that of "bottom-up" causation. . . . So it is legitimate to describe the realities postulated

as existing at the higher levels (the wholes, the "top" of the "top-down" terminology) to be causally interactive, in both directions, with the realities postulated as existing at the lower ones (the parts, the "bottom")—while continuing, of course, to recognize the often provisional nature of our attempted depictions of reality at both levels.[18]

Therefore, based on the "top-down" aspect of this model in which the system-as-a-whole influences its constituent parts, God may be conceived to genuinely influence events and behaviors at all levels in the hierarchy of created being in a whole-part fashion. However, based on the "bottom-up" aspect of this model, in which the constituent parts influence the system-as-a-whole, the inherent finitude, behavior, and intentionality of the parts of the cosmos may also be understood to exert a part-whole effect and even constraint on the intentions and influences of its personal Creator. Because, in an evolutionary framework, creation retains autonomy and freedom in its relationship with the Creator, it is conceivable that God's capacity to influence the cosmos may encounter resistance and rejection in the creaturely realm, most especially in the realm of the human. Moreover, because the Divine remains free and autonomous, as well as loving and just in relation to creation, it is conceivable that God, too, may resist or refuse participation in the freely chosen actions of human persons that are inimical to the divine will and intentions. In either case, within a model of whole-part/part-whole interaction between God and the cosmos, the cosmos clearly has the capacity to influence and affect the Divine, even to the point that I am suggesting—that such processes cause God to suffer in, with, and under the entities, structures, and processes of the cosmos in their costly unfolding in time.

In view of this dynamic, it is clear that the understanding of God as Continuous Creator in whole-part/part-whole interaction with the cosmos provides a critical element in the affirmation of the creative suffering of the Triune God. If God is Continuous Creator, sustaining, preserving, vivifying, and transforming the cosmos through immanent creativity and whole-part influence, "then God has entered into the very life of things. Every quark, every particle, every aspect of matter and energy is connected to God's desire and hope for the world."[19] However, if this creative relationship is bidirectional, then God does not remain in isolation from the events, entities, and processes of the cosmos. Rather, God exists and acts in intimate and immanent involvement with these cosmic realities, to the extent that these realities can exert their effects on God. If this is the case, then God does not remain unaffected by cosmic realities, even those that include pain and death with the suffering that attends them. What is more, as transcendent and immanent Creator, God embraces and permeates these entities, processes, and structures of the cosmos in all their pain and suffering, false starts, and dead ends. But in God's gracious doing so, these very painful events become the means through which the Triune God intimately draws near and passes by, disclosing Godself as transcendently, immanently, and incarnately present and active in the travail of cosmic history.[20]

The Anthropic Principle of Cosmic Development

Although God is not *a* person or even three *persons*, according to most contemporary understandings of the term, in view of the apparent fine-tuning of the universe toward human life termed the anthropic principle, one can infer that the nature of God is "at least personal," "suprapersonal," or even "transpersonal" if God is to be the transcendent ground of personal subjectivity. Based on this anthropic principle and on the assessment of humanity as the most highly developed, complex, and sensitive entity in the cosmos, the least misleading way of speaking about the God who created such complex beings is to use language that expresses the uniqueness of this creature, the language of personhood. Furthermore, human personhood not only represents a distinctive kind of entity in the universe but also provides a distinctive type of explanation in the universe, namely, the explanation of personal agency.

Hence, if the personal is the most irreducible entity in the cosmos and if personal agency is the most irreducible type of explanation for events in the cosmos, then one could conclude that only a God conceived as personal could be considered the ultimate source of a cosmos that includes human personhood and personal agency at the summit of its hierarchy of being and behavior. However, not all theologians agree. Some have suggested that an extrapolation of the anthropic principle to the personal nature of God raises "theological doubt" and serves to create God in humanity's image rather than the converse.[21] Even Peacocke cautioned that such a theological move "personalises God too much, that is, speaks in an excessively extrapolated manner of the ultimately ineffable Divine Being."[22] However, the notion of an unequivocally personal God finds strong support in the powerful words of Paul Tillich:

> Why must the symbol of the personal be used at all? The answer can be given through a term used by Einstein himself: the supra-personal. The depth of being cannot be symbolized by objects taken from a realm which is lower that the personal, from the realm of things or sub-personal living beings. The supra-personal is not an "It," or more

exactly, it is a "He" as much as it is an "It," and it is above both of them. But if the "He" element is left out, the "It" element transforms the alleged supra-personal into a sub-personal, as usually happens in monism and pantheism. And such a neutral sub-personal cannot grasp the center of our personality; it can satisfy our aesthetic feeling or our intellectual needs, but it cannot convert our will, it cannot overcome our loneliness, anxiety, and despair. . . . This is the reason that the symbol of the Personal God is indispensable for living religion.[23]

Acknowledging both the limits of language and the power of the personal for a living religion, I support the affirmation of the personal nature of God as essential to the notion of the suffering of God. This support stems from three lines of thought concerning the nature of the personal derived from Peacocke's work. First, it is of the nature of the personal to be purposive and to communicate those purposes through goal-directed agency. If this is also true of the personal nature of God, then, in view of the indeterminate free process of the cosmos and the arbitrary free will of its human creatures, it is logical to infer that the purposeful and goal-directed agency of God within the cosmos is arguably an agency at risk of delay, frustration, and even rejection. Consequently, the risk and frustration incurred through this dynamic and purposeful relationship with the cosmos may well entail for God what "in a human context, might well be described as suffering."[24] Second, it is of the nature of the personal to be conscious and self-conscious. If this is true of the personal nature of God, then, in view of the coincidence of consciousness and suffering in human personhood—a coincidence associated with, but distinguishable from, physical pain—it is logical to infer that the preeminent consciousness and self-consciousness of God must have a preeminent capacity to experience personal suffering. Third, it is of the nature of the personal to be capable of love. If this is true of the personal nature of God, then, in view of the association of suffering with human love and of the self-offering and self-emptying love communicated through the personhood of God in Jesus the Christ, it is logical to infer that the God whose personal nature is unconditional love possesses the capacity to suffer unconditionally in that love. In Peacocke's own words,

> risking love on behalf of another who remains free always entails suffering in the human experience of love. . . . So our "model" of God as the personal agent of the creative process has to be amplified to include an awareness of him as the Creator who suffers in, with, and through his creation as it brings into existence new and hazardous possibilities.[25]

Transcendent and Immanent Creativity

As I have made evident by the sheer volume of repetition, there is perhaps no theological concept that Peacocke tried as fiercely to maintain and defend throughout his theology as the concept of the radical transcendence and immanence of God as Creator in relation to the cosmos. Throughout his writings, this radical transcendence and immanence of God as Creator has been held together in a variety of ways by means of the Christian concept of the Triune God.[26] In his earliest writings, Peacocke's emphasis focused on the primacy of the Triune God as transcendent and immanent Creator of and in the cosmos. At that time, Peacocke expressed this notion in explicitly traditional categories. Pointing to the Nicene Creed as theological grounding for the Triune creativity of God, Peacocke maintained,

> God the Father is believed in as "Maker of heaven and earth, and of all things visible and invisible"; God the Son as he "by whom all things were made"; and God the Holy Spirit as "the Lord, the Giver of life".... [It] is notable that in this Creed one God is said to be creator, but that each "Person" of the Triune God is explicitly involved with creation.[27]

Expanding this insight in terms of the evolutionary development of the cosmos, Peacocke affirmed,

> God is one and acts fully, completely, in all his manifestations (he is "coinherent") yet... is distinguishable in three forms. As transcendent, God (the Father) initiates by his will the whole cosmic development; as incarnate, God (the Son) focuses and reduces his being into the confines of a human personality; as immanent, God (the Holy Spirit) works through the whole cosmic development, which culminates in the life "in Christ."[28]

In subsequent writings, Peacocke explored alternative theological models that functioned to maintain this balance of divine transcendence and immanence. These models included that of the *Logos* as the expression of God in creative activity, the Wisdom (*Sophia*) of God active at the creation of the world and powerfully immanent in the cosmos and in humanity, the Spirit of God "not as referring to a divine hypostasis... but as indicating God himself active towards and in his human creation," and ultimately the model of panentheism in specifically female terms.[29] In addition, *God and the New Biology* explicitly unfolds Peacocke's sacramental view of the universe, "which incorporates the Christian understanding of God's trinity of being and which takes seriously the scientific perspective." Finally, in terms that clearly reflect philosophical categories, Peacocke expressed this integrated view of the universe thus:

> The world is created and sustained in being by the will of God. . . . The Son, or Word of God (the *Logos*), is the all-sufficient principle and form of this created order. At every level, this order reflects in its own measure something of the quality of the deity. . . . The continuing creative power which is manifest as a *nisus* at all levels of existence to attain its intended form is . . . God as "Holy Spirit."[30]

In his most recent works, however, Peacocke largely abandoned his attempts to correlate his evolutionary theology of God with the traditional categories and models of Christianity. Inexorably drawn by the classical Christian tradition, Peacocke admitted, "It is tempting to relate the triply-formulated concepts which denote ways in which God is understood to relate to the world specifically to the three traditional *personae* of the Trinity, that is to Father, Word/*Logos*/ 'Son' and Holy Spirit."[31] However, rather than engaging in such "intellectual vertigo," Peacocke preferred "not to speculate about the relationship of the three to each other . . . [and] to remain reticent about any more positive, ontological affirmations concerning the, by definition, ineffable and inaccessible Godhead."[32] Hence, one does not find inferences concerning the "immanent" and "economic" Trinity or concerning God *in se* and God in creation. Rather, one increasingly finds in Peacocke an understanding of the One God distinguished as personally Transcendent, personally Incarnate, and personally Immanent and characterized in panentheistic relation to the cosmos.

Although Christian theology has not historically resorted to a panentheistic formulation of the concept of the Trinity to hold together the transcendence and immanence of God in relation to the world, I find the use of the panentheistic paradigm compelling.[33] First, the panentheistic formulation of God as Trinity enables one to embrace and to balance significant beliefs in Christianity concerning the nature and attributes of the Triune God. Such beliefs include the understanding of God as transcendent, incarnate, and immanent; as Creator and Source of cosmic being; as infinite, necessary, and free; and as omnipotent, omniscient, and faithful sustainer of the cosmos. At the same time, panentheism has the power to engage with integrity the creative and necessary task of reconstructive theology in response to the compelling insights of contemporary science. These insights include the elements of evolutionary cosmology and biology; the freedom, autonomy, and self-creativity of the cosmos and its creatures; and the ubiquity of pain, suffering, and death inherent and inflicted in the cosmos. Finally, a reformulation of the notion of God as Trinity in terms of panentheism and in terms of God's creative relationship to the cosmos as transcendent, incarnate, and immanent has significant implications for a divine response to the pervasiveness of cosmic suffering.

Three consequences of a panentheistic theology of God as transcendent and immanent Creator deserve emphasis in dialogue with the notion of a suffering God. First, if one conceives the Trinity in terms of God's relation to the cosmos as Transcendent, Incarnate, and Immanent, then classical distinctions between God *in se* and God in relation to creation do not apply in such an evolutionary theology. Therefore, no distinction needs to be made concerning the capacity for divine suffering in God *ad intra* as opposed to God *ad extra*. Second, if the Trinity as Transcendent, Incarnate, and Immanent is understood in panentheistic terms and, thus, in inextricable relation to the cosmos, then no aspect of the Trinity is detached from the God-world relationship. Therefore, cosmic and human images for the suffering of the Divine remain, however inadequately and falteringly, appropriate venues for expressing this cosmic and human experience of the Divine.[34] Third, if the Trinity as Transcendent, Incarnate, and Immanent is conceived in panentheistic terms, then the being and becoming of the cosmos is integral to the Being and Becoming of the Divine. Hence, events in the life of the cosmos, including events of pain, suffering, and death, are events in the life of God. "All that is created is embraced by the inner unity of the divine life of the Creator—Transcendent, Incarnate, and Immanent."[35]

The Panentheistic Paradigm of the God-World Relationship

As evident from the preceding discussion, the overarching philosophical concept of the panentheistic paradigm of the God-world relationship draws together multiple elements of scientific and theological thought. This paradigm effectively integrates into one cohesive model the evolutionary and quantum insights disclosed through the sciences—the costliness of evolution, cosmic indeterminacy, whole-part interaction, and the anthropic principle—and the Christian concept of the Triune God as transcendent, incarnate, and immanent. One uses this metaphor fully cognizant that " 'words strain, crack and sometimes break, under the burden' of trying to speak in the least misleading way possible about the divine nature."[36] Nevertheless, the panentheistic model of God-world relationship has the remarkable capacity to entwine the manifold strands of my theological argument intelligibly and productively. This is especially true of the argument for the creative suffering of the Triune God.

Peacocke's own selection of the panentheistic model of God-world relationship results from his perception of the inadequacy of Western classical theism in conceptualizing the Creator God of Christianity in transcendent, incarnate, and immanent relation to the cosmos. This inadequacy of classical theism stems in part from its insistence on maintaining the ontological distinction between the Creator and creation in terms of discrete "substances." Because of the ontological impossibility of the interpenetration of different substances, the created realm was conceived as "outside" God, and thus God's ongoing influence on creation could be conceived only in terms of interventions from outside the world. This conception carries with it three difficulties for evolutionary theology. First, this concept's excessive emphasis on God as transcendent tips the balance with God as incarnate and immanent that trinitarian theology seeks to maintain. Furthermore, it precludes the concept of the self-creativity of the cosmos as the immanent creativity of God-*qua*-Creator. Finally, it suggests that God's creativity in the cosmos is interventionist, which provokes acute difficulties from a scientific perspective. A different model for expressing the intimate presence of the Divine in, with, and under the cosmos and its processes must be employed that yet maintains the distinction between Creator and the created.

The movement from substance ontology to relational finds echoes in theologians such as Walter Kasper, Catherine LaCugna, and Denis Edwards. According to Walter Kasper, "the ultimate and highest reality is not substance but relation."[37] Denis Edwards has written similarly, suggesting "reality . . . is more a network of relationships than a world of substances."[38] Catherine LaCugna cites the ontological traditions of Greek and Latin theology to suggest, "*personhood is the meaning of being.* To define what something is, we must ask who it is or how it is related. . . . We need now to specify the ontology appropriate to this insight, namely an ontology of relation or communion."[39] Hence, a critical element in appropriating the panentheistic model is to make the move away from "substance" ontology to "personal" or "relational" ontology. As described by LaCugna,

> A relational ontology understands both God and the creature to exist and meet as persons in communion. . . . The meaning of to-be is to-be-a-person-in-communion. . . . God's To-Be is To-Be-in-relationship, and God's being-in-relationship-to-us *is* what God is. A relational ontology focuses on personhood, relationship, and communion as the modality of all existence.[40]

For Peacocke, the effectiveness of this move is found in countering the critique by Christian theology that, in the panentheistic model, there is no distinction between God and creation. Such a lack of distinction would suggest either that God is pantheistically identified with creation or that creation is incorporated into the divine.[41] However, if one asserts that the ontological distinction between the Creator and created is best conceived as "personal" or "relational," then this suggests a distinction of "subjects" rather than "substances." Hence, one can maintain the intimate, internal, and interpenetrating relationship between God and creation while still upholding both the ontological distinction between Creator and created "subjects" and the balance of the Transcendent, Incarnate, and Immanent "subjects" of the Triune God.

The imagery of intimacy, internality, and interpenetration in the creative process suggests to Peacocke that the language of human procreation might offer a viable means by which to talk about God as transcendent, incarnate, and immanent Creator. However, search as he might among traditional theological images of God-world relationship—images that predominantly reflect a patriarchal imagination and symbol system—Peacocke was not able to find a model that adequately communicated the understanding of the interpenetration of God in the cosmos and the cosmos within God in ontologically distinctive, yet internal ways. According to Peacocke, traditional Western models of God's creative activity place "too much stress on the externality of the process—God . . . regarded as creating rather in the way the male fertilises the female from outside." In response to this theological difficulty, Peacocke suggested that a "more fruitful" model derived from the female procreative process and, thus, from female imagery.

> Mammalian females nurture new life within themselves and this provides a much needed corrective to the purely masculine image of divine creation. God, according to panentheism, creates a world other than Godself and "within herself" (we find ourselves saying for the most appropriate image)—yet another reminder of the need to escape from the limitations of male-dominated language about God.[42]

In Peacocke's procreative model, God as Ground of being—indeed, pregnant mother—brings the cosmos to birth *within* her. According to Ian Barbour, "this seems to represent a degree of unity intermediate between that of a mother's relation to her own body, on the one hand, and that of her relation to a growing child . . . on the other." Like his own process model, Barbour claims, Peacocke's procreative model safeguards the distinct identities of God, of the cosmos as a whole, and of individual creatures, while yet recognizing their interdependence and relatedness.[43]

At this point, it is important to consider the ramifications of this panentheistic-procreative model on the evolution of Peacocke's concept of the suffering of God. For the most part, the link between the suffering of God and the suffering of the cosmos in Peacocke's thought has been forged through the life, suffering, and death of Jesus Christ and expressed in the acclamation of God as self-emptying Love. The introduction of the panentheistic-procreative paradigm, however, fashions another means by which to conceive of God's suffering in relation to the suffering world. Despite the growing affirmation of the suffering of God in Christian circles, "in the classical perception God as transcendent and as existing in a space distinct from that of the world, there is an implied detachment from the world in its suffering."[44] However, a panentheistic-procreative paradigm yields no such implication. Moreover, if the classical perception of the Divine provoked the dilemma of God's response to evil and suffering as a clash between divine power and divine benevolence exercised beyond the pale of cosmic existence, no such dilemma exists here.

On this point, nonetheless, critics like John Polkinghorne contend that if God is understood panentheistically as both transcendent ground of all being and immanent participant in the creative processes of the cosmos, then God must be conceived as actively and receptively participative in the suffering of the cosmos, a conclusion that Polkinghorne associates with process theology.[45] In an attempt to differentiate and defend his understanding of panentheism in opposition to process theology, however, Peacocke suggested that "process theology has tended to over-emphasize God's *total* receptivity to all events in the world in a way that seems to allow God little discrimination." By contrast, Peacocke asserted that, in his own usage of the panentheistic model, "I have not wanted to imply an equally direct involvement of God in all events nor that all events equally and in the same sense affect God."[46]

Despite this qualification by Peacocke, Polkinghorne continues to insist that invoking different levels of involvement and effect does not seem to resolve the conflict. In his later works, however, Peacocke suggested,

> when the natural world, with all its suffering, is panentheistically conceived of as "in God," it follows that the evils of pain, suffering, and death in the world are internal to God's own self: God must have experience of the natural. This intimate and actual experience of God must also include all those events that constitute the evil intentions of human beings and their implementation—that is, the moral evil of human society.[47]

Hence, in further response to Polkinghorne's critique, Peacocke clearly affirms the *receptivity* of God in Divine Being and Becoming to all manner of existential reality, both well and ill, while at the same time implicitly rejecting God's *active* or *volitional* involvement in cosmic travail by invoking notions such as cosmic indeterminacy.

Consequently, the proposal of the panentheistic-procreative paradigm proves to be an especially apt way not only of modeling the God-world relationship in which the world is conceived "as being given existence by God in the very 'womb of God' " but also of "evoking an insight into the suffering of God in the very processes of creation. God is creating the world from within and, the world being 'in' God, God experiences its sufferings directly as God's own and not from the outside."[48] This is an insight pregnant with possibility that I explore in the final chapter of this book.

Evaluation

Having identified, analyzed, and assessed the key concepts that contribute to Arthur Peacocke's evolutionary theology of the suffering of God, I now move to an evaluation of Peacocke's proposals specifically in terms of the creative suffering of the Triune God. Contending that the concept of the creative suffering of the Triune God is theoretically defensible, theologically viable, and pastorally crucial in view of this suffering world, I now test this proposal by means of four principal criteria: (1) fit with data, (2) simplicity, (3) fecundity, and (4) pastoral efficacy. The *data* with which such proposals must *fit* are threefold: the broad features of the entities, structures, and processes of the evolving cosmos; the fundamental insights of the Christian tradition; and the panentheistic paradigm of the God-world relationship. The *simplicity* of a proposal is judged by the directness and clarity of its expression, free of circumlocution and convolution that serves to evade the logical consequence of an experience or of its inference. The *fecundity* of a proposal requires that it have generativity, a vitality about it that has the capacity to foster new ideas and creative responses about God and the God-world relationship regarding suffering. Finally, these ideas and responses must demonstrate *pastoral efficacy*, the capacity to inspire, transform, and liberate human persons and the universe in ways that promote the full flourishing of all manner of being in the midst of a suffering world.

Fit with Data

As just indicated, the criterion of *fit with data* addresses three elements with which Peacocke's proposals must show coherence. These elements are the insights of evolutionary science, the Christian theological tradition, and the panentheistic paradigm of the God-world relationship.

EVOLUTIONARY SCIENCE

As the basis for Peacocke's theology of God, the insights of evolutionary science prove more than fitting for Peacocke's postulate of God as suffering and Triune

Creator. Several core notions provide this fit. One begins with the free and autonomous self-creativity of the cosmos that inherently entails the death of old forms for the emergence of new forms of life. The presence of pain in the sentient creatures of the cosmos both accompanies this death and serves as a means by which to protect creatures from death, in that pain functions as a warning signal for danger and disease. In sentient, conscious, and self-conscious creatures, however, this pain is further attended by the experience of suffering. Although pain is an odious physical sensation, suffering implies the "conscious endurance of pain or distress"[49] or the awareness of "the disruption of inner harmony" that results from physical, mental, emotional, and/or spiritual forces.[50] It is the experience of sentient creatures and conscious persons "induced by the loss of integrity, intactness, cohesiveness, or wholeness" or by the destruction and frustration of purposive behavior.[51] It may be a consequence of cosmic processes operating freely and autonomously through law and chance and within the reality of cosmic indeterminacy. It may also be a consequence of human persons operating freely and autonomously through action and intentions that have results deleterious to persons and purposes other than their own.

By these measures, the affirmation of God as suffering Creator coheres with affirmations of God as rational, as personal, and as purposive in relation to the cosmos and thus, analogously, as capable of suffering the disruption of harmony and the frustration of purpose that produce distress in human persons. This affirmation is amplified when the concept of God as rational, personal, and purposive is integrated with the notion of God as Triune Creator of the cosmos. With this integration, one can conceive of God not only as suffering the disharmony and destruction of divine purpose brought about by human persons operating freely and autonomously through action and intentions that have results harmful to the cosmos and its creatures but also as suffering the pain, suffering, and death ubiquitous in the cosmos through the creative processes identified with God-*qua*-Creator. Hence, "Any serious consideration of the creative action of God as dynamic and evolutionary," as the continuous, integral, and pervasive action of God-*qua*-Creator, "is inexorably led to face the fact of death, pain, and suffering in that process and so come to an understanding of God as the suffering Creator."[52]

THE CHRISTIAN TRADITION

Although much has been made of the fact that Peacocke's affirmation of the suffering of God conflicts with the classical theological tradition of Christianity, Peacocke indisputably incorporated Christianity's core theology of the Triune nature of God; its long-established belief in the transcendence, incarnation, and immanence of God in relation to the cosmos; the biblical tradition; and its central doctrines of creation and incarnation into his affirmation of the suffering of God. The affirmation of the suffering of God links to the Christian tradition through an understanding of divine suffering in Trinitarian terms. While choosing not to suffer the "intellectual vertigo" that so many theologians take upon themselves in their metaphysical speculations concerning the Immanent and Economic Trinity, Peacocke unequivocally accepted the trinitarian God as disclosed through the entities, structures, and processes of the cosmos. This Trinity is manifest as transcendent, as incarnate, and as immanent creativity in, with, and under the creative processes of the cosmos with its costly unfolding in time. Moreover, because this creativity is the activity of God's very self in the cosmos, this Triune God is also intimately involved in the costly consequences of that creativity for well or ill.

Peacocke also set forth a strong case that suggests significant biblical support for the notion of the divine dynamism and *pathos* of the "living God" and has made salient connections between the creative immanence of the suffering God in the cosmos and the groaning of the Spirit in bringing the cosmos to birth. However, the most powerful argument for consonance between the suffering of God in the cosmos and the Christian tradition, of course, centers on the paschal mystery of Jesus the Christ. Forged from the earliest stages of Peacocke's reflections on the suffering of God, this link is all the more fortified by his subsequent scientific insights. Affirming both the Christ *and* the cosmos as the self-communications of the self-offering, self-emptying, and self-limiting God of Love, Peacocke articulated this dual affirmation forcefully and poignantly:

> The God whom Jesus obeyed and expressed in his life and death is indeed, therefore, a "crucified God," and the cry of dereliction can be seen as an expression of the anguish of God in creation . . . the tragedy of his actual human life can be seen as a drawing back of the curtain to unveil a God suffering in and with the sufferings of created humanity and so, by natural extension, with those of all creation.[53]

Although one may clearly wish to temper the implication that it was through obedience to his God that Jesus endured the cross, one must recognize the indisputable fit between the affirmation of the suffering of God and the event of the cross. Furthermore, it fits with the pervasive cruciformity of the cosmos in, with, and under which God continually suffers in cosmic history.

One certainly sees in this formulation how Peacocke's conviction concerning the relationship of science and theology leads to efforts to discover consonance between evolutionary cosmology and biology and Christian faith without subjugating one to the other. On this point, however, some disagree. Alister McGrath, for example, expresses a general unease with Peacocke's "theological discernment" and suggests that Peacocke evaluates the Christian tradition according to his scientific needs rather than evaluating his theoretical work on the basis of Christianity.[54] Elmer W. Brewer echoes McGrath's sentiment, suggesting that Peacocke's approach attempted to integrate scientific and theological concepts. Brewer contends that Peacocke did not maintain the integrity of the two disciplines and that, invariably, "science holds the trump card" in this interaction.[55]

The remarks of both McGrath and Brewer, however, misrepresent Peacocke's methodology as an attempt at integration and, in so doing, misconstrue Peacocke's understanding of science and theology as interacting and mutually illuminative approaches to the same reality. According to John Polkinghorne, to conceive of Peacocke's methodology as solely the integration—or as Polkinghorne terms it, the "assimilation"—of the ideas of science into theology is to miss an equally strong tendency in Peacocke toward attempting to maintain consonance between the two disciplines.[56] Based on an accurate understanding of Peacocke's enterprise, one realizes that Peacocke sought neither to "theologize science" nor to concede theology to science.[57] However, in this scientific world, he did intend to speak "to those who would like to follow the Christian way but thought they could not do so with intellectual integrity."[58]

Beyond these methodological issues, Peacocke was also criticized for the understanding of Incarnation that underlies some of his inferences. These inferences include "if God was present in and one with Jesus the Christ, then we have to conclude that *God* also suffered in and with him in his passion and death"; "if Jesus is indeed the self-expression of God in a human person, then the tragedy of his actual human life can be seen as a drawing back of the curtain to unveil a God suffering in and with the sufferings of created humanity and so, by natural extension, with those of all creation";[59] and further, "the life and death—in conjunction with the teaching—of Jesus provide a profounder revelation than that afforded by the evolutionary process of the truth that God as creator suffers in and with his creation."[60] Although inferences such as these solidly forge the link between the suffering of God from an evolutionary perspective and from a Christian perspective, scholars such as Alister McGrath and John Polkinghorne question the ontology that grounds such statements.

McGrath wonders if Peacocke's "reductionist concept of incarnation" can bear the weight it needs to without some reference to the notion of the transcendence and immanence of God. Peacocke's notion of the Incarnation suggests that, in his human personhood, Jesus the Christ is the instantiation of both the transcendence and immanence of God. This, however, is a notion that McGrath indicts as "theologically vulnerable."[61] For his part, Polking-horne's critique centers on the fact that Peacocke seemed to present two differ-ent and ultimately conflicting interpretations of Incarnation. The first is the interpretation of Jesus as the instantiation of the transcendence and imma-nence of God; the second is that of Jesus the Christ as an example of emergent humanity.[62] Jim McPherson also raises this point. According to McPherson, if Jesus is emergent from the natural processes of creation, if Incarnation does not imply any descent from above, then it begs the question of whether Jesus the Christ can be considered the second person of the Trinity.[63]

In response, one must concede that Peacocke displayed a proclivity for ex-ploring a variety of theological and Christological interpretations based on his evolutionary insights, some of which inherently conflict with each other. Nevertheless, he was firm in the conclusion concerning the interrelation be-tween the self-disclosure of God in the cosmos and in Jesus the Christ. One might suggest that Peacocke's own expression, "Divine Being Becoming Hu-man," best articulated Peacocke's Christological understanding:

> If Jesus the Christ really is a self-communication *from* God and the self-expression *of* God in a human person . . . [then] what were glim-mers of light on a distant horizon might in him become shafts of the uncreated light of the Creator's own self. Hints and faint echoes of the divine in nature might then in Jesus the Christ become a reso-nating word to humanity from God's own self, a manifest revelation of God . . . in his person.[64]

In addition to these Christologically focused critiques, Peacocke's affirmation of the self-emptying and suffering of God—whether creative in nature, Triune in attribution, or loving in purpose—does not escape the variety of existential, philosophical, and theological critiques raised by Christian theologians con-cerning suffering in God discussed at the beginning of this book. In fact, to some extent, it exemplifies them. In Peacocke's perspective, the association of suffering with the divine does tend to entangle God in time, to inhibit God's freedom, and to subject the Creator to the vicissitudes of the created order. Moreover, his affirmation of divine suffering does radically contest the asser-tions of divine immutability, impassibility, omniscience, and omnipotence that are characteristic of classical theism. Furthermore, as implied by both McGrath and Brewer, Peacocke's assertion of suffering in God does loom as a potential liability to every classical Christian doctrine that considers these philosophical and theological predicates axiomatic.

Although Peacocke did not address such issues in his theological reflec-tions, his theology itself provides viable responses. First, it is clear that his continuous emphasis on the transcendence *and* immanence *and* Incarnation of God in relation to the cosmos serves to mitigate the force of these critiques. Because of the radical balance that Peacocke insists on maintaining among the trinity of divine modes of relation to the cosmos, God remains *both* temporal *and* atemporal, *both* free *and* freely self-restrained, *both* subject to *and* Subject beyond the vagaries of the created order. Furthermore, in his explicit intention to examine the impact of evolutionary and quantum science on the nature, attributes, and purposes of God, Peacocke was willing to bear the theological consequences of thinking within a novel paradigm. As Peacocke contended,

> Theology has been most creative and long-lasting when it has responded most positively to the challenges of its times. . . . It is in this spirit that we . . . attempt to shape a contemporary expression of the Christian experience of God in terms—metaphors, models, analogies and symbols—that might be believable and usable by a "Western" humanity now deeply and irreversibly, and quite properly, influenced by the sciences.[65]

As to further criticism of the concept of suffering in God—that it eternalizes or universalizes suffering, that it glorifies and commends suffering, or that it militates against action for justice and liberation—one looks to Peacocke's evolutionary insights for response. Peacocke made it clear that the suffering that attends pain and death is an existential aspect of a cosmos created by God in autonomy and freedom, through chance within law, with the capacity for self-creativity and the emergence of sentience and consciousness. Moreover, suffering is a given in a cosmos in which the ultimate emergent of that cosmos, a being who possesses self-consciousness and personal subjectivity in addition to sentience and consciousness, has the autonomy and freedom not only to assent to participation in the loving and creative purposes of the Creator of the cosmos but also to dissent from participation in these intentions.

Hence, given the existential reality of pain, suffering, and death that subsist as inevitabilities in a cosmos that evolves through free processes and free will, Peacocke's attribution of suffering to God does not glorify or commend suffering in the cosmos and in its creatures. Rather, it seeks to offer a morally acceptable and coherent response to the suffering of the cosmos and its creatures in their existential situation.[66] Moreover, as suggested before, although God does not prevent the occurrence of the inherent and inflicted evil that results from the freedom and autonomy of the cosmos and its creatures, neither does the creativity of God's suffering love intend that pain, suffering, and death endlessly endure or eschatologically triumph.

THE PANENTHEISTIC PARADIGM

Peacocke's theological affirmation of the transcendent, incarnate, and immanent Triune God, coupled with his emphasis on the doctrines of creation and
Incarnation, led him to affirm the panentheistic model of God-world relation as
the most appropriate model through which to model such a God-*qua*-Creator in
relation to creation. This model possesses an especially fine fit with the notion
of the suffering of God. By using the panentheistic paradigm with his concept
of God as transcendent, incarnate, and immanent in relation to the cosmos,
Peacocke provides a further means by which to affirm the suffering of God in
all aspects of divine relation to the cosmos. For Peacocke, there is neither need
nor justification to preserve the transcendence of God from being scathed by
the experience of suffering. To do so would be a morally incoherent response to
the ubiquitous suffering of the cosmos. By employing the panentheistic paradigm of the Trinity in relation to the world, however, Peacocke found a model
that adequately offers the moral and coherent response that he desired. For in
the panentheistic paradigm of divine transcendence, Incarnation, and immanence, God embraces, participates in, and permeates the cosmos in its costly
unfolding. As God does so, God freely suffers any and all things that the cosmos
itself endures and willingly suffers any and all things to bring the cosmos to life.

Simplicity

Clearly, the emergence of Peacocke's concept of the suffering of God in dialogue with evolutionary science often exemplifies the circuitous route of the
evolutionary path itself. Like the process of evolution, there is no straight shot
from origin to end. However, Peacocke's affirmation of the creative suffering of
God demonstrates both simplicity and directness of thought. For the most part,
there is no attempt on Peacocke's part to avoid the logical consequences that
flow from his evolutionary understandings to his theology of the suffering of
God, despite the fact that he articulates these consequences with all the reserve
and dissembling warranted by his critical realist approach to language about
God. There is, however, one notable exception to this assessment, and that
exception is in his rationale for the self-limitation and suffering of God, namely,
for the "overarching purpose" of the emergence of "freely responsive" humanity
in the cosmos.[67]

As discussed previously, Peacocke's postulate of this overarching purpose
seems to be unnecessarily convoluted and speculative because the free and

autonomous self-creativity of the cosmos seems to entail the self-limitation and suffering of its Creator far before the emergence of humanity in the universe. Furthermore, the postulate of an overarching intention is anthropocentric rather than cosmocentric in nature and implicitly depreciates the intrinsic value of the cosmos to an instrumental value as the conduit for the emergence of the human person. Having noted this exception in Peacocke's theology of the suffering of God, however, I must point out that Peacocke's articulation of his rationale for divine suffering has undergone development since its first expression in *Creation and the World of Science*. In more recent writings, he maintains that God "suffers the natural evils of the world along with ourselves because...God purposes to bring about a greater good thereby, that is, the kaleidoscope of living creatures, delighting their Creator, and eventually free-willing, loving persons who also have the possibility of communion with God and with each other."[68] With this development in his thought, Peacocke reinstates his cosmocentric approach and places humanity once again in its appropriate nexus within the cosmos. In so doing, Peacocke regains the simplicity and directness that is most characteristic of his discourse. Moreover, he avoided the suggestion that there is a hierarchical ordering of divine value and favor in the cosmos, an impropriety concerning the God who arrays the lilies of the fields that neither toil nor spin and who feeds the birds of the air that neither sow nor reap.[69]

Fecundity

One of the most significant features of Peacocke's theology in general and of his theology of the suffering of God in particular is the fecundity of his proposals. By situating his theology within an evolutionary worldview and within the panentheistic paradigm, Peacocke generated a myriad of new perspectives and possibilities for contemplating and symbolizing God, the cosmos and its creatures, and the God-world relationship. The concepts of the Divine as Cosmic Composer and as Improvisor of Unsurpassed Ingenuity; of the Triune nature of God as personally Transcendent, Incarnate, and Immanent in, with, and under the creative processes of the cosmos; of the cosmos as freely and autonomously self-creative, as characterized by kaleidoscopic fecundity and ubiquitous suffering, and as evolving through free process and free will; of its creatures as irreducibly emergent and of humanity as inextricably interwoven into the nexus of cosmic life; of the world as within God and of God within, but not exhausted by, the world; and of the procreative model of God birthing the world in anguish and in joy—each and all of these images of God and of the cosmos are pregnant with the promise of deeper and broader theological insight and discourse. Moreover, Peacocke's theology expands the settings in which his symbols of God, the cosmos, and their interrelation function, especially his symbol of God as suffering Creator. God does not suffer solely for creation's human emergents—for the atonement of human sin, for the salvation of human souls, for ransom from human bondage, or even for liberation from human oppression. God suffers in, with, and under the creative processes of the cosmos for the healing, the salvation, the transformation, and the liberation of the *whole of the cosmos* itself. Moreover, God does so as a mother who yearns to bring to new and abundant life the child of her womb.

Because of this, Peacocke's theology of the suffering of God addresses not only the obstacles that hinder classical theology in its efforts to respond morally and coherently to the ubiquity of pain, suffering, and death in the cosmos and in its creatures but also the concerns of those served by feminist theology, liberation theology, and ecological theology. It does so by not only addressing morally and coherently the sources of suffering visited upon and experienced by women, the subjugated, and the cosmos but also by lifting the burden of philosophical and theological paradigms of God and suffering that have only added weight to their experience of oppression. Furthermore, it does so in a way that respects the insights of science that reject an interventionist model of God-world interaction and that respect the core elements of the Christian tradition concerning the God who is self-emptying and vulnerable Love disclosed in Jesus the Christ. By affirming the concept that *God* suffers transcendently, incarnately, and immanently in, with, and under the inherent and inflicted pain, suffering, and death of the cosmos and its creatures, Peacocke's theology offers to all who suffer the promise of a God who is not only a companion in their suffering but also an incessantly creative impetus and catalyst for the transformation of pain, suffering, and death into new and emergent life.

Pastoral Efficacy

In the earlier examination of the effect of cosmic indeterminacy on the concept of the suffering of God, significant questions arose concerning the pastoral efficacy of such a concept to alleviate the experience of existential suffering endemic in the cosmos. These questions concerned whether the attribution of self-limitation and suffering in God served to solve the problem of suffering and whether a self-limited and suffering Creator was worthy of human trust. Although my responses at that point centered on a clear understanding of Peacocke's postulates concerning the Triune nature of God and the steadfast and unwavering creativity of God, these issues require further examination and response. In the perspective I set forth in this study, it is not the *affirmation* of the suffering of God that renders the Divine impotent and unworthy of trust. Rather, it is the *denial* of suffering in God that renders the Divine ineffective and irrelevant in the face of the existential reality of suffering in human and nonhuman creation. If one is left with the theodicy's dilemma of attempting to defend either the omnipotence or the benevolence of God or of trying to reconcile the two by means of divine omniscience—in other words, left with the understanding that God arbitrarily can intervene but refuses to do so for some reason known only to God—then Christians "are the most pitiable people of all."[70] However, for Peacocke, there was no such dilemma. Rather, through the insights of evolutionary science and the Christian tradition, Peacocke set forth a pastorally efficacious understanding of a Triune God who in transcendent, incarnate, and immanent vulnerability is familiar with suffering and bears cosmic grief. Moreover, he further identified a God who in transcendent, incarnate, and immanent creativity moves toward life and offers healing liberation. This pastorally efficacious response, therefore, centers on two pairs of insights in his theology of the suffering of God: the evolutionary process and the paschal mystery of Jesus the Christ and the Triune nature of God within the panentheistic-procreative model of God-world relationship.

"LIFE IS CHANGED, NOT ENDED": THE EVOLUTIONARY PROCESS AND THE PASCHAL MYSTERY

I have continuously noted throughout this work that the evolutionary process of the emergence of new life and novel forms in a closed universe frequently entails the death, the passing, or the transformation of old forms of life in order for the new to appear and develop. This dynamic process varies. At times it involves the death or extinction of species through natural selection or through the natural process of aging; at other times, it involves the incorporation of more rudimentary forms into more complex forms through the process of eating. Sometimes this process takes place through geologic or atmospheric events—through earthquakes, through volcanic eruption, through inclement weather conditions, and through tsunamis—with often calamitous results. In contrast, there are ubiquitous occasions when pain, suffering, and death are not part of natural evolutionary processes but are inflicted by the exercise of human freedom and autonomy upon the "other"—through starvation, through violence, through genocide, through warfare, and through despoliation. Hence, whether the source is inherent in the natural evolution of the universe or inflicted by human iniquity, in a cosmos characterized by free process and free will, pain, suffering, and death happen. The essential question is what the juxtaposition of this cosmic reality with the paschal mystery of Jesus the Christ has to tell humanity about the responsiveness and potency of God in the face of such existentials in the cosmos and in human experience. I suggest that what the cosmos reveals is thoroughly consonant with what the paschal mystery of Jesus the Christ reveals: that pain, suffering, and death are within the liberating and transforming embrace of the creative Love of God and that this creative Love of God has the capacity to bring forth from the most deleterious of events in cosmic and human history new and emergent modes of life. Fundamentally, the evolutionary process and the event of Jesus the Christ remind human beings that, ultimately, life is changed and not ended. Moreover, Peacocke's theology of the suffering of God discloses that the efficacious, creative, and salvific Love of God has the potential to be all the more effective because of its incarnate and immanent suffering in, with, and under cosmic history, a suffering that communicates to conscious and self-conscious creatures not separation, but companionship; not apathy, but empathy; not absence, but intimacy; and not arbitrariness, but steadfast love.

"IN, WITH, AND UNDER": THE TRINITY AND THE PANENTHEISTIC-PROCREATIVE PARADIGM

The evolutionary process and the paschal mystery as previously discussed provided a *dynamic* through which to assess the pastoral efficacy of Peacocke's theology of the suffering of God. Now, as this section considers God as Trinity and the panentheistic-procreative paradigm, one sees that Peacocke also provided *images* or *models* through which to assess pastoral efficacy. Beginning with the conceptual image of the Triune nature of God, Peacocke's understanding of God as transcendent, incarnate, and immanent suggests that God relates to the cosmos and to its creatures in three distinguishable yet unified modes. This is an understanding that Peacocke shared with the Christian tradition, albeit in a distinctly different way.

Whether one talks about the Trinity as Father, Son, and Holy Spirit or as Transcendent, Incarnate, and Immanent in relation to the cosmos, this affirmation of God as Trinity by Peacocke and by the Christian tradition springs from and leads to a differentiation of activities appropriate to each. For Peacocke and for the Christian tradition, each member of the Triune God shares in a distinctive way in the life of the cosmos. As the Nicene Creed affirms, the Father or God Transcendent is the "Maker of heaven and earth," the Son or God Incarnate is the one "through whom all things were made," and the Holy Spirit or God Immanent is the "Giver of Life." Although Peacocke did not suggest a similar differentiation with regard to divine suffering, there is logic in the assumption that, if members of the Trinity are distinguishable in terms of their modes of *creativity*, they are also distinguishable in terms of their modes of *suffering*.[71] Using Peacocke's own relational distinctions, the Incarnate, Transcendent, and Immanent God may be said to suffer *in, with,* and *under* the suffering of the cosmos and its creatures.

What is the point of distinguishing the modes of suffering in the Trinity? The point is precisely a pastoral one. The understanding that God as Triune has the capacity to suffer with the cosmos and its creatures in distinctive ways responds to the experiential reality of human suffering that is itself variously distinguished as sympathetic, empathetic, and protopathetic.[72] Distinguishing such modes of suffering in God enables human persons to identify their own suffering with the sufferings of God and to do so with the certain faith of the Hebrew psalmist who prayed, "O God, you know me . . . you understand my thoughts from afar . . . with all my ways you are familiar. Even before a word is on my tongue . . . you know it all."[73] Moreover, distinguishing modes of suffering in God offers different ways in which to find one's suffering relieved, for example, through sympathetic companioning, through empathetic identification, or through protopathetic resistance to suffering and evil in human and cosmic existence.

In addition to implying the Triune nature of God, the understanding that God suffers *in, with,* and *under* the cosmos led Peacocke to another pastorally efficacious means by which to model the divine travail, that of the panentheistic-procreative model of female pregnancy and birthing. By using such a model, one is able to image with unparalleled simplicity and clarity the profound intimacy and mutuality of creation and its Creator, the God whose essence is Love. Like a mother with the child of her womb, God in this model envelops, enfleshes, and permeates the very being of the cosmos. God provides for the cosmos of her womb a fecund environment in which to thrive, the matter and structures by which to develop, and the vitality and nourishment by which to flourish. Moreover, "when the natural world, with all its suffering, is panentheistically conceived of as 'in God,' it follows that the evils of pain, suffering, and death in the world are internal to God's own self: God must have experience of the natural."[74] And so it follows when the cosmos is imaged embryonically in the womb of God. Whatever the child suffers in its wholeness or in its most minute parts, the mother suffers as well in painstaking sensitivity until the health and well-being of her offspring are restored.

The pastoral efficacy of the panentheistic-procreative model also extends to the concerns of contextual theologies such as feminist theology and ecological theology. With regard to the aims of feminist theology, the use of female images and metaphors for the being and becoming of God and of the cosmos addresses a significant imbalance in the theological tradition of Christianity with its almost exclusive use of male imagery and language for God. Furthermore, this model stresses the value of embodiment, particularly *female* embodiment. In accentuating the value of female embodiment, this model unequivocally affirms the capacity of female experience and subjectivity to bear the image of the Divine. In so doing, it inherently critiques and condemns the subordination, denigration, and abuse of women and encourages an ethics of worth, equality, and mutuality within Christianity and within the world as a whole.

Ecologically, the panentheistic-procreative model stresses the profound connection between creation and its Creator, between the cosmos and the source of its being and becoming. Imaging the cosmos within God and God within and around the cosmos graphically demonstrates that what is experienced by the cosmos and by its creatures is immediately and acutely experienced by God. Earthquakes and tsunamis reverberate within God. Toxicity and pollution poison the offspring of God's womb. Rain forest depletion and strip mining disfigure the form of God's beloved creation. Through this realization, the panentheistic-procreative model effectively denounces the despoliation and devastation of the cosmos through human choices and behavior, accentuates the intrinsic rather than instrumental value of the cosmos, and urges humanity "to be co-creator with God ... acting for the good of both humanity and the Earth's eco-systems ... in such a way that it can go on being the medium through which life can continue and explore new forms of existence under the guidance of God."[75]

Summary

Informed by the panentheistic paradigm of the God-world relationship and by the evolutionary theology of Arthur Peacocke, the concept of the creative suffering of the Triune God has shown itself to be theoretically defensible, theologically viable, and pastorally efficacious in view of this suffering world. Arriving at this determination by examining the fecundity and pastoral efficacy of Peacocke's proposals, however, unquestionably stirs the desire to further develop his fertile ideas. Therefore, my final chapter of this book does just that.

In that chapter, I expand three aspects of Peacocke's theology of the suffering of God. The first is Peacocke's proposition that the suffering of God in, with, and under the entities, structures, and processes of the cosmos is best expressed through the use of female procreative imagery in the panentheistic model. Hence, I attempt to develop a female model of the suffering of God using the theological, mystical, and biblical notions of God as She Who Is, the

Source of all being;[76] as *Shekhinah*, the indwelling hypostatization of God with the poor and the suffering of Israel; and as *Sophia*, the pervasive spirit of divine Wisdom that permeates and impels creation toward fullness of life. The second is Peacocke's proposition concerning the suffering of God and ecological ethics. Thus, I explore Peacocke's own insights concerning the ecological ethics that spring from his concept of the creative suffering of the Triune God and suggest an additional ecological ethic of "midwifery," one consonant with the female procreative model developed and set forth. Finally, I unpack Peacocke's proposition of the suffering of God as *in, with,* and *under* the cosmos. In so doing, I attempt to find consonance between distinctive forms of human suffering as sympathetic, empathetic, and protopathetic and to suggest ways in which such forms of suffering might be predicated analogously to the Triune God. And at the end, when this present exploration must cease, I hope to find, like Peacocke himself, that "with the drawing of this Love and the voice of this Calling . . . the end of all our exploring will be to arrive where we started and know the place for the first time."[77]

6

Feminist, Ecological, and Pastoral Explorations

As I approach the end of this theological undertaking, "the drawing of this Love and the voice of this Calling" lead me to delve more deeply in this final chapter into three applications of an evolutionary theology of the creative suffering of the Triune God that demonstrate the praxical value of the theoretical exploration undertaken thus far.[1] These contexts are feminist theology, ecological ethics, and pastoral efficacy. Within the feminist theological context, I expand on Peacocke's proposal that the most appropriate imagery through which to articulate the creative suffering of God within a panentheistic paradigm is the female procreative experience. In so doing, I formulate a model of the creative suffering of the Triune God in terms of three female images for God drawn from the theological, mystical, and biblical traditions of Christianity and of its progenitor, Judaism. The first of these images is that of She Who Is, the Matrix of all being, which is based on Elizabeth Johnson's reading of the theological understandings of Thomas Aquinas. The second is that of *Shekhinah*, the indwelling hypostatization of God with the poor and the suffering of Israel, which is based on the kabbalist tradition of mystical Judaism. The third is that of *Sophia*, the pervasive spirit of divine Wisdom that permeates and impels creation toward fullness of life, which is based on the sapiential tradition of Hebrew Scriptures and on the Pauline tradition in the Christian Scriptures. Within the ecological context, I examine Peacocke's own insights concerning the ethical stance associated with his theology of the creative suffering of the Triune God.

These insights include the image of the human person as priest of creation and as cocreator with the Triune God. I then develop an additional model of ecological ethics for an evolving cosmos that is consistent with my female procreative-panentheistic paradigm based on the activity of midwifery.[2] Finally, within the pastoral context, I follow Peacocke's lead of differentiating the modes of divine creativity that each member of the Trinity has with the cosmos, and I conjecture that a similar differentiation might be made with regard to divine suffering. On the basis of such a conjecture, I propose that the suffering of God in relation to the cosmos may be understood in terms of transcendent sympathy, incarnate empathy, and immanent protopathy and support this proposal by suggesting the pastoral efficacy of such a differentiation.[3] Immediately following each of the three proposals is an evaluation that makes use of the fourfold criteria set by this study: fit with data, simplicity, fecundity, and pastoral efficacy. I then conclude this chapter and this study with remarks concerning the impact of these proposals on future theological discourse and praxis.

Explorations in Feminist Theology

The Panentheistic Procreative Model of the Creative Suffering of the Triune God

Based on his commitment to afford equal emphasis to each aspect of the triune relationship of God to the cosmos and underscored by his recognition that such a relationship implies intimacy, embodiment, and vivification in the creative process, Peacocke suggested throughout his writings that the language of human procreation might offer a viable means by which to talk about God as transcendent, incarnate, and immanent Creator. In so doing, he further proposed that the most fruitful model of this creative relationship derives from the female procreative process and, thus, from female imagery. According to Peacocke, in the female panentheistic-procreative model, "God . . . creates a world other than Godself and 'within herself.'"[4] Moreover, Peacocke contended, integrating the understanding of the Triune God as suffering into this procreative paradigm "gives an enhanced significance to this feminine pan*en*theistic model."[5] In view of these insights about the consonance of a female panentheistic-procreative paradigm with the suffering of God as Triune, I ask whether the traditions of Christianity or Judaism provide data through which to develop this insight and find three female images of God drawn from their theological, mystical, and biblical traditions. These are the theological appellation She Who Is, the mystical manifestation *Shekhinah*, and the biblical personification *Sophia*. Each image corresponds to one of the Trinitarian relations, each image has an integral relation to the others, and each image resonates with the timbre of divine suffering in response to the travail of the cosmos.

GOD IN TRANSCENDENCE: SHE WHO IS—DIVINE SUFFERING *WITH* THE COSMOS

In her influential text *She Who Is: The Mystery of God in Feminist Theological Discourse*, Elizabeth Johnson states that the appellation "SHE WHO IS can be spoken as a robust, appropriate name for God. With this name we bring to bear in a female metaphor all the power carried in the ontological symbol of absolute, relational livingness that energizes the world."[6] She grounds this proposal in two interrelated elements of the Jewish and Christian traditions. The first is the Hebrew designation of God as YHWH, biblically translated as I AM WHO AM, the God of the burning bush, of holy ground, of Moses and the Israelite people. Although Johnson acknowledges the range of exegetical difficulties that surround the interpretation of this appellation, she contends, "Of all the interpretations of the name given at the burning bush, however, the one with the strongest impact on subsequent theological tradition links the name with the metaphysical notion of being. YHWH means 'I am who I am' or simply 'I am' in a sense that identifies divine mystery with being itself."[7] The second is the related Thomistic theological proposal that, because the very essence and existence of God is Being itself, then the most appropriate name for God is HE WHO IS. Noting, however, that the original Latin reads *"qui est,"* translatable as "who is" or "the one who is," Johnson contends:

> In English the "who" of *qui est* is open to inclusive interpretation. . . . If God is not intrinsically male, if women are truly created in the image of God, if being female is an excellence, if what makes women exist as women in all difference is participation in divine being, then there is a cogent reason to name toward . . . God, "the one who is," with implicit reference to an antecedent of the grammatically and symbolically feminine gender.[8]

In Johnson's theological formulation, the image of God as She Who Is signifies in female terms the God who is "pure aliveness in relation, the unoriginate welling up of fullness of life in which the whole universe participates."[9] This signification clearly echoes Peacocke's own expression of the Divine Being of God as transcendent source of cosmic life. In terms of a panentheistic-procreative model, the Creator She Who Is mothers all creation. She envelops in her womb its *entities*, stars and planets, earth and sky, creatures of the land

and sea, all races of humanity; its *structures*, subatomic and atomic, molecular and organic, communal and societal, global and universal; and its *processes*, natural selection and evolutionary emergence, regularities of law and randomness of chance, quantum indeterminacy and special relativity. "All is created through her; all is created for her. In her everything continues in being."[10]

Nonetheless, the being and the becoming of all things in the cosmos is inevitably attended by pain, suffering, and death in the movement toward emergent existence. The cosmic child of this Mother's womb endures these pangs of pain, suffering, and death that life may be birthed anew. The transcendent Mother of the universe therefore inherently senses and intimately suffers the least bit of distress that afflicts the growing life within her. Moreover, the transcendent Mother suffers her own travail in the birthing process.

> The processes of creation are immensely costly to God in a way dimly shadowed by and reflected in the ordinary experience of the costliness of creativity in multiple aspects of human creativity.... [The] processes of creation through biological evolution ... involved God's costly, suffering involvement in them on behalf of their ultimate fruition ... and in their ultimate consummation.[11]

Nevertheless, a mother often has a suffering distinctively her own. Although "the pain of childbirth ... is accompanied by a powerful sense of creativity and ... joy," it is nonetheless a creative suffering unlike any other.[12] In the process of pregnancy, the transcendent Mother bears the unimaginable weight of a cosmos laden with inherent and inflicted pain and death. She is sickened morning and evening by the violence, oppression, and exploitation that ravages the developing life within her, the offspring of her love. In the labor of birthing, she cries out, gasping and panting, unable to restrain herself.[13] As Johnson explains, "The loud birthing cries evoke a God who is in hard labor, sweating, pushing with all her might to bring forth ... the fruit of her love."[14] What's more, this labor is for all created time, for the birth of the cosmos in its fullness is an eschatological event to be completed only in the new creation in which all weeping and suffering and death will be no more. Until that time, the transcendent Mother of Peacocke's panentheistic-procreative paradigm suffers *with* the cosmos and its processes, enduring the passion of the process of bringing forth new life. In Divine Being and creativity, the transcendent Mother God is both "God as abyss of livingness ... the matrix of all that exists, mother and fashioner of all things ... absolute holy mystery of love"[15] and God as cosmos-bearer, suffering and laboring, expanding and contracting, gasping and panting, stretching and straining, pushing and burning with love-driven passion for the life of the world.

GOD INCARNATE: *SHEKHINAH*—DIVINE SUFFERING IN THE COSMOS

According to Gershom Scholem, a prominent twentieth-century scholar in the study of Jewish mysticism, "The *Shekhinah* . . . is a concept that has intimately accompanied the Jewish people for some two thousand years, through all phases of its turbulent and tragic existence . . . itself undergoing manifold developments and transformations."[16] The term *Shekhinah*[17] is derived from the Hebrew *shakan*, meaning "presence" or "act of dwelling," and is expressed as a feminine-gendered substantive. It was used to refer to an aspect of the deity perceived by humanity[18] and appears in the Talmud, the Midrash, and the mystical Kabbalah.[19] The Talmud refers to *Shekhinah* as a visible and audible manifestation of the presence and activity of God in the world.[20] In the Midrash of the rabbis, *Shekhinah* is recognized as an independent divine entity, female in form, who dwells with the chosen in times well or ill, who intercedes compassionately with God for humanity, and who is present within the humblest circumstances and with the most insignificant of creatures.[21] In kabbalist sources, *Shekhinah* attains a fuller sense and significance as a completely female hypostatization.[22]

Interpretations of *Shekhinah* differ over time, but each acknowledges *Shekhinah* as divine, as identified with God's very self, and as an independent entity. She is recognized as existent within the Godhead, within creation as a whole, and with the suffering in particular. In terms of a panentheistic-procreative model of the Triune God, *Shekhinah* corresponds to God Incarnate in the cosmos, the firstborn of creation. In terms of a female model of the suffering of God, *Shekhinah* correlates in particularly striking ways with the identification of the suffering of God with the life, suffering, death, and resurrection of Jesus the Christ.[23]

Reflecting one of Peacocke's own incarnational understandings, commentators suggest that awareness of *Shekhinah* arose as a consequence of the attempt to reconcile the duality of God's transcendent and immanent presence in relation to the world.[24] While philosophers debated the relationship of the transcendence and immanence of the Divine, the witness of the people of Israel testified that this existence of God in the world was experienced not only as presence but also as intimacy and immediacy. This indwelling omnipresence of God was called by the name *Shekhinah* and was clearly understood as the link between the eternal and temporal worlds, as one who had been sent by God as the very presence of the Divine.[25] In rabbinic literature, *Shekhinah* was both an appellation interchangeable with God and a quality or possession of the Deity, given to the world solely because of Israel.[26] According to the Hasidim, God produced a created light, the *kavod*, as "the first of all creation," from which resounds the voice and word of God to the prophets and holy ones.[27] Shortly before the appearance of Christianity, *Shekhinah* began to develop as an independent entity, and her spiritual presence took substance. *Shekhinah* could be localized in a particular place, and her movements became discernible. *Shekhinah* speaks and acts, sings with joy and cries with grief, admonishes and encourages, and becomes angry and appeased. She is considered to have an opinion, a mind, a will, and a personality.[28] Thus, *Shekhinah* develops into a mediator between humanity and God, heaven and earth. Through her, God enters the world; she is the medium through which God is accessible to human beings.

Countless tracts from the rabbinic and kabbalist literature affirm that *Shekhinah* shares the joys and the affliction of both the community and the individual person of Israel to the extent that the Divine feels the pain of the human.[29] "When a human being suffers, what does the *Shekhinah* say? 'My head is too heavy for me; my arm is too heavy for me.' And if God is so grieved over the blood of the wicked that is shed, how much more so over the blood of the righteous?"[30] As the wounded one, *Shekhinah* not only weeps for the suffering of her people, crying out when someone undergoes punishment, but also suffers their persecutions with them, "like Israel's twin."[31] Like Jesus, the firstborn of all creation, *Shekhinah*, the cosmic offspring in the womb of She Who Is, suffers intimately with and in the same manner as those who bear the sufferings that often attend the inherent and inflicted pain and death of the cosmos. In their respective traditions, both Jesus and *Shekhinah* participate as co-sufferers with God's people. As God Incarnate, both Jesus and *Shekhinah* manifest and involve the Divine in the life of the cosmos and its creatures with intimacy and immediacy. In their indwelling among and advocacy for those on the margins of civic and religious society, both Jesus and *Shekhinah* embrace and enter into the fate of the afflicted, experiencing their suffering, pain, and death and groaning with their anguish.[32]

Clearly, the conception of *Shekhinah* as God Incarnate provides a means by which to envision the Divine within the history of a suffering cosmos. Coupled with the tradition of Jesus the Christ, *Shekhinah* reveals herself in intimate involvement with the suffering of the world, an involvement that suggests the suffering presence of God Incarnate. However, the integration of these traditions also testifies to the liberating action of Jesus and of *Shekhinah* as God Incarnate on behalf of the suffering and the oppressed. As the intercession of *Shekhinah* and the resurrection of Jesus symbolize, suffering and death can be mitigated and transformed through the vivifying and liberating presence and power of the God of Jesus and of *Shekhinah*, whose unending life and unconditional love alone bring salvation. Although God's self-limited power may not prevent all manner of evil endured by these Incarnate Ones, neither are they overcome by such evil. Rather, *Shekhinah* and the Christ of God move through suffering and death toward new life, liberation, and transformation. This is the good news of salvation and the hope for liberation inherent in God Incarnate in *Shekhinah*.

GOD IN IMMANENCE: *SOPHIA*—DIVINE SUFFERING *UNDER* THE COSMOS

In his schema of the Trinity of God in relation to the cosmos, Arthur Peacocke correlated the Immanence of the Creator God with the doctrine of the Holy Spirit.[33] According to Peacocke, this doctrine enables Christian thought to conceive of God as creatively and dynamically present and active in the whole of the created cosmos and in the cosmic processes themselves. Moreover, the doctrine of the Holy Spirit is "peculiarly consonant" with that scientific perspective of the cosmos as emergent, that is, "of a cosmos in which creativity is ever-present" through a "directing agency" that leads to the emergence of humanity.[34] In the panentheistic-procreative model explored here, this presence and action of the Holy Spirit permeates and pervades the Incarnate One, "the firstborn of creation," the offspring of the Divine Mother's womb. Within the female model of divine travail being developed, this presence and action of the Holy Spirit is particularly consonant with the female personification of the suffering creativity of God known as *Sophia*.

The appellation *Sophia* represents the Greek translation of "wisdom," which is grammatically feminine in gender not only in Greek but also in Hebrew (*hokmah*) and in Latin (*sapientia*). According to the authors of *Wisdom's Feast*, a study of the sapiential tradition in the Hebrew and Christian Scriptures, *Sophia* initially appears to be a relatively minor figure in the biblical tradition. However, when one attends more closely to her presence, one finds that only four other personalities are written about with greater depth throughout all of Scripture.[35]

Although the meaning of her name is explicitly "wisdom," the purview of *Sophia* is decidedly creativity. At the moment of *creatio ex nihilo*, *Sophia* was present, delighting in the work of creation, delighting in the creatures of the earth.[36] When Solomon pleaded for the gift of *Sophia*, she revealed herself as the source of "all good things":

> Therefore I prayed, and understanding was given me;
> I called upon God, and the spirit of *Sophia* came to me,
>
> . . . .
>
> I loved her more than health and beauty,
> and I chose to have her rather than light,
> because her radiance never ceases.
> All good things came to me along with her,
> and in her hands uncounted wealth.
> I rejoiced in them all, because *Sophia* leads them;
> but I did not know that she was their mother.[37]

Not only is *Sophia* source and mother of creation, but in the unfolding process of *creatio continua*, "she reaches mightily from one end of the earth to the other, and she orders all things well."[38] She is "a breath of the power of God, and...can do all things, and while remaining in herself, she renews all things."[39] As Immanent Creator under the evolving cosmos, *Sophia* participates in the creative process, gives order to existence itself, and continually renews and transforms all creation. *Sophia* communicates the mysteries of God through the works of the cosmos. As she who is the "designer of all," *Sophia* has knowledge "of signs and wonders, of the unfolding of the ages and the times."[40] As immanent creativity of the universe, *Sophia* comprehends

> The organization of the universe and the force of its elements,
> The beginning and the end and the midpoint of times,
> the changes in the sun's course and the variations of the seasons.
> Cycles of years, positions of the stars, natures of animals,
>   tempers of beasts,
> Powers of the winds and thoughts of men,
> uses of plants and virtues of roots—
> Such things as are hidden...and such as are plain;
> For *Sophia*, the artificer of all, taught me.
> For in her is a spirit
> intelligent, holy, unique,
> Manifold, subtle, agile,
> clear, unstained, certain,
> Not baneful, loving the good, keen, unhampered, beneficent,
>   kindly,
> Firm, secure, tranquil,
> all-powerful, all-seeing,
> And pervading all spirits,
> though they be intelligent, pure and very subtle.

> For *Sophia* is mobile beyond all motion,
> and she penetrates and pervades all things by reason of her purity.[41]

Nonetheless, the processes through which such mysteries are communicated and such creativity is accomplished do not always manifest such power, order, and delight. As evolutionary science demonstrates, the continuous creativity of the cosmos identified with the immanent creativity of *Sophia*-God involves fits and starts, culs-de-sac and dead ends, trials and errors, pain and death. The operations of both free process and free will are costly ones, fraught with risk and uncertainty. The guiding and purposeful activity of *Sophia* is diverted, resisted, and sometimes rebuffed on the path to the emergence of fullness of life in the eschaton. And the scriptures witness to her passionate response. "The evil way . . . I hate," *Sophia* proclaims, "and all who hate me love death."[42] She flees from deceit and withdraws from the senseless; injustice she cannot bear.[43] She groans within the bowels of emergent creation and bemoans resistance to liberation and change. She rails against those who squander opportunities for life and rages against those who reject transformation. Her heart breaks over those who rebuff her invitation to flourish and mourns over those whose self-will leads to death. She suffers the rejection of her creative agency and flares forth in righteous anger:

> I called and you refused,
> I extended my hand and no one took notice;
> you disdained all my counsel, and my reproof you ignored—
>
> . . . .
>
> Then they call me, but I answer not; they seek me, but find me not;
>
> . . . .
>
> And in their arrogance they preferred ignorance,
> and like fools they hated knowledge:
>
> . . . .
>
> The self-will of the simple kills them,
> the smugness of fools destroys them.[44]

Such is the lament of a suffering God, the cry of *Sophia* when her creative dynamism is resisted and refused. Such is the image of *Sophia* as the self-limited God of Peacocke's evolutionary theology, as she passionately responds to the vagaries and vicissitudes of cosmic and human freedom and autonomy.

Nevertheless, in her righteous passion and suffering, the Immanent *Sophia*-God definitively "stands . . . as a permanent sign of protest . . . as a permanent witness against" cosmic and human suffering.[45] Though, in an evolving universe, "light must yield to night . . . over *Sophia* evil can never triumph."[46]

Through her incessant creative dynamism, *Sophia* enters into creation and its creatures and "from age to age she produces friends of God and prophets" against dysteleological suffering and death within the cosmos.[47] Inspiring humanity and exercising creativity in the cosmos,

> *Sophia* calls aloud in the streets,
> she raises her voice in the public squares;
> she calls out at the street corners,
> she delivers her message at the city gates.[48]

And the message *Sophia* delivers is a message of life: life that endures in the face of suffering, life that emerges through the travail of suffering, life that wells up in the midst of suffering through the creative dynamism of the immanent creativity of *Sophia*-God.

Evaluation

In terms of the assessment criteria proposed, the development of the panentheistic-procreative model of the creative suffering of the Triune God both fits and exceeds the data derived from evolutionary theology. The model of She Who Is, *Shekhinah*, and *Sophia* as the God who suffers transcendently, incarnately, and immanently in relation to the cosmos fits both a trinitarian God-world relationship and the affirmation of the suffering of God in, with, and under the creative processes of the cosmos with their costly unfolding in time. Moreover, in following through the proposal of the viability of a female metaphor for God as Creator of the cosmos, this model both fits and expands Peacocke's own conjectures by developing a model in which all three relationships of the Triune God in this panentheistic-procreative model are presented through female imagery extracted from the Jewish and Christian traditions. Furthermore, the facility with which these images function individually and in concert to communicate a Trinitarian understanding, the inference of the creative suffering of God, and the use of female imagery tends toward a positive assessment of the simplicity of this model. This also suggests a favorable judgment of the fecundity of this model as it sets forth a novel interpretation of God's transcendent, incarnate, and immanent relationship to the cosmos in a panentheistic paradigm. By doing so, it is to be hoped that it encourages other innovative formulations of this Triune relationship as well as creative concepts of the Divine in alternate female imagery.

Finally, the criterion of pastoral efficacy appears to be fulfilled in three areas. First, this female procreative model affirms female embodiment and celebrates the natural processes of pregnancy and birthing. However, in view of the patriarchal imagination that often predominates in society and in theology, those who propose the image of God as mother must take care not to "undermine women's search for identity in their whole person apart from the relationship and role of mothering" by circumscribing its female imagery for God within the sole construct of motherhood.[49] Commenting on the use of the image of God as mother in Sallie McFague and Elizabeth Johnson, among others, Tricia Sheffield cautions,

> The metaphor of God as mother can fall into an essentialized category
> of women as nurturing, life-giving, and sacrificial . . . a typical de-
> scription of the gendered female. . . . God as mother is helpful to shock
> a complacent society out of its male metaphors for God, but care must
> be given not to participate in this same society by falling back on
> stereotypes of the mother.[50]

Johnson herself warns against uncritically appropriating the patriarchal idealization of motherhood as normative that relegates women to the private sphere of society. She also points out the ambiguous intricacies in the nature of the parent-child relationship and emphasizes the limits of all such predications about God as Creator drawn from the realm of creation because of the analogous nature of speech toward the mystery of God. Nevertheless, Johnson adds, "there is . . . powerful and largely untapped truth available in the range of women's experience of having and being mothers that can reshape speech about the mystery of God" as Creator in relation to the cosmos and its creatures.[51] Second, the female procreative model shows the accessibility of female imagery and models for God drawn from the Jewish and Christian traditions for theological reflection and discourse. Third, the female panentheistic-procreative model demonstrates the dynamic of creativity and suffering in God that is core to Peacocke's evolutionary theology of the suffering God. Clearly, the transcendent She Who Is, the incarnate *Shekhinah*, and the immanent *Sophia* do not remain mired in suffering in a weakened and vitiated theism, but move in, with, and under suffering toward full and emergent life.

Explorations in Ecological Ethics

The Role of Humanity in an Evolving Cosmos according to Arthur Peacocke

In *Creation and the World of Science*, Arthur Peacocke asked what the appropriate response and role of humanity might be in relation to creation if conceived within the paradigm of the panentheistic God-world relationship within the scientific perspective. Peacocke cautioned against roles such as dominion, steward, and manager as hierarchical in nature and liable to distortion and abuse. To communicate humanity's integral and caring role within the cosmos, Peacocke proposed seven other roles or clusters of roles to express the proper relationship of "man in creation" conceived in panentheistic relation to its Creator. These roles are (1) priest of creation, (2) symbiont, (3) interpreter, (4) prophet, (5) lover, (6) trustee and preserver, and (7) cocreator, coworker, or co-explorer with God the Creator.[52] Table 6.1 summarizes Peacocke's proposed roles of humanity within the cosmos, the theological presupposition that underlies each, and the ecological values and ethical actions commensurate with each role.

The Model of Midwifery in the Process of Procreation

Undoubtedly, each of the models of humanity's role in the cosmic ecosystem suggested by Peacocke has merit and consonance within his theoretical and theological framework. However, in keeping with the procreative model of the creative suffering of the Triune God I developed, I wish to put forward an additional model of humanity's role in relation to the cosmos, the role of the midwife in the process of procreation. Its theological basis derives from the proposal of the God-world relationship as panentheistic and procreative, especially as conceived through female images of God. In this conceptual paradigm, God as Mother is conceived as birthing forth the creation toward fullness of life through the natural self-creativity of the cosmos. This birthing takes place through natural processes and structures within God-as-Mother and within the cosmos-as-firstborn and is best facilitated through the symbiotic interrelation of cosmic creatures.

The procreative model of cosmic creation with its emphasis on natural processes and structures and its stance of interdependence parallels that model of the human procreative process facilitated through the practice of midwifery. In this model, pregnancy and birth are regarded and respected as normal and natural life processes that, under most circumstances, do not require the intervention of technological and scientific methods or the use of chemical agents. Based on ancient wisdoms that trust the mother's instincts and intentions for her child, midwifery exercises a holistic model of care that attends to every aspect of the physical, psychological, emotional, and cognitive well-being of the expectant mother, the developing child, and her vigilant loved ones.[53] Those who exercise the role of the professional midwife learn and embrace the values of education and expertise, vigilance and attentiveness, nurturance and gentleness, and sensitivity and respect for the interrelated persons and processes involved in the emergence of new life.

TABLE 6.1. Human Roles, Ecological Values, and Ethical Action toward Creation

Humanity's Cosmic Role	Theological Basis	Ecological Values	Ethical Action
Priest of creation	Immanent presence of God in the cosmos as creative agent; derived sacredness of creation = world as sacrament	Respect and reverence for creation as mediating the presence of God	Mediate between insentient nature and God; seek to further and fulfill God's purposes in creation
Symbiont	Panentheistic God-world relation; sacredness of all life; creation as sanctuary	Gentle, reverent, and discriminating attitude toward creation, its creatures, and its use	Partner with cosmic creatures in adaptive and sustaining relationships
Interpreter	God as self-communicating agent, expressing purposes and meanings through the sacrament of creation	Attentiveness to God's revelation of Self, purposes, and meanings in creation	Discern, articulate, and communicate God's purposes and meaning for creation and its creatures
Prophet	God's intention that creation respond to divine communication of Self and meaning in creation	Attentiveness to God's revelation of Self, purposes, and meanings in creation	Call humanity to recognize and respond to the communication of the Divine in creation
Lover of nature	Unfathomable richness, uniqueness, connectivity, and complexity of God's creativity in the cosmos	Sensitivity to the interdependent and emergent complexity of the cosmic organism	Cultivate I-Thou relation with creation in its irreducible mystery and splendor
Trustee and preserver	God's creation of the cosmos at each level of complexity for its own sake and not for human utility	Appreciation and understanding of the uniqueness and irreplaceability of each created being	Care "before God" for what is of intrinsic value to God
Cocreator Coworker Co-explorer	God as continuous Creator, as Composer of the cosmic fugue, and as Explorer of cosmic possibilities	Creativity, cooperation, and innovation with regard to the cosmic potentialities	Participate with God harmoniously in the dynamic evolution of the opus of the cosmos

Source: Peacocke, *Creation and the World of Science*, 295–306.

These values lead, of course, to a series of ethical actions undertaken by trained midwives. The first ethical action is *respectful treatment* that fosters gentle nurturance and care for all those involved in the event of pregnancy and birth. It includes the willingness to support natural processes as they unfold uniquely in each emergence of new life and to promote the autonomy and freedom of both the mother and the child as they participate in these processes. The second is *personal attention* that explores the questions involved in the process of birth, that attempts to resolve fears and concerns, and that develops trusting and nurturing relationships among family members. It also involves vigilant care and support attuned to the mother's needs and desires before, during, and after birth. The *acquisition and dissemination of information* is the third ethical action of the midwife. She collects and shares information pertinent to pregnancy and birth and provides practical suggestions for the care and nutrition of mother and child. She researches the various tests, procedures, and interventions that might be undertaken so that informed choices may be made as to their necessity, their effects, and their risks. Finally, the midwife acts as *monitor, advocate,* and *companion.* She carefully evaluates the progress of pregnancy and birth and exercises her expertise in differentiating normal, natural processes and events from those that require diagnostic or remedial interventions. In the event of difficulties, she knows the appropriate specialists from whom to enlist aid. The midwife also empowers the mother to value her own embodiment, to discover her own life-giving capacities, and to move through a healthy process of laboring and birthing free from imposed timetables. Ultimately, the midwife serves as a "sympathetic female companion," mothering the mother as the life within her comes to full term.[54]

From this overview of the role of midwifery in the human process of procreation, certain values and actions present themselves as ecologically and ethically consistent with the panentheistic-procreative paradigm of God-world relation and with the multiple models that Peacocke proposed. With regard to a cosmos conceived in procreative terms, the model of midwifery offers the values of *education and expertise* critical to understanding the entities, processes, and structures of an evolving cosmos and promotes active *acquisition and dissemination of information* crucial to facilitating the emergence and survival of the world's fragile ecosystems. It encourages an *attentiveness* to those choices that facilitate the healthy growth and development of the cosmos and its creatures and a *vigilance* that guards against the incursion of elements that are deleterious to its well-being. In so doing, it urges the human person to act ethically as *monitor of* and *advocate for* the full flourishing of all forms of life in the cosmos and encourages particular attention to the misuse or abuse of the environment caused by unregulated technology or chemical pollutants. The model of midwifery further supports attitudes of *nurturance and gentleness* toward the cosmos that result in *respectful treatment* of creation and its creatures, thus militating against approaches to the biosphere and atmosphere that trigger abuse, despoliation, and destruction of ecosystems and their inhabitants. Ultimately, the model of midwifery fosters *respect and reverence* for transcendent Mother, incarnate Firstborn, and immanent Creativity and inspires the human person to be an active *companion* in creative travail of the Trinity who, in a labor of tireless and unconditional love, strains toward the emergence of fullness of life in the new creation.

Evaluation

The model of midwifery that I set forth as an ecologically responsible and ethically viable response to an evolutionary understanding of the relationship of the human person to the cosmos has great consonance with Peacocke's own models of "man in creation." It demonstrates a sound fit with the ecological values and ethical actions that are essential to the flourishing of an evolutionary cosmos, while at the same time augmenting Peacocke's examples to include a specifically female model that is consonant with the procreative paradigm. The simplicity of the model of midwifery derives from its direct connection to the procreative paradigm and from its emphasis on inherent, natural processes for the fostering and emergence of life. Although the model demonstrates simplicity, there is also a novelty to it that suggests fecundity in its use and interpretation. This model seems able to address issues that affect the transcendent mother, the incarnate firstborn, and the immanent processes in the procreative paradigm and shows intrinsic vigilance concerning abuse of the body of the cosmos through misuse of technology and chemical pollutants. As far as its pastoral efficacy is concerned, the model of midwifery, like the procreative paradigm itself, affirms female embodiment and celebrates the natural processes of pregnancy and birthing. Moreover, it advances a specifically female form of advocacy and praxis into ecological theology and environmental ethics. Finally, the ecological and ethical model of midwifery solidifies the connection between the life and processes of human existence and the life and processes of cosmic existence, of which humanity is an integral and inextricable part.

A further practical way of evaluating the midwife model of ecological ethics might be to demonstrate its fit, simplicity, fecundity, and pastoral efficacy with the values and actions deemed vital to the sustainability of the cosmos at this juncture in history. These values and actions are effectively expressed in the Earth Charter, "a declaration of fundamental principles for building a just, sustainable, and peaceful global society in the 21st century." An outgrowth of the Earth Charter Initiative, the charter was "created by the largest global consultation process ever associated with an international declaration, endorsed by thousands of organizations representing millions of individuals." Clearly in tune with the relational emphasis of the midwife model of care, the charter "seeks to inspire in all peoples a sense of global interdependence and shared responsibility for the well-being of the human family and the larger living world. The Earth Charter is an expression of hope and a call to help create a global partnership at a critical juncture in history." Moreover, the mission of the Earth Charter Initiative is precisely an ethical one: "To establish a sound ethical foundation for the emerging global society and to help build a sustainable world based on respect for nature, diversity, universal human rights, economic justice and a culture of peace."[55]

Although the charter is not a theological document, it resonates with the insights of the premier thinkers in the ecology-theology dialogue and derives from the wisdom of the world's great religious traditions. Table 6.2 parallels the ecological values and actions suggested by a midwife model of care with some of those proposed by the Earth Charter. Like the model of midwifery, the charter *advocates study and knowledge* concerning ecological systems and sustainability and stipulates that such *knowledge be available* as it relates to human and environmental well-being. The charter urges individuals and groups to *adopt lifestyles* that safeguard the regenerative capacity of the earth and that provide for a quality of life consistent with a finite world. The charter also insists on a vigilance that *protects and restores Earth's ecological systems*, with emphasis on the natural processes that sustain and promote life. Both the model of midwifery and the charter warn about the necessity of *protecting existing and emerging life from harm* caused by pollution, toxins, or environmentally hazardous technology to promote the full flourishing of all members of the cosmic community. Each endorses a stance of *care and respect toward all cosmic life* by recognizing its intrinsic value and its interdependent diversity. Finally, both the model of midwifery and the Earth Charter accentuate that in an evolving cosmos, from the microlevel to the macrolevel, "*relationships* are not just interesting . . . they are all there is to *reality*."[56]

Fundamentally, it is this reality of relationship within a panentheistic paradigm that the midwife model affirms and promotes ecologically, ethically, and theologically. Ecologically, the midwife model of care preserves and protects the relationships that exist between the beings and processes of human and nonhuman life in the cosmos. It also stresses the profound relationship between creation and its Creator, between the cosmos and the source of its being and becoming. Imaging the cosmos within God and God within and around the cosmos graphically demonstrates that what is experienced by the

TABLE 6.2. Comparison of Values and Actions of the Model of Midwifery and the Earth Charter as Ecological Ethic

The Model of Midwifery	The Earth Charter
Education and expertise concerning the entities, processes, and structures of an evolving cosmos.	*Advance the study and exchange of the knowledge* about ecological systems and sustainability.
Acquisition and dissemination of information regarding the emergence and survival of the world's fragile ecosystems.	*Ensure the availability* of information of vital importance to human health and environmental protection.
Attentiveness to those choices that facilitate the healthy growth and development of the cosmos and its creatures.	*Adopt lifestyles* that safeguard Earth's regenerative capacities and emphasize quality of life and sufficiency in a finite world.
Vigilance against the incursion of elements that are deleterious to cosmic well-being.	*Protect and restore the integrity of Earth's ecological systems* with special concern for biological diversity and the natural processes that sustain life.
Monitor the misuse or abuse of the environment caused by unregulated technology or chemical pollutants.	*Prevent harm to any part of the environment* caused by pollutants, radioactivity, toxins, or environmentally hazardous technology.
Advocate the full flourishing of all forms of life in the cosmos.	*Uphold the right of all without discrimination* to a natural and social environment supportive of the flourishing of Earth's human and ecological communities.
Nurturance and gentleness toward the cosmos and its creatures.	*Care for the community of life* with understanding, compassion and love.
Respectful treatment of creation that safeguards against abuse, despoliation, and destruction of ecosystems and their inhabitants.	*Respect Earth and life* in all its diversity, interdependence, and intrinsic value.
Companion in the creative travail of the Trinity, who, in a labor of tireless and unconditional love, strains toward the emergence of fullness of life and new creation.	*Live in right relationship* with oneself, other persons, other cultures, other life, Earth, and the larger whole of which all are a part.

Source: "Midwives' Model of Care" and "What to Expect from a Caregiver Who Provides the Midwifery Model of Care," Citizens for Midwifery, accessed 12 February 2005; available from http://www.cfmidwifery.org.

cosmos and by its creatures is immediately and acutely experienced by God. Earthquakes and tsunamis reverberate within God. Toxicity and pollution poison the offspring of God's womb. Rain forest depletion and strip mining disfigure the form of God's beloved creation. This realization fosters an ethical response that inspires and promotes values and actions consistent with the interdependent and supportive relationships essential to the cosmos. Ethically, the midwife model effectively denounces the despoliation and devastation of the cosmos through human choices and behavior. It accentuates the intrinsic rather than instrumental value of the cosmos and urges humanity "to be co-creator with God . . . acting for the good of both humanity and the Earth's eco-systems . . . in such a way that it can go on being the medium through which life can continue and explore new forms of existence under the guidance of God."[57] Theologically, the midwife model of ecological ethics sustains and nurtures the gracious and gratuitous relationship between creation and its Creator God, that larger life and Ground of Being of which the cosmos is an intimate part. Furthermore, it generates myriad new perspectives and possibilities for contemplating and symbolizing God, the cosmos and its creatures, and the God-world relationship, and it expands the settings in which symbols of God, the cosmos, and their interrelation function. The midwife model of care in a panentheistic paradigm explicitly asserts that God's creative activity not only extends to the full flourishing of creation's human emergents but also ceaselessly labors in, with, and under the very processes of the cosmos for the healing, the salvation, the transformation, and the liberation of the *whole of the cosmos* itself. Moreover, God does so as a mother who yearns to bring to new and abundant life the child of her womb.

Explorations in Pastoral Ministry

Differentiated Trinitarian Creativity in the Evolutionary Theology of Arthur Peacocke

In the final section of this chapter, I return to Arthur Peacocke's conceptual image of the Triune nature of God "in, with, and under" the cosmos and its creative, costly processes.[58] Returning to this image of threefold suffering, I once again note that Peacocke's understanding of God as transcendent, incarnate, and immanent suggests that God relates to the cosmos and to its creatures in three distinguishable yet unified modes. This is an understanding that Peacocke shared with the Christian tradition, albeit in a distinctly different way. Hence, whether one talks about the Trinity as Father, Son, and Holy Spirit; as Transcendent, Incarnate, and Immanent in relation to the cosmos; or, now, as She Who Is, *Shekhinah*, and *Sophia*, the affirmation of One God in Three Divine Persons by the Christian tradition springs from the human experience of God's activities in the economy of salvation and leads to the theological differentiation of activities appropriate to each. Though the Godhead is One, each member of the Triune God shares in a distinctive way in the life of the cosmos. As explained by William Hill in *The Three-Personed God*, "What is in reality a common prerogative of the trinitarian members is predicated of one alone to manifest his personal uniqueness in the Godhead. But this cannot be done arbitrarily; some mysterious affinity between a person and an action *ad extra*, or an essential attribute, lies at the base of this kind of speech."[59] Taking a different approach to this interplay of unity and diversity in the Trinity, Peacocke, in his affirmation of the One God as Creator, pointed out the Nicene Creed's identification of the Father as the Maker of heaven and earth, of the Son as the one through whom all things were made, and of the Holy Spirit as the Giver of Life. Although Peacocke did not suggest a similar differentiation with regard to the divine suffering of the Three Persons in One God, I would contend that there is logic in the assumption that, if members of the Trinity are distinguishable in terms of their modes of *creativity*, they are also distinguishable in terms of their modes of *suffering*.[60] Using Peacocke's own relational distinctions, the Incarnate, Transcendent, and Immanent God may be said to suffer *in*, *with*, and *under* the suffering of the cosmos and its creatures.

Differentiated Suffering in the Triune God

What is the point of distinguishing the modes of suffering in God as Trinity? One might point to Hill's theological suggestion that "some mysterious affinity" exists between a particular Person of the Trinity and an action or an attribute disclosed by God through the economy of salvation. Taking the most obvious application of Hill's suggestion, God-Incarnate in Jesus the Christ must surely be regarded as suffering *in* the world. Moreover, with regard to Moltmann's crucified God, the Father could be said to suffer *with* the Son in suffering his death on the cross. Finally, in the Pauline reference to the travail of creation, the Spirit could be regarded as the groaning *under* the birthing of creation toward full flourishing and liberation. However, it is my claim that, in addition to its theological validity in the economy of salvation, the point of distinguishing modes of suffering in God is also precisely pastoral. The understanding that God as Triune has the capacity to suffer with the cosmos and its creatures in distinctive ways responds to the experiential reality of human suffering that is itself variously distinguished as sympathetic, empathetic, and protopathetic. Distinguishing such modes of suffering in the Persons of God enables human persons to identify their own suffering with the unique sufferings of God in Trinity and to do so with the certain faith of the Hebrew psalmist who prayed, "O God, you know me . . . you understand my thoughts from afar . . . with all my ways you are familiar. Even before a word is on my tongue . . . you know it all."[61] Moreover, distinguishing modes of suffering in the Trinity offers different ways in which to find one's own suffering relieved and by which to relieve another's suffering, for example, through sympathetic companioning, through empathetic identification, or through protopathetic response and resistance to the pain, suffering, and death in cosmic and human existence associated with a distinctive Person of the Triune God.

Therefore, using my female panentheistic-procreative paradigm, I affirm first that, because God is One in relationship to the cosmos, the distinctive types of suffering suggested here are experienced by each and all Persons of the Trinity in relation to the cosmos. In the process of birthing the creation, the Transcendent Mother certainly suffers protopathetically *under* the pangs of labor; in her indwelling, the Incarnate *Shekhinah*, like Jesus the Christ, truly suffers sympathetically *with* the ostracized and oppressed of the cosmos; and in her participation in the costly creative processes that bring forth new life, the Immanent *Sophia* surely suffers empathetically *in* the trials and errors of cosmic self-creativity. Nevertheless, I contend further that, in Hill's words, there exists a mysterious affinity between the sympathetic, empathetic, and protopathetic forms of suffering and God as Transcendent, Incarnate, and Immanent that could facilitate healing and liberative relationships among the suffering of the cosmos and its inhabitants and the specific persons of the Triune God. Although the descriptions of suffering I present neither exhaust the range of human and cosmic affliction nor expend the possible avenues of healing and liberation, they do suggest in a triune fashion the ways in which divine suffering might be understood to provide a liberative and transformative response to the travail of the cosmos. Furthermore, while I propose these attributions for the female panentheistic-procreative Trinity of She Who Is, *Shekhinah*, and *Sophia*, these forms of suffering may also manifest an affinity with other Trinitarian formulations, including the Trinity of Father, Son, and Holy Spirit of the classical Christian tradition.

SHE WHO IS: GOD IN TRANSCENDENT SYMPATHY

According to the *Oxford English Dictionary*, the suffering of *sympathy* is "the quality or state of being . . . affected by the suffering or sorrow of another; a feeling of compassion or commiseration."[62] In the female panentheistic-procreative paradigm, this type of suffering has particular affinity with the experience of She Who Is, Transcendent Mother of the Cosmos. Because of the suffering or sorrow of the other, the cosmos and its creatures, She Who Is responds sympathetically, suffering passionately as a mother who does not forget the child of her womb, suffering compassionately *with* the afflicted firstborn of her womb through all of the inherent and inflicted travail of its history.[63] This sympathetic suffering of She Who Is provides solace, strength, and liberation to those who, in their human suffering, need the knowledge that there is one who companions them in their suffering. It is not necessary that these sufferers find

She Who Is in the same state of suffering in which they find themselves. The one thing necessary is that the sufferers find She Who Is with them and available to them in their time of suffering. In this way, such sufferers may experience the unconditional presence and support of this sympathetic companion who encourages and upholds them on their passage through their suffering and death to healing and new life.

SHEKHINAH: GOD IN INCARNATE EMPATHY

There are other sufferers, however, who experience solace and strength in the sure knowledge that someone has experienced or now experiences suffering and pain akin to their own. Their liberation springs from the realization that they can identify their suffering with that of another and that another identifies with them in their pain. This experience is reflected in the description of suffering as *empathy*, which entails the capacity of "understanding, being aware of, being sensitive to, and vicariously experiencing the feelings, thoughts, and experience of another of either the past or present without having the feelings, thoughts, and experience fully communicated in an objectively explicit manner."[64] It connotes a type of suffering rooted in and shaped by one's own present or past experience of suffering in oneself, by means of which one is able to experience an "identification with and understanding of another's situation, feelings, and motives."[65] Thus, it is an experience uniquely attributable to *Shekhinah*, God-Incarnate *in* the cosmos, who, like Jesus the suffering servant of God, "was despised and rejected," a bearer of sorrows, and acquainted with grief.[66] Like Jesus, *Shekhinah* shares natural being and becoming and, like other incarnate ones, experiences firsthand the ubiquity of pain, suffering, and death in the cosmos. Hence, there is no need for human sufferers to communicate explicitly to *Shekhinah* the sufferings they are enduring. *Shekhinah* knows their sufferings incarnately and experientially. She has known the rejection they have known; she has suffered their exile and yearned like them for liberation. In this intimate, incarnate, and experiential knowledge of their affliction, *Shekhinah* is able to move with those who suffer and who identify their suffering with *Shekhinah*'s own through their trials and travail to liberation and resurrection.

SOPHIA: GOD IN IMMANENT PROTOPATHY

Finally, liberation and healing comes to some sufferers through experiences of a dynamic spirit of resistance to suffering and an unrelenting urgency toward right relationship and life within themselves or within another. Such sufferers recognize that there is a particular form of suffering that is associated with experiences and events that obstruct creativity and the emergence of life in the cosmos and in its creatures—events of oppression and exploitation, events of violence and injustice, events of destruction and despoliation. It is *not* a suffering *with* another or a suffering *in* union with another. It is a primal and immediate suffering that wells up *under* and through the passions of those who yearn and strive for the full flourishing of human and cosmic being whenever that full flourishing is at risk of frustration or demise. This is a suffering described as *protopathy* and defined as a primary suffering that is immediately produced, one that is not consequent or produced by another's suffering.[67] This is the suffering of *Sophia,* the God who is Immanent within the cosmic processes. Protopathy is the suffering of *Sophia*-God, who experiences with unparalleled immediacy the events within creation and its history that militate against that movement toward the new creation in which life and right relations within the universe come to fulfillment in the reign of God. This primal suffering, moreover, is one that reverberates with the righteous rage, resolute resistance, and ethical activity of *Sophia*-God in opposition to all that hinders the creativity of the cosmos and everything that spawns the senseless suffering inflicted against its communion of life. Empowered by the suffering of *Sophia* immanent in the being and becoming of the cosmos, these sufferers find healing and liberation in that vivified suffering toward new creation that no dysteleological suffering can ultimately thwart. In the words of Elizabeth Johnson, Holy *Sophia*

> keeps vigil through endless hours of pain while her grief awakens protest. The power of this divine symbol works not just to console those who are suffering, but to strengthen those bowed by sorrow to hope and resist. If God grieves with them in the midst of disaster, then there may yet be a way forward.[68]

Evaluation

The pastoral model of the threefold differentiation of suffering in the Triune God represents a novel application of the data of evolutionary and trinitarian theology. In its fit with these positions, this pastoral model affirms the oneness of Divine Being that makes the activities of God essentially unified in relation to the cosmos, as well as the diversity of Divine Becoming that makes such activities distinctive in relation to the cosmos. This unity-in-diversity leads with theoretical simplicity, therefore, to the possibility of appropriating specific forms of suffering to the Persons of the Trinity on the basis of that "mysterious affinity" that rises from *personal* analogy and *personal* experience toward the attributes of God conceived as *personal*. There is, moreover, fecundity in this attempt to attribute different forms of suffering to the Persons of God, in that the proposals set forth here represent only preliminary steps toward further explorations of the mystery of God in the experience of cosmic and human suffering. Finally, the pastoral efficacy of this proposal is clear. The threefold differentiation of suffering within the Triune relationship of God to the cosmos and its creatures enables human persons to identify their own suffering with the unique sufferings of God in Trinity, to experience their own suffering mitigated or transformed in ways appropriate to the needs of each creature and the desires of each human heart, and to find models through which they might respond to the suffering of others in the cosmic community.

Despite this affirmation of the pastoral efficacy of differentiating types of suffering within God, there is clearly a need to struggle with the way in which the suffering of the Triune God may be conceived in response to the pain, suffering, and death that is *inherent* in the processes of the cosmos in contrast to that which is *inflicted* through the exercise of human free will. As noted earlier, Peacocke did not distinguish between the suffering of God in relation to the creative processes of the cosmos and the suffering of God in relation to the exercise of human free will. For Peacocke, the suffering of God in relation to free process and free will stems from God's transcendent, incarnate, and immanent relation to the cosmos and its creatures within a panentheistic paradigm. Whether the source of this pain, suffering, and death is associated with the evolutionary creativity of the cosmos or with the human capacity to hinder or thwart such creativity through the exercise of free will is inconsequential to Peacocke. The fact that pain, suffering, and death per se exist in the cosmos provides a sufficient basis for him to infer that a God who relates transcendently, incarnately, and immanently to the cosmos and its creatures in a panentheistic paradigm suffers in, with, and under the sufferings of the cosmos with its costly unfolding in time.

However, one who sets out to differentiate forms of suffering in God, as I have done here, must wrestle with the notion that divine suffering in response to cosmic processes that tend toward new life may be different than divine suffering in response to human choices and actions that are inimical to the emergence of such life. Careful to avoid generalization, one might suggest that, in response to the pain, suffering, and death that is generated by natural evolutionary processes, God may be conceived as suffering sympathetically and empathetically with those affected by the vagaries of cosmic processes—by earthquakes and tsunamis, by tornadoes and droughts, by predation and natural selection, by cell mutations and disease. However, because such events do not arise from processes that are essentially contrary to the self-creativity of the cosmos, they may not be conceived as arousing the protopathetic suffering associated with the obstruction of divine purpose. On the other hand, in response to the pain, suffering, and death that *are* associated with the hindrance of the divine impetus toward life and full flourishing, one might suggest that God not only suffers sympathetically and empathetically, but also suffers protopathetically because such decisions are detrimental to the divine thrust toward fullness of life in the universe. Indisputably, further reflection and exploration of the interplay between inherent and inflicted suffering in the cosmos and differentiated suffering in God are clearly warranted. Such reflection and exploration could demonstrate the fecundity of this concept by entering more deeply into the suffering of God in relation to evolutionary processes in contrast with imposed afflictions that cry out for justice. Moreover, it could augment the pastoral efficacy of these proposals by proposing an array of responses modeled on the creative suffering of the Triune God that are available to human persons in their striving to address wisely and effectively the suffering inherent in an evolutionary cosmos, as opposed to the suffering triggered by humanity's abuse of free will.

Conclusion

Speaking Rightly of God?

Through words that "strain, crack and sometimes break under the burden" of the mysteries of God, of cosmic suffering, and of the relation between the two, I have set forth an evolutionary theology of the creative suffering of the Triune God as a means to speak rightly about the mystery of God in the midst of a suffering world. Using the approach of evolutionary theology in contrast to a biblical model of the suffering God, I offered a broader point of entry than that of revelation in a religiously and theologically pluralistic world. Expanding liberation theologies of the cross, I set forth a cosmocentric perspective in which the suffering cosmos, as well as suffering humanity, mediates and communicates the ultimately ineffable mystery of the suffering of God. While incorporating this cosmocentric approach, I nonetheless maintained the distinction between God and the cosmos through a panentheistic model of God-world relationship rather than pantheistically identifying creation with Creator. Furthermore, an evolutionary compass permitted me to utilize data derived from the full range of entities, structures, and processes of cosmic life, rather than from metaphysical, philosophical, or phenomenological principles, such as those of classical or process theology. Because of this, I was able to demonstrate the appropriateness and viability of using an alternate paradigm to frame theological analysis concerning the suffering of God, one that validates ongoing creativity and transformation within cosmic history. Moreover, my use of such an approach increased the defensibility of my proposals for persons who live in an age when science and personal experience shape the personal and social consciousness of humanity concerning itself and the cosmos as much as religion or philosophy.

Beyond this comparison with specific biblical, liberation, ecological, and process approaches to the suffering of God, an evolutionary theological approach enabled me to integrate scientific understandings with the insights of the Christian tradition. Evolutionary science permitted possibilities for imaging the Triune God and God-world relationship through human experience in a continually creative cosmos. At the same time, it maintained a consistency with core Christian concepts such as the transcendence and immanence of God, the doctrine of the Trinity, the doctrine of creation, and the doctrine of the Incarnation of God in Christ. Moreover, through the use of a panentheistic paradigm, I was able to reenvision a balanced, interactive, and dialogical relationship between theological and scientific concepts often presumed at odds. The panentheistic paradigm maintained the balance between divine transcendence and divine immanence, as well as the balance between the notion of Trinity and the variously nuanced ways in which God as Transcendent, Incarnate, and Immanent in the cosmos reveals Godself and the God-world relationship. It empowered connections between the notion of God as Creator and images drawn from the female procreative experience, as well as between the revelation of God in the paschal mystery of Christ and divine self-disclosure in the travail and transformation of the cosmos. Adopting an epistemological stance of critical realism allowed me to integrate classical and contemporary discourse concerning God and the God-world relationship, while acknowledging the limitation of theological discourse derived from the created order and asserting the validity of human speech about God through the analogical nature of theological language.

At the close of this study, the question remains whether the concept of the creative suffering of God can adequately respond to the experience of existential suffering endemic in the cosmos. As noted earlier, I believe that it is not the denial of suffering in God that mitigates existential and experiential misery in the cosmos and its creatures. Rather, it is the affirmation of the suffering of God that renders the Divine as trustworthy and efficacious in the face of the existential reality of suffering in human and nonhuman creation. A theology of the suffering God based on an evolutionary perspective does not leave the sufferer with the dilemma of whether God can arbitrarily intervene but refuses to do so for some reason known only to God. Rather, such a theology sets forth a pastorally efficacious understanding of a Triune God who in transcendent, incarnate, and immanent vulnerability is familiar with suffering and bears cosmic grief. It is a theology that functions to disabuse Christians of the notion that God or the will of God is the source of cosmic, systemic, or personal suffering. Rather, Christians are drawn to recognize that God as transcendent, incarnate, and immanent is the companion-sufferer who intimately understands and deeply participates in the plight and the pain of the afflicted. Moreover, this model does not eternalize or glorify suffering but reveals that suffering in the cosmos and in its inhabitants grieves the Creator as it grieves the created. By sharing the suffering of the beloved creation, the Triune God demonstrates that suffering itself is not redemptive and salvific. Rather, it is the love, the creativity, and the infinite possibility within the Divine that are redemptive through continuous creativity, unconditional presence, and freely offered grace. This is an affirmation rooted in both evolutionary science and Christian theology. It arises from the theological understanding that the Creator God is immanent and incarnate within suffering creation and at the same time infinitely transcends it. Moreover, it arises from the evolutionary insight that the Creator and creation do not remain mired in pain, suffering, and death but, in infinite creativity, possess the capacity to move continuously toward transformation, liberation, and new life. In addition, because it is the cosmos and not just humanity that participates in the being, life, and creativity of the Divine in the panentheistic model, this model functions to inspire an ethics of care that is not only personal and communal but also ecological. As Christians grow to contemplate and emulate the God who embraces, permeates, and suffers with both human being *and* cosmic being, action for restoration, transformation, and liberation will extend creatively, sympathetically, empathetically, and protopathetically not only to all manner of abused and violated persons but also to all levels of the abused and violated cosmos itself.

Persuaded by the evolutionary theology of Arthur Peacocke and his notion of the suffering of God in transcendent, incarnate, and immanent relation to creation, I have offered my own tentative proposals in dialogue with feminist theology, ecological ethics, and pastoral ministry. These proposals met the standards set forth by the study itself, but the true validation of their efficacy will come when the insights I set forth produce resonances within the minds, hearts, and practices of those who suffer as a result of the ubiquitous pain and death inherent and inflicted in the cosmos. I desire and encourage such validation of my proposals. In so doing, I hope that these insights will bear fruit for transformation, liberation, emergence, and resurrection toward fullness of life for the cosmos that bears the sufferings and death of Christ in its being and becoming even to this day.

Notes

CHAPTER I

1. Ronald Goetz, "The Suffering of God: Rise of a New Orthodoxy,"
Christian Century 103 (April 1986): 385–389 at 387.

2. Dietrich Bonhoeffer, *Letters and Papers from Prison*, trans. Reginald H.
Fuller (New York: Macmillan, 1962), 219–220.

3. Goetz, "Suffering of God," 385–389.

4. Edward Schillebeeckx, *Christ: The Experience of Jesus as Lord*, trans.
John Bowden (New York: Crossroad, 1999), 725, italics in the original.

5. Kenneth Surin, "The Impassibility of God and the Problem of Evil,"
Scottish Journal of Theology 35, no. 2 (1982): 97–115 at 103–104.

6. John Haught, *God after Darwin: A Theology of Evolution* (Boulder, CO:
Westview, 2000), 46.

7. Mary Daly, *Beyond God the Father* (Boston: Beacon, 1973).

8. Joanne Carlson Brown and Rebecca Parker, "God So Loved the World?"
in *Violence against Women and Children: A Christian Theological Sourcebook*, ed.
Carol J. Adams and Marie M. Fortune (New York: Continuum, 1995), 36–59.

9. Schillebeeckx, *Christ*, 727, italics in the original.

10. Edward Schillebeeckx, *Jesus: An Experiment in Christology*, trans.
Hubert Hoskins (New York: Seabury, 1979), 267.

11. Schillebeeckx, *Christ*, 728.

12. Johann Baptist Metz, *A Passion for God: The Mystical-Political Dimension of Christianity* (New York: Paulist, 1998), 69, italics in the original.

13. Ibid., 70.

14. Arthur Peacocke, "The Cost of New Life," in *The Work of Love:
Creation as Kenosis*, ed. John Polkinghorne (Grand Rapids, MI: Eerdmans,
2001), 37.

15. Arthur Peacocke, *Theology for a Scientific Age: Being and Becoming: Natural, Divine and Human* (hereafter *TSA*) (Minneapolis: Augsburg Fortress, 1993), 126.

16. Jürgen Moltmann, *The Crucified God: The Cross of Christ as the Foundation and Criticism of Christian Theology*, trans. R. A. Wilson and John Bowden (Minneapolis: Fortress, 1993), 270–271.

17. Ibid., 219–223 at 219.

18. Ibid., 227.

19. Ibid., 243.

20. Ibid., 203.

21. Ibid., 192.

22. Ibid., 248.

23. Jürgen Moltmann, *The Church in the Power of the Spirit: A Contribution to Messianic Ecclesiology*, trans. Margaret Kohl (New York: Harper & Row, 1977), 64.

24. Ibid., 200–278.

25. Jürgen Moltmann, *The Trinity and the Kingdom: The Doctrine of God*, trans. Margaret Kohl (Minneapolis: Fortress, 1993), 23–60. See also Moltmann's essays, "God's Kenosis in the Creation and Consummation of the World," in *The Work of Love: Creation as Kenosis*, and "*Shekhinah*: The Home of the Homeless God," in *Longing for Home*, ed. Leroy S. Rouner (Notre Dame, IN: Notre Dame University Press, 1996).

26. Ephraim E. Urbach, *The Sages: Their Concepts and Beliefs*, trans. Israel Abrahams (Cambridge, MA: Harvard University Press, 1987), 40.

27. Max Kadushin, *The Rabbinic Mind* (New York: Jewish Theological Seminary of America, 1952), 227.

28. Abraham Heschel, *God in Search of Man: A Philosophy of Judaism* (New York: Harper & Row, 1955), 21.

29. Moltmann, "*Shekhinah*," 175.

30. Moltmann, *Trinity and the Kingdom*, 30.

31. Moltmann, *Crucified God*, 271.

32. See Franz Rosenzweig, *The Star of Redemption*, trans. William W. Hallo (New York: Holt, Rinehart, Winston, 1971), 192.

33. Jon Sobrino, *Jesus the Liberator: A Historical-Theological Reading of Jesus of Nazareth*, trans. Paul Burns and Francis McDonagh (Maryknoll, NY: Orbis, 2001).

34. Ibid., 234.

35. Schillebeeckx, *Jesus*, 317.

36. Sobrino, *Jesus the Liberator*, 238.

37. Ibid., 235.

38. Ibid., 242.

39. Ibid., 243.

40. Ibid.

41. Ibid., 244.

42. Jon Sobrino, *Christology at the Crossroads: A Latin American Approach*, trans. John Drury (Maryknoll, NY: Orbis, 1978), 371.

43. Sobrino, *Jesus the Liberator*, 245–246, italics in the original.

44. Leonardo Boff, *Jesucristo*, in Sobrino, *Jesus the Liberator*, 246.

45. Sobrino, *Jesus the Liberator*, 247.

46. Ibid., 249.

47. Ibid., 250.

48. Ibid., 251.

49. Bonhoeffer, *Letters and Papers from Prison*, 224–225.

50. Pedro Casaldáliga, *Todavia estas Palabras*, trans. Paul Burns and Francis McDonagh (Navarra, Spain: Editorial Verbo Divino, 1990), 45.

51. Sobrino, *Jesus the Liberator*, 243. See also Karl Rahner, *Foundations of Christian Faith: An Introduction to the Idea of Christianity* (New York: Seabury, 1978), 86–89; and Schillebeeckx, *Christ*, 31–54.

52. Daniel Day Williams, *God's Grace and Man's Hope* (New York: Harper, 1949), 125.

53. Daniel Day Williams, *The Spirit and the Forms of Love* (New York: Harper & Row, 1968), 122–123.

54. Williams, *Spirit and the Forms of Love*, 124.

55. Ibid., 126.

56. Ibid., 126–127.

57. Ibid., 128.

58. Ibid., 185.

59. Sallie McFague, *Models of God: Theology for an Ecological, Nuclear Age* (Philadelphia: Fortress, 1988), and *The Body of God: An Ecological Theology* (Minneapolis: Fortress, 1993).

60. McFague, *Body of God*, 131, italics in the original.

61. McFague, *Models of God*, 72.

62. Ibid., 71. According to McFague, who acknowledges John Cobb's thinking on the subject, human persons are essentially spirits that possess a body. For McFague, this does not suggest a kind of dualism but simply acknowledges that, while one's body expresses both unconscious and conscious elements of one's personhood, humans are capable of self-reflective distance from their bodies. This, according to Cobb, is especially true when the human person is ill, enslaved, debilitated, or dying. See *Models of God*, 201, n. 14.

63. Ibid., 72.

64. Ibid., 75.

65. Ibid.

66. Ibid., 148–150.

67. McFague, *Body of God*, 131–132. McFague's notion of theology from the "backside of God" is based on her reflections on Exodus 33:23b. Moses requests that God show him the divine glory, but God warns Moses that no one can see the face of God and live. However, God agrees to allow Moses a glimpse of the back of God— a notion that inspires McFague's insights on the transcendence and immanence of God.

68. Ibid., 131, italics in the original.

69. Ibid., 155, italics in the original.

70. Ibid., 133.

71. Ibid., 135.

72. Ibid., 160–164.

73. Ibid., 175–176. McFague cites Arthur Peacocke on this point; see *Body of God*, 258, n. 12.

74. Ibid., 179.

75. Ibid., 195.

CHAPTER 2

1. "Suffering," *Merriam-Webster Online Dictionary*, accessed 14 March 2005; available from http://www.m-w.com/cgi-bin/dictionary?book=Dictionary&va=distress.

2. Mary Ann Fatula, "Suffering," in *The New Dictionary of Theology*, ed. Joseph A. Komonchak, Mary Collins, and Dermot A. Lane (Wilmington, DE: Glazier, 1988), 990.

3. Peacocke, "Cost of New Life," 37, italics in the original.

4. Arthur Peacocke, "The Challenge and Stimulus of the Epic of Evolution to Theology," in *Many Worlds*, ed. Stephen Dick (Philadelphia: Templeton Foundation, 2000), 89, italics in the original.

5. Ibid., 91.

6. Isaac Newton, *The Mathematical Principles of Natural Philosophy*, trans. A. Motte, *Internet Modern History Sourcebook*; accessed 1 April 2007; available from http://www.fordham.edu/halsall/mod/newton-princ.html.

7. "Newton," University of Dallas, accessed 4 May 2004; available from http://phys.udallas.edu.

8. Peacocke, *TSA*, 29–30.

9. Richard Schlegel, "The Impossible Spectator in Physics," *Centennial Review* 19 (1975): 217–231 at 218.

10. Niels Bohr, *Atomic Theory and Description of Nature* (Cambridge: Cambridge University Press, 1934), 119.

11. Karl Heim, *The Transformation of the Scientific World View* (London: SCM, 1953), 24.

12. Charles Darwin, *On the Origin of Species by Means of Natural Selection, or the Preservation of Favoured Races in the Struggle for Life* [book online] (London: John Murray, 1872), accessed 4 May 2004; available from http://www.literature.org/authors/darwin-charles/the-origin-of-species-6th-edition/.

13. Ibid., http://www.literature.org/authors/darwin-charles/the-origin-of-species-6th-edition/preface.html.

14. Ibid., http://www.literature.org/authors/darwin-charles/the-origin-of-species-6th-edition/introduction.html.

15. Ibid., http://www.literature.org/authors/darwin-charles/the-origin-of-species-6th-edition/chapter-03.html.

16. Ibid., http://www.literature.org/authors/darwin-charles/the-origin-of-species-6th-edition/introduction.html.

17. "Neo-Darwinism," *ISCID Encyclopedia of Science and Philosophy,* International Society of Complexity, Information, and Design, accessed 5 May 2004; available from http://www.iscid.org.

18. Arthur Peacocke, *God and the New Biology* (hereafter *GNB*) (London: J. M. Dent and Sons, 1986), 41–47 at 43.

19. Niles Eldredge and Stephen J. Gould, "Punctuated Equilibria: The Tempo and Mode of Evolution Reconsidered," *Paleobiology* 3 (1977): 115–151.

20. Named for its original proponent, French biologist Jean-Baptiste Pierre Antoine de Monet, Chevalier de Lamarck (1744–1829).

21. Richard Lewontin, "Gene, Organism, and Environment," in *Evolution from Molecules to Men,* ed. D. S. Bendall (Cambridge: Cambridge University Press, 1983), 273–285.

22. Peacocke, *GNB,* 47.

23. Arthur Peacocke, *Science and the Christian Experiment* (hereafter *SCE*) (London: Oxford University, 1971), 33.

24. Arthur Peacocke, "Articulating God's Presence in and to the World Unveiled by the Sciences," in *In Whom We Live and Move and Have Our Being: Panentheistic Reflections on God's Presence in a Scientific World,* ed. Philip Clayton and Arthur Peacocke (Grand Rapids, MI: Eerdmans, 2004), 141.

25. Arthur Peacocke, "Theology and Science Today," in *Cosmos and Creation: Science and Theology in Consonance,* ed. Ted Peters (Nashville, TN: Abingdon, 1989), 30.

26. Brian Swimme and Thomas Berry, *The Universe Story: From the Primordial Flaring Forth to the Ecozoic Era—A Celebration of the Unfolding of the Cosmos* (San Francisco: HarperSanFrancisco, 1994), 7.

27. John Polkinghorne, *One World: The Interaction of Science and Theology* (London: SPCK, 1986), 56.

28. Peacocke, *SCE,* 84–91.

29. Jennifer Cobb Kreisberg, "A Globe, Clothing Itself with a Brain," *Wired Magazine.* Terra Lycos Network, accessed 5 May 2004; available from http://www.wired.com/wired/archive/3.06/teilhard.html?pg=2.

30. Arthur Peacocke, "The New Biology and Nature, Man and God," in *The Experiment of Life: Proceedings of the 1981 William Temple Centenary Conference,* ed. F. Kenneth Hare (Toronto: University of Toronto Press, 1983), 56–58. The research of Prigogine and Eigen is also applicable to the discussion of the interplay of chance and necessity in the evolutionary process discussed later.

31. Ilya Prigogine and Gregoire Nicolis, "Biological Order, Structure and Instabilities," *Quarterly Review of Biophysics* 4 (1971): 107–148.

32. Manfred Eigen and Ruthild Winkler, *The Laws of the Game: How the Principles of Nature Govern Chance,* trans. Robert Kimber (New York: Knopf, 1981).

33. Manfred Eigen, "*Molekulare Selbstorganisation und Evolution,*" *Naturwissenschaften* 58, no. 10 (1971): 519. Translation by Arthur Peacocke, with italics in the original.

34. Arthur Peacocke, "God as the Creator of the World of Science," in *Interpreting the Universe as Creation,* ed. V. Brummer (Kampen, Netherlands: Kok Pharos, 1991), 103.

35. Peacocke, *SCE*, 82.

36. Ibid., 77–88.

37. Kenneth Denbigh, *An Inventive Universe* (London: Hutchinson, 1975), 156.

38. Arthur Peacocke, *Creation and the World of Science: The Bampton Lectures 1978* (hereafter *CWS*) (Oxford: Clarendon, 1979), 90–93.

39. Christopher Southgate, "Different Understandings of Chance," *Meta-Library* of the *Metanexus Online Journal*, accessed 10 May 2004; available from http:// www.meta-library.net, italics in the original.

40. Stanley L. Jaki, *God and the Cosmologists* (Washington, DC: Regnery Gateway: 1989), 142–145; and David Hume, *An Enquiry concerning Human Understanding* (La Salle, IL: Open Court, 1958), 104.

41. Peacocke, *TSA*, 117.

42. Julian Huxley, *Evolution in Action* (Middlesex, England: Penguin, 1963), 43–44.

43. Peacocke, *CWS*, 93.

44. See Theodosius Dobzhansky, "Teilhard de Chardin and the Orientation of Evolution: A Critical Essay," in *Process Theology: Basic Writings*, ed. Ewert Cousins (New York: Newman, 1971).

45. Jacques Monod, *Chance and Necessity* (New York: Vintage, 1972), 112–113.

46. Henry P. Stapp, *Mind, Matter, and Quantum Mechanics* (Berlin: Springer-Verlag, 1993), 91.

47. David J. Bartholomew, *God of Chance* (London: SCM, 1984), 97.

48. Richard Dawkins, *The Blind Watchmaker* (Harlow, England: Longmans: 1986).

49. Peacocke, "God as the Creator of the World of Science," 102.

50. Stephen J. Gould, *Wonderful Life: The Burgess Shale and the Nature of History* (London: Penguin, 1989), 35.

51. See Dobzhansky, "Teilhard de Chardin and the Orientation of Evolution," 229–248.

52. Karl Popper, *A World of Propensities* (Bristol, England: Thoemmes, 1990), 12, italics in the original.

53. George G. Simpson, *The Meaning of Evolution: A Study of the History of Life and Its Significance for Man* (London: Oxford University Press, 1950).

54. Ibid., c. 15.

55. Ibid., 248–260.

56. Peacocke, *TSA*, 67.

57. Pierre Teilhard de Chardin, *The Phenomenon of Man*, trans. Benjamin Wall (Harper & Row, 1975), 301: "Reduced to its ultimate essence, the substance of these long pages can be summed up in this simple affirmation: that if the universe, regarded sidereally, is in process of spatial expansion (from the infinitesimal to the immense), in the same way and still more clearly it presents itself to us, physico-chemically, as in process of organic *involution* upon itself (from the extremely simple to the extremely complex)—and, moreover, this particular involution 'of complexity' is experimentally bound up with a correlative increase in interiorisation, that is to say in the psyche or consciousness."

58. Peacocke, "Challenge and Stimulus," 106, italics in the original.

59. Peacocke, "Cost of New Life," 32.

60. Simpson, *Meaning of Evolution*, 260.

61. Michael Polanyi, *The Tacit Dimension* (London: Routledge and Kegan Paul, 1967), 47.

62. Simpson, *Meaning of Evolution*, 292, italics in the original.

63. Brandon Carter, "Large Number Coincidences and the Anthropic Principle in Cosmology," in *Confrontation of Cosmological Theories with Observational Data: Copernicus Symposium II*, ed. M. S. Longair (Boston: D. Reidel, 1974).

64. Such constants include the "Sommerfield fine-structure constant" that represents the strength of interaction between electrons and photons, the number of dimensions in the universe, and the variously interpreted "cosmological constant," proposed and later repudiated by Einstein and yet revived in studies of the dynamics and expansion of the universe.

65. Carter, "Large Number Coincidences," 291.

66. Ibid., 294.

67. John D. Barrow and Frank T. Tipler, *The Anthropic Cosmological Principle* (Oxford: Oxford University Press, 1986).

68. Ibid., 16.

69. Ibid., 21–22.

70. Hugh Montefiore, *The Probability of God* (London: SCM, 1985), and John Polkinghorne, *Science and Creation* (London: SPCK, 1988).

71. "In the beginning there was nothing.... By chance there was a fluctuation, and a set of points, emerging from nothing and taking their formation from the pattern they formed.... From absolute nothing, absolutely without intervention, there came into being rudimentary existence." Peter W. Atkins, *Creation Revisited* (New York: Freeman, 1992), 149.

72. Bartholomew, *God of Chance*, 64–65.

73. Montefiore, *Probability*, 38.

74. Peacocke, *CWS*, with internal quote by Bernard Lovell, "In the Centre of Immensities," 68.

75. Peacocke, *TSA*, 87.

CHAPTER 3

1. This question reflects the oft-quoted maxim of Elizabeth A. Johnson, "The symbol of God functions," which emphasizes in part the fact that models and symbols of God carry significant personal, communal, societal, and political ramifications for those who profess a particular belief. See Elizabeth A. Johnson, *She Who Is: The Mystery of God in Feminist Theological Discourse* (New York: Crossroad, 1993), 4.

2. Sir Francis Bacon, *The Advancement of Learning*, in Peacocke, "Rethinking Religious Faith in a World of Science," in *Religion, Science, and Public Policy*, ed. Frank T. Birtel (New York: Crossroad, 1987), 4.

3. Robert J. Russell, "A Critical Appraisal of Peacocke's Thought on Religion and Science," *Religion and Intellectual Life* 2 (1985): 48–58.

4. Peacocke, "Rethinking Religious Faith," 11–12.

5. Peacocke, *CWS*, 33–34.

6. Mary Hesse, *Revolutions and Reconstructions in the Philosophy of Science* (Brighton, England: Harvester, 1981), xii.

7. Ibid., xii.

8. Thomas S. Kuhn, *The Structure of Scientific Revolutions* (Chicago: University of Chicago Press, 1962).

9. Arthur Peacocke, *Intimations of Reality: Critical Realism in Science and Religion* (hereafter *IR*) (South Bend, IN: University of Notre Dame Press, 1984), 17–19.

10. Michael Mulkay, *Science and the Sociology of Knowledge* (London: Allen and Unwin, 1979), 59–62.

11. Peacocke, *IR*, 21–22.

12. Ian A. Barbour, *Religion and Science: Historical and Contemporary Issues* (San Francisco: HarperSanFrancisco, 1997), 109–110, 118.

13. Ernan McMullin, "The Case for Scientific Realism," in *Essays on Scientific Realism*, ed. Jarrett Leplin (Berkeley: University of California Press, 1984), 26, italics in the original.

14. Leplin, "Introduction," in *Essays on Scientific Realism*, 1.

15. Joseph A. Bracken, "Images of God within Systematic Theology," *Theological Studies* 63, no. 2 (June 2002): 362–373 at 365.

16. Peacocke attributes this phrase to R. M. Harré, *Theories and Things* (New York: Sheed & Ward, 1961).

17. Peacocke, *CWS*, 21–22.

18. An often-quoted example of this experimental argument involves the discussion by Ian Hacking of the conceptual shift in how scientists have thought of the "electron" between 1900 and today. Although scientific belief about electrons has undergone many changes in the last century, "scientists are committed, on the basis of past evidence and current experience, to 'believing in' electrons—that is, they cannot organize their current observations without asserting that electrons exist. *What they believe about electrons . . . changes*, but it is electrons to which they still refer, by long social links that go back to the first occasions on which they were 'discovered' and the referring term 'electron' was introduced." See Peacocke, "Rethinking Religious Faith," 17.

19. Peacocke, *IR*, 28, italics in the original.

20. Ibid., 25–29.

21. Nancey C. Murphy, "Review: *Intimation of Reality*," *Zygon* 20, no. 4 (December 1985): 464–466.

22. Nancey C. Murphy, "Relating Theology and Science in a Postmodern Age," *CTNS Bulletin* 7, no. 4 (Autumn 1987): 1–10.

23. Philip Hefner, "Just How Much May We Intimate about Reality? A Response to Arthur Peacocke," *Religion and Intellectual Life* 2, no. 4 (1985): 32–38 at 32–33.

24. Ibid., 33–38, at 33 and 38.

25. Peacocke, *IR*, 27, italics in the original.

26. Ian Hacking, *Representing and Intervening* (Cambridge: Cambridge University Press, 1983), 275, italics added.

27. Peacocke, *IR*, 45.

28. Vitor Westhelle, "Theological Shamelessness? A Response to Arthur Peacocke and David A. Pailin," *Zygon* 35 (March 2000): 165–172 at 169–170.

29. Wentzel van Huyssteen, *Theology and the Justification of Faith* (Grand Rapids, MI: Eerdmans, 1989), 162–163.

30. Ibid., 41.

31. This position and potential are clearly articulated by Sallie McFague throughout *Models of God: Theology for an Ecological, Nuclear Age* (Philadelphia: Fortress, 1988).

32. Ian Barbour, *Myths, Models and Paradigms* (London: SCM, 1974), 69.

33. Ian Barbour, *Religion and Science: Historical and Contemporary Issues* (San Francisco: HarperSanFrancisco, 1997), 117.

34. Janet M. Soskice, *Metaphor and Religious Language* (Oxford: Oxford University Press, 1984), 210–211.

35. Ian Barbour, *Issues in Science and Religion* (New York: Harper Torch, 1971), 158.

36. McMullin, "Case for Scientific Realism," 39.

37. Peacocke, *IR*, 31.

38. Ibid., 30.

39. Ibid., 30–33.

40. McMullin, "Case for Scientific Realism," 39.

41. N. R. Campbell, "The Structure of Theories," in Peacocke, *IR*, 31.

42. Soskice, *Metaphor*, 181–182.

43. Peacocke, *CWS*, 39.

44. Peacocke, *TSA*, 14.

45. Ibid., 14.

46. Thomas Aquinas, *Summa Contra Gentiles*. Book One: God. Trans. A. C. Pegis (Notre Dame, IN: University of Notre Dame Press, 1975), 140–148.

47. Bracken, "Images of God within Systematic Theology," 365. This understanding of Bracken is reminiscent of Rahner's axiom concerning the Economic and Immanent Trinity. Bracken crafts his statement, however, with disclaimers that are in keeping with the conditional and qualified presuppositions of critical realism.

48. Peacocke, "Rethinking Religious Faith," 22.

49. Sallie McFague, *Metaphorical Theology* (Philadelphia: Fortress, 1983), 104.

50. Thomas Fawcett, *The Symbolic Language of Religion* (London: SCM, 1970), 82.

51. Soskice, *Metaphor*, 176.

52. Peacocke, *IR*, 44.

53. E. L. Mascall, "Review: *Creation and the World of Science*," *Religious Studies* 16, no. 3 (1980): 357–359 at 358–359. It is interesting to note that McFague herself includes the assessment of "usefulness" among her criteria for evaluating particular models of God arising from her metaphorical theological approach. See *Models of God*, 26–27.

54. Peacocke notes that, when applied to God, the term *cause* in his own or in Soskice's argument is not used in such a way as to imply that God is one cause among others in the nexus of events that constitute the created order. He suggests qualifying the notion by conceiving God as "that which gives being to all-that-is, and so, in this sense, is a cosmos-explaining-being; he is that which renders all-that-is intelligible." See *IR*, 87–88, n. 69.

55. Thomas Aquinas, *Summa Theologiae: Existence and Nature of God*. Vol. 2 (Ia. 2–11). Trans. Timothy McDermott (Manchester, England: Blackfriars, 1964), 13–14.

56. George Lindbeck, *The Nature of Doctrine: Religion and Theology in a Postliberal Age* (Philadelphia: Westminster, 1984), 32.

57. Schillebeeckx, *Christ*, 31–54.

58. Ibid., 32, italics in the original.

59. Soskice, *Metaphor*, 139, italics in the original.

60. Hefner, "Just How Much May We Intimate about Reality?" 36, italics in the original.

61. Augustine, *Sermo* 52, c. 6, n. 16: PL 38:360, in "Creeds, Trinity, and Providence," *Catechism of the Catholic Church*, accessed 8 June 2004; available from http://www.illinoisknights.org.

62. Aquinas, *Summa Theologiae*, Ia. 13. 2, 60.

63. Ibid., Ia. 13, a. 5, 64.

64. Acts 17:28 (*RSV*).

65. Aquinas, *Summa Theologiae*, Ia. 13. 2, 60–62.

66. Ibid., Ia. 13. 3, 62.

67. Ibid., Ia. 13. 12, 71–72.

68. Ibid., Ia. 13. 6, 65.

69. Jim McPherson, "The Integrity of Creation: Science, History, and Theology," *Pacifica* 2 (1989): 333–355 at 346.

70. Peacocke, *IR*, 47.

71. Ian Barbour, "Review: *Intimations of Reality: Critical Realism in Science and Religion*," *Religion & Intellectual Life*, II, no. 4 (Summer 1985): III–114 at 112.

72. Peacocke, *IR*, 47.

73. Peacocke, *TSA*, 16.

74. Ibid., 15.

75. Peacocke, *CWS*, 35.

76. Peacocke, *TSA*, 13.

77. Aquinas, *Summa Contra Gentiles*, 29: 2, 138.

78. Ibid., *Summa Theologiae*, Ia. 2. 2:2, 12.

79. Robert J. Russell, "The Theological Scientific Vision of Arthur Peacocke," *Zygon* 26 (December 1991): 505–517.

80. Soskice, *Metaphor*, 139, italics in the original.

81. John Polkinghorne, *Science and Theology: An Introduction* (Minneapolis: Fortress, 1998), 22–24.

82. McFague, *Models of God*, 26.

83. Peacocke, *TSA*, 17.

84. These writers include B. G. Mitchell, *The Justification of Religious Belief* (London: Macmillan, 1973), and D. Pailin, "Can the Theologian Legitimately Try to Answer the Question: Is the Christian Faith True?" *Expository Times* 84 (1973): 321–329. In his work *Axiomatics and Dogmatics* (Belfast: Christian Journals, 1982), J. R. Carnes employs the alternate terms "existential relevance" ("fit"), "adequacy" ("cogency"), and "economy" ("simplicity"). Peacocke himself presents two somewhat different lists within *Theology for a Scientific Age*, 15 and 91. The fourth criterion relates to the aims of my present work and is characterized in terms appropriated from the goals of feminist liberation theology.

85. Barbour, *Religion and Science*, 109–110.

86. McFague, *Models of God*, 27.

87. As Aquinas indicates in his *Summa Theologiae*, "Since therefore God is outside the whole order of creation, and all creatures are ordered to Him, and not conversely, it is manifest that creatures are really related to God Himself; whereas in God there is no real relation to creatures, but a relation only in idea, inasmuch as creatures are referred to Him. Thus there is nothing to prevent these names which import relation to the creature from being predicated of God temporally, not by reason of any change in Him, but by reason of the change of the creature; as a column is on the right of an animal, without change in itself, but by change in the animal" (*ST* Ia. 13. 7). And further, "Therefore there is no real relation in God to the creature; whereas in creatures there is a real relation to God; because creatures are contained under the divine order, and their very nature entails dependence on God" (*ST* Ia. 28. 1), 66 and 152.

88. F. L. Cross and E. A. Livingstone, eds., *Oxford Dictionary of the Christian Church*, 2nd edition (Oxford: Oxford University Press, 1983), 1027.

89. Barbour, *Religion and Science*, 329–332, 357–360.

90. Curtis L. Thompson, "From Presupposing Pantheism's Power to Potentiating Panentheism's Personality: Seeking Parallels between Kierkegaard's and Martensen's Theological Anthropologies," *Journal of Religion* 82, no. 2 (April 2002): 225–251 at 234.

91. Bracken, "Images of God within Systematic Theology," 367, italics added.

92. Peacocke, *TSA*, 96, italics in the original.

93. Doctrinal Commission of the Church of England, *We Believe in God* (London: Church House Publishing, 1987), 66.

94. David Pailin, *God and the Processes of Reality* (New York: Routledge, 1989), 81.

95. Barbour, *Religion and Science*, 322–332.

96. Michael W. Brierley, "Naming a Quiet Revolution: The Panentheistic Turn in Modern Theology," in *In Whom We Live and Move and Have Our Being*, 1–15. It is interesting that in his article Brierley parallels his notion of the "quiet revolution" with the surreptitious "rise of the new orthodoxy" of the suffering God, so characterized by Ronald Goetz.

97. McFague, *Body of God*, and Grace Jantzen, *God's World, God's Body* (London: Darton, Longman, and Todd, 1984).

98. Peacocke, "Articulating God's Presence," 137–154 at 151.

99. Philip Clayton, "Emerging God: Theology for a Complex Universe," *Christian Century* 12, no. 1 (13 January 2004): 26–30.

100. John Macquarrie, *In Search of Deity: An Essay in Dialectical Theism: The Gifford Lectures 1983–1984* (London: SCM, 1984), 36–37.

101. Philip Clayton, *The Problem of God in Modern Thought* (Grand Rapids, MI: Eerdmans, 2000), 490–493.

102. Peacocke, "Articulating God's Presence," 151–152.

103. Peacocke, *TSA*, 301, italics in the original.

104. Peacocke, "Articulating God's Presence," 147, italics in the original.

105. Concerning the ontology of relationality from a scientific context, see Thomas F. Torrance, *Reality and Scientific Theology* (Edinburgh: Scottish Academic Press, 1985). On such ontology from a theological perspective, see, inter alia, Isabel Carter Heyward, *The Redemption of God: A Theology of Mutual Relation* (Washington, DC: University Press of America, 1982), and *Touching Our Strength: The Erotic as Power and the Love of God* (San Francisco: Harper & Row, 1989), as well as Jürgen Moltmann, *The Trinity and the Kingdom.*

106. Johnson, *She Who Is,* 234–235.

107. Peacocke, *PSG,* 139.

CHAPTER 4

1. Peacocke, *TSA,* 100–101.

2. In this proposal, Peacocke links his understanding of the distinction between the Being and the Becoming of the Divine to the distinction between the essence and the energies of God articulated in the theological tradition of Eastern Orthodoxy. In Eastern Orthodoxy, Peacocke suggests, there is a distinction made between the "essence" of God, what God is in Godself or God's being, and the "energies" of God, what God does or God's becoming in relation to the cosmos. In the light of his overall project, Peacocke suggests that this distinction is the most explicit way of holding together the transcendence and immanence of God in relation to the cosmos. Cf. Peacocke, "Articulating God's Presence," 152. On this point, Peacocke points to the work of Kallistos Ware. In his description of "Palamite Panentheism," Bishop Ware writes,

In his teaching concerning the immanent energies of God, omnipresent throughout his creation, Saint Gregory Palamas sets before us a doctrine of God that is intensely dynamic. The emphasis is clearly upon "becoming" rather than "being." Permeating the world, the divine energies are precisely the life and power of God, directly and immediately active throughout the natural order.... Yet while permeating the created universe through his energies, God also transcends the universe in his ineffable essence, which remains forever unknowable.... Palamas in this way is a maximalist: the whole of God is radically transcendent in his essence, and the whole of God is radically immanent in his omnipresent energies.

See Kallistos Ware, "God Immanent Yet Transcendent: The Divine Energies according to Saint Gregory Palamas," in *In Whom We Live and Move and Have Our Being*, 157–168 at 165–166. Despite some resonance between the thinking of Peacocke on Divine Being and Becoming and that of Eastern Orthodoxy on divine essence and energies, however, a close examination of Peacocke's understanding of divine transcendence and immanence reveals such a marked difference from that of Eastern Orthodoxy that caution must be taken in presuming facile parallels between the two concepts. See, for example, Aristotle Papanikolaou, "Divine Energies or Divine Personhood: Vladimir Lossky and John Zizioulas on Conceiving the Transcendent and Immanent God," *Modern Theology* 19, no. 3 (2003): 357–385.

3. Peacocke, *TSA*, 101.

4. Peacocke, *CWS*, 74–75.

5. Peacocke, *TSA*, 101–102.

6. Peacocke, *GNB*, 95.

7. Arthur Peacocke, "Chance and Law in Irreversible Thermodynamics, Theoretical Biology, and Theology," in *Chaos and Complexity: Scientific Perspectives on Divine Action*, ed. Robert J. Russell, Nancey Murphy, and Arthur Peacocke (Vatican City State: Vatican Observatory Foundation, 1995), 138.

8. Peacocke, *CWS*, 77–78.

9. Peacocke, "Theology and Science Today," 30.

10. Peacocke, *TSA*, 102.

11. This inference clearly references the Christian concept of the Triunity of God, a reference that Peacocke points out only parenthetically at this stage of his proposal.

12. Peacocke, *TSA*, 102–103, italics in the original.

13. Peacocke, *SCE*, 132.

14. Albert Einstein, *Out of My Later Years* (Westport, CT: Greenwood, 1970), 61.

15. Peacocke, *TSA*, 103.

16. Peacocke, *CWS*, 65.

17. Peacocke, *TSA*, 103–104.

18. Gunther Stent, *Nature, Lond.*, in Peacocke, *GNB*, 60.

19. See Michael J. Behe, *Darwin's Black Box: The Biochemical Challenge to Evolution* (New York: Touchstone Books, 1996); William Dembski, *The Design Inference: Eliminating Chance through Small Probabilities* (Cambridge: Cambridge University Press, 1999); and Kenneth E. Himma, "Design Arguments for the Existence of God, in *The Internet Encyclopedia of Philosophy*, accessed 20 December 2004; available from http://www.iep.utm.edu/d/design.htm.

20. Peacocke, *IR*, 63.

21. Peacocke, *CWS*, 204, italics in the original.

22. Peacocke, *TSA*, 104.

23. Cf. Aquinas, *Summa Theologiae*, Ia.2.3, 13.

24. Frederick C. Copleston, *Aquinas* (Baltimore, MD: Penguin Books, 1961), 118–120.

25. Aquinas, *Summa Theologiae*, Ia:28:1, 152.

26. Peacocke, *TSA*, 105.

27. Peacocke, *GNB*, 95–96.

28. Peacocke, *IR*, 63.

29. See Donald T. Campbell, " 'Downward Causation' in Hierarchically Organized Systems," in *Studies in the Philosophy of Biology: Reduction and Related Problems*, ed. Francisco J. Ayala and Theodosius G. Dobzhansky (London: Macmillan, 1974); and Roger W. Sperry, *Science and Moral Priority* (Oxford: Blackwell, 1983).

30. See chapter 2 of this book.

31. James A. Wiseman is critical of Peacocke's whole-part approach for its lack of stress on part-whole influence, which Wiseman construes as emphasizing divine transcendence and de-emphasizing divine immanence. See *Theology and Modern Science: Quest for Consonance* (New York: Continuum, 2002), 116–117. However, a closer reading of Peacocke's work reveals that Peacocke is most clear about the dual character of these influences. See Peacocke, *TSA*, 54–55.

32. Peacocke, *TSA*, 158.

33. This insight is echoed in Karl Rahner's notion of God as essentially self-communicating Being.

34. Barbour, *Religion and Science*, 315.

35. Once again, Peacocke's position clearly resonates with Karl Rahner's notion of the mediated immediacy of God through categorical reality. See Rahner, *Foundations of Christian Faith*, 81–86.

36. Peacocke, *TSA*, 206–207.

37. Ibid., 160–161 at 161.

38. Polkinghorne, *Science and Theology*, 87–89.

39. Wiseman, *Theology and Modern Science*, 117.

40. Philip Clayton, *God and Contemporary Science* (Edinburgh, Scotland: Edinburgh University, 1997), 21–24.

41. Peacocke, *GNB*, 96.

42. Peacocke, *TSA*, 112.

43. Peacocke, *SCE*, 176.

44. Peacocke, *TSA*, 98.

45. Peacocke, *CWS*, 131–133, italics in the original.

46. Peacocke, "Challenge and Stimulus of the Epic of Evolution," 110, italics in the original.

47. Peacocke, *TSA*, 91–93.

48. Richard Swinburne, *The Existence of God* (Oxford: Clarendon, 1979), 8.

49. Richard Swinburne, "Mackie, Induction, and God," *Religious Studies* 19 (1983): 385–391 at 385.

50. Peacocke, *PSG*, 140–141.

51. Peacocke, *TSA*, 160.

52. Peacocke, *PSG*, 70.

53. Peacocke, *PSG*, 71.

54. Peacocke, *CWS*, 70, italics in the original.

55. Peacocke, *TSA*, 111–112, italics in the original.

56. Ibid., 112.

57. Ibid., 112–113.

58. Ibid., 114–115.

59. Peacocke, "Cost of New Life," 36, italics in the original.

60. Genesis 1:31 (*NAB*).

61. Peacocke, CWS, 108–111.

62. Ibid., 110. See also Haridas Chaudhuri and Frederic Spiegelberg, eds., *The Integral Philosophy of Sri Aurobindo: A Commemorative Symposium* (London: Allen & Unwin, 1960).

63. Cf. Proverbs 8:27–31.

64. Harvey Cox, *The Feast of Fools* (Cambridge, MA: Harvard University, 1969), 151.

65. Jürgen Moltmann, *Theology and Joy,* trans. Reinhard Ulrich (London: SCM, 1973), 38.

66. Peacocke, *TSA*, 115.

67. Peacocke, *CWS*, 104–105.

68. Peacocke, *SCE*, 83.

69. Peacocke, *CWS*, 95.

70. David Pailin, "Review: *Theology for a Scientific Age,*" *Journal of Theological Studies* 42 (1991): 814–819 at 816.

71. Peacocke, "New Biology and Nature, Man and God," 58.

72. Peacocke, *TSA*, 119.

73. Barbour, "Review: *Intimations of Reality,*" 113.

74. Peacocke, *IR*, 70–71.

75. Nancey Murphy, "Review: *Theology for a Scientific Age,*" *Cross Currents* 41, no. 3 (1991): 416.

76. Peacocke, *CWS*, 95.

77. Eugene M. Klaaren, "Review: *Creation and the World of Science,*" *Zygon* 16, no. 2 (1981): 193.

78. Peacocke, *CWS*, 105.

79. Peacocke, "New Biology and Nature, Man and God," 59.

80. Peacocke, *TSA*, 174–175.

81. Montefiore, *Probability,* 98.

82. Barbour, "Review: *Intimations of Reality,*" 113.

83. Peacocke, *TSA*, 176, italics in the original.

84. Peacocke, "Theology and Science Today," 35.

85. Danny R. Stiver, "Review: *God and the New Biology,*" *Review and Expositor* 85 (Winter 1988): 167–168.

86. These unpredictabilities include not only those at the subatomic level resulting from random mutation or explained by the Heisenberg uncertainty principle but also those at the level of the cosmos, in which environmental factors and human freedom come into play.

87. Peacocke, *TSA*, 121.

88. Peacocke, "Theology and Science Today," 37–38.

89. Peacocke, *PSG*, 41, italics added.

90. Peacocke, *TSA*, 121.

91. Lucien Richard, *Christ the Self-Emptying God* (New York: Paulist, 1997), 136.

92. Peacocke, "Cost of New Life," 37.

93. Ron Highfield, "Divine Self-Limitation in the Theology of Jürgen Moltmann: A Critical Appraisal," *Christian Scholar's Review* 32, no. 1 (2002): 63.

94. Polkinghorne, *Science and Theology*, 95.

95. Highfield, "Divine Self-Limitation," 63.

96. Peacocke, *SCE*, 137. Philosopher Søren Kierkegaard agrees and proclaims in his *Christian Discourses*, "A human cannot bear that his 'creatures' should be something directly over and against him. . . . But God who creates out of nothing and says 'Be!' lovingly adds, 'Be something even over and against me.' Wonderful love, even God's omnipotence is under the power of love!" See *Christian Discourses*, trans. Walter Lowrie (Princeton, NJ: Princeton University Press, 1971), 132–133.

97. Peacocke, *TSA*, 121–123 at 123.

98. Arthur R. Peacocke, *Paths from Science Towards God: The End of All Our Exploring* (hereafter *PSG*) (Oxford: Oneworld, 2001), 59, italics in the original.

99. James Salmon, "Review: *Theology for a Scientific Age*," *Theological Studies* 53, no. 4 (1992): 791.

100. Highfield, "Divine Self-Limitation," 49.

101. Nicholas Saunders, *Divine Action & Modern Science* (Cambridge: Cambridge University Press, 2002), 150, n. 27.

102. Peacocke, *TSA*, 142–143, italics in the original.

103. Jonathan Doye, Ian Goldby, Christina Line, Stephen Lloyd, Paul Shellard, and David Tricker, "Contemporary Perspectives on Chance, Providence, and Free Will," *Science and Christian Belief* 7, no. 2 (1995): 129–132; and Stiver, "Review: *God and the New Biology*," 168.

104. Peacocke, *PSG*, 122.

105. Highfield, "Divine Self-Limitation," 61.

106. Peacocke, *PSG*, 59, emphasis added. This definition, as well as that of *omnipotence*, reflects Richard Swinburne's conception of God mentioned in the previous discussion of the personal nature of God. See *TSA*, 92, and Swinburne, *Existence of God*, 8.

107. Peacocke, *TSA*, 122, italics in the original.

108. William Lane Craig, *Divine Foreknowledge and Human Freedom: The Coherence of Theism: Omniscience* (Leiden: E. J. Brill, 1991), 12. Craig indicates that foreknowledge of contingent future events is assumed in biblical theism.

109. Arthur R. Peacocke, "God's Interaction with the World: The Implications of Deterministic 'Chaos' and of Interconnected and Interdependent Reality," in *Chaos and Complexity: Scientific Perspectives on Divine Action*, ed. Robert J. Russell, Nancey C. Murphy, and Arthur R. Peacocke (Vatican City State: Vatican Observatory Foundation, 1995), 280.

110. Ibid.

111. The questions posed with regard to divine omnipotence and limitation as contingent or necessary apply here as well.

112. Peacocke, *PSG*, 59.

113. Peacocke, *TSA*, 122–123.

114. John Polkinghorne, *Science and Christian Belief: Reflections of a Bottom-up Thinker* (London: SPCK, 1994), 81.

115. Keith Ward, *Religion and Creation* (Oxford: Clarendon, 1996), 188.

116. Aquinas, *Summa Theologiae*, 1a. 10. 2, 41, italics in the original.

117. Boethius, *De Consol.* V, in Aquinas, *Summa Theologiae*, 1a.10.1, 40–41 at 40.

118. Aquinas, *Summa Theologiae*, 1a.14.13, 82–84 at 83.

119. John Jefferson Davis, "Quantum Indeterminacy and the Omniscience of God," *Science and Christian Belief* 9, no. 2 (1997): 129–144 at 133–134.

120. Denis Edwards, "The Discovery of Chaos and the Retrieval of the Trinity," in *Chaos and Complexity*, 170–171.

121. Davis, "Quantum Indeterminacy," 134, italics in the original.

122. Peacocke, *SCE*, 123–124.

123. Ibid., 124–130 at 130.

124. Peacocke, *CWS*, 80–81, n. 53, italics in the original. On the points raised by Peacocke, see, inter alia, J. R. Lucas, *A Treatise on Space and Time* (London: Methuen, 1973), and Nelson Pike, *God and Timelessness* (London: Routledge and Kegan Paul, 1970).

125. See Peacocke, "Cosmos and Creation," in *Cosmology, History, and Theology*, ed. W. Yourgrau and A. D. Breck (New York: Plenum, 1977), 379.

126. J. R. Lucas, "The Temporality of God," in *Quantum Cosmology and the Laws of Nature: Scientific Perspectives on Divine Action*, ed. Robert J. Russell, Nancey Murphy, and C. J. Isham (Vatican City State: Vatican Observatory Foundation; Berkeley, CA· CTNS, 1993), 235.

127. Ibid., 236.

128. Peacocke, *TSA*, 130–132 at 131, italics in the original.

129. John Polkinghorne, *Belief in God in an Age of Science* (New Haven: Yale University, 1998), 74.

130. Pailin, "Review: *Theology for a Scientific Age*," 816.

131. Peacocke, *TSA*, 132.

132. Doctrine Commission of the Church of England, *We Believe in God*, 160. Quoted by Peacocke in *TSA*, 132–133.

133. Peacocke, *TSA*, 124, italics in the original.

134. Ibid., 123, italics in the original.

135. Peacocke, *CWS*, 197.

136. Ibid., 198–199.

137. James E. Huchingson, "Review: *Theology for a Scientific Age*," *Zygon* 31 (1996): 355.

138. This resemblance to Teilhard has also been noted by John Haught in his review of *Science and the Christian Experiment* in *Theological Studies* 33 (1972): 558–559.

139. D. G. Trickett, "Review: *Creation and the World of Science*," *Journal of Religion* 61, no. 2 (1981): 207.

140. Peacocke references the work of Jürgen Moltmann in this area. See Moltmann, "God's Kenosis in the Creation and Consummation of the World," in *The Work of Love*, 137–151 at 146. The internal quote is taken from Gershom Scholem, "*Schöpfung aus Nichts und Selbstverschränkung Gottes*," in Moltmann, 146.

141. Peacocke, *PSG*, 86–87.

142. Peacocke, "Cost of New Life," 38, italics in the original.

143. Polkinghorne, *Belief in God*, 74.

144. Peacocke, "Cost of New Life," 37, italics in the original.

145. Peacocke, *TSA*, 125.

146. Polkinghorne, *Belief in God*, 14.

147. Peacocke, *TSA*, 125. One must note that Peacocke refers to these events as "natural *evils*" or "*pointless* suffering and tragedy" that are "inimical to human health, welfare and happiness, and indeed life," despite the fact that the evolutionary emergence of novel forms of life takes place through these very events. Denis Edwards suggests that such events must be regarded in nonanthropomorphic and nonmoral terms as objective processes in nature, rather than as manifestations of evil. See Edwards' discussion "Original Sin and Saving Grace in an Evolutionary Context," in *Evolutionary and Molecular Biology: Scientific Perspectives on Divine Action*, ed. Robert John Russell, William R. Stroeger, and Francisco J. Ayala (Berkeley: Center for Theology and the Natural Sciences, 1998), 377–392.

148. Peacocke, *TSA*, 125.

149. Peacocke, "Cost of New Life," 37, italics in the original.

150. Ibid., 39.

151. Peacocke, *TSA*, 126. Again, Peacocke evaluates evolutionary events as "evils."

152. Peacocke, *PSG*, 87. The expression of this insight in this volume of Peacocke's writings suggests some expansion of his anthropocentric notion of God's "overarching purpose" for the cosmos. Moreover, in a footnote to *Theology for a Scientific Age*, Peacocke indicates that his assertion of God's suffering in order to "bring about a greater good thereby" reflects his "broad acceptance" of the Irenaean theodicy of natural evil as expressed by John Hick in "An Irenaean Theodicy," in *Encountering Evil*, ed. Stephen T. Davis (Edinburgh, Scotland: T. & T. Clark, 1981), 39–52, and in *Evil and the God of Love* (London: Macmillan, 1966). See Peacocke, *TSA*, 363, n. 72.

153. Peacocke, "Cost of New Life," 41, italics in the original, and Revelation 13:8 (*NAB*).

154. Ibid., 41–42.

155. Ibid., 42, italics in the original. The reference to the "crucified God" is, of course, that of Jürgen Moltmann in *The Crucified God*.

156. Peacocke, "Cost of New Life," 42.

157. Ibid., 37.

158. Cf. Romans 8:19–22 (*RSV*).

159. Peacocke, "Articulating God's Presence," 151–152.

160. Peacocke, *PSG*, 88.

161. Peacocke, *TSA*, 126.

162. A gloss on T. S. Eliot's "Four Quartets 4: Little Gidding," *American Poems*, accessed 4 January 2005; available from http://www.americanpoems.com. These are verses that Peacocke himself was fond of quoting.

163. Peacocke, *TSA*, 300.

CHAPTER 5

1. Portions of this chapter appear in the article "The Creative Suffering of the Triune God: An Evolutionary Panentheistic Paradigm," *Theology & Science* 5, no. 3 (2007): forthcoming.

2. Peacocke, *SCE*, 135.

3. Alfred Tennyson, "In Memoriam, A.H.H." *Tapestry: The Institute for Philosophy, Religion, and the Life Sciences, Inc.*, accessed 17 November 2004; available from http://www.tapestryweb.org/tornado/tennyson.html.

4. Peacocke, *SCE*, 137.

5. Peacocke, *TSA*, 309.

6. Ibid.

7. Recall that predictability served as one of the criteria by which scientists judged the level of critical realism attributable to a theory.

8. E.g., Heisenberg's uncertainty principle.

9. Frederic R. Howe, "Review: *God and the New Biology*," *Bibliotheca Sacra* 145 (1988): 459.

10. Saunders, *Divine Action*, 209.

11. Ibid., 351.

12. Doye et al., "Contemporary Perspectives on Chance," 132.

13. Highfield, "Divine Self-Limitation," 61.

14. Klaaren, "Review: *CWS*," 193.

15. Doye et al., "Contemporary Perspectives on Chance," 138.

16. Davis, "Quantum Indeterminacy," 134.

17. As noted earlier, Wiseman criticizes Peacocke's approach as lacking the component of part-whole influence, which Wiseman construes as emphasizing divine transcendence and de-emphasizing divine immanence. See *Theology and Modern Science*, 116–117.

18. Peacocke, *TSA*, 54–55.

19. Jeffrey C. Pugh, *Entertaining the Triune Mystery: God, Science, and the Space Between* (Harrisburg, PA: Trinity, 2003), 53.

20. This conclusion resonates with Karl Rahner's notion of the mediated immediacy of God, the notion that God, as the infinite and transcendental source and term of all reality, is present in and disclosed through finite categorical reality. See Rahner, *Foundations of Christian Faith*, 81–86.

21. McPherson, "Integrity of Creation," 346.

22. Arthur Peacocke, in a personal communication with this writer, December 1, 2004.

23. Paul Tillich, *Theology of Culture* (New York: Oxford University Press, 1959), 131–132.

24. Peacocke, *IR*, 67.

25. Ibid., 78.

26. Peacocke, *CWS*, 206.

27. Peacocke, *SCE*, 120.

28. Ibid., 176.

29. Peacocke, *CWS*, 204–207 at 207.

30. Peacocke, *GNB*, 125.

31. Peacocke, *TSA*, 348.

32. Peacocke, *PSG*, 167–168.

33. John C. Polkinghorne, "*Creatio Continua* and Divine Action," *Science & Christian Belief* 7 (1995): 101–108 at 103.

34. This is a fundamental corollary of the critical realist approach. Cf. Peacocke, *Intimations of Reality*.

35. Peacocke, "New Biology and Nature, Man and God," 35.

36. Peacocke, *CWS*, 199. Enclosed quote from T. S. Eliot, "Burnt Norton V," from *Four Quartets*. *Art of Europe*, accessed 7 December 2004; available at http://www.artof europe.com.

37. Walter Kasper, *The God of Jesus Christ* (London: SCM, 1983), 156.

38. Denis Edwards, "The Discovery of Chaos and the Retrieval of the Trinity," in *Chaos and Complexity*, 60.

39. Catherine M. LaCugna, *God for Us: The Trinity and Christian Life* (San Francisco: Harper Collins, 1991), 248–249, italics in the original.

40. Ibid., 250, italics in the original.

41. John Polkinghorne, *Science and the Trinity: The Christian Encounter with Reality* (New Haven: Yale University Press, 2004), 95.

42. Peacocke, *PSG*, 139.

43. Barbour, *Religion and Science*, 242.

44. Peacocke, *PSG*, 141.

45. Polkinghorne, "*Creatio Continua* and Divine Action," 102–103.

46. Peacocke, *TSA*, 372, italics in the original.

47. Peacocke, "Articulating God's Presence," 151.

48. Peacocke, *PSG*, 142.

49. "Suffering," *Merriam-Webster Online Dictionary*, accessed 14 March 2005; available from http://www.m-w.com/cgi-bin/dictionary?book=Dictionary&va=distress.

50. Fatula, "Suffering," 990.

51. Cassell, "Pain and Suffering," in *Encyclopedia of Bioethics*. Vol. 4, ed. William T. Reich (New York: Macmillan, 1995), 1899–1900.

52. Peacocke, *CWS*, 200.

53. Peacocke, "Cost of New Life," 42.

54. Alister McGrath, "Old Theology and the New Biology," *Science and Christian Belief* 1, no. 2 (1989): 168.

55. Elmer W. Brewer, "The Approaches of John Polkinghorne, Arthur Peacocke, and Ian Barbour for the Integration of Natural Science and Christian Theology," Ph.D. diss. (Southern Baptist Theological Seminary, 1995), 148.

56. Polkinghorne, *Science and Theology*, 118–119. According to Polkinghorne, those who move toward assimilating the insights of science and theology attempt to discover as close a conceptual relationship as possible between the two realms of thought. However, in opposition to Brewer's suggestion, these theorists

resist surrendering the integrity of one to the other. On the other hand, those who move toward consonance between science and theology stress the "conceptual autonomy" of theology while realizing that a consistency with science must be achieved. In Polkinghorne's mind, Peacocke's thought represents elements of each approach as Peacocke attempts to maintain continuity with the Christian tradition in step with the advance of science.

57. Ibid.

58. James Salmon, "Review: *Theology for a Scientific Age*," *Theological Studies* 53, no. 4 (1992): 790.

59. See, e.g., Peacocke, *TSA*, 310, and "Cost of New Life," 42, italics in the original.

60. Peacocke, *GNB*, 107.

61. McGrath, "Old Theology and the New Biology," 168.

62. Polkinghorne, *Science and Theology*, 111.

63. McPherson, "Integrity of Creation," 346–347.

64. Peacocke, *TSA*, 290–311 at 300, italics in the original. In this chapter, Peacocke lays out a wonderful presentation of the consonance between the revelation of God in the cosmos and of God in Jesus the Christ, centered on the attributes of Divine Being and Becoming.

65. Peacocke, *TSA*, 7.

66. Polkinghorne, *Science and Theology*, 93–94.

67. Cf. Peacocke, *CWS*, 198–199.

68. Peacocke, *PSG*, 87.

69. Cf. Luke 12:24–28.

70. Cf. 1 Corinthians 15:19. The quote itself concerns resurrection: "But if Christ is preached as raised from the dead, how can some among you say there is no resurrection of the dead? If there is no resurrection of the dead, then neither has Christ been raised. And if Christ has not been raised, then empty too is our preaching; empty, too, your faith. Then we are also false witnesses to God, because we testified against God that he raised Christ, whom he did not raise if in fact the dead are not raised. For if the dead are not raised, neither has Christ been raised, and if Christ has not been raised, your faith is vain; you are still in your sins. Then those who have fallen asleep in Christ have perished. If for this life only we have hoped in Christ, we are the most pitiable people of all." See 1 Corinthians 15:12–19 (*NAB*).

71. One thinks of the proposal by Jürgen Moltmann (*Crucified God*, 243), whom Peacocke references on multiple occasions with regard to the suffering of God: "The Son suffers dying, the Father suffers the death of the Son."

72. According to the *Oxford English Dictionary*, *protopathy* is a "primary suffering; pain or other sensation immediately produced, i.e. one not produced by or consequent on another . . . a term for a first or original suffering, opposed to sympathy." Cf. "Protopathy," *Oxford English Dictionary Online*, accessed 14 February 2005; available from http://dictionary.oed.com.

73. Psalm 139:1–4, passim, adapted from the *NAB*.

74. Peacocke, "Articulating God's Presence," 151.

75. Peacocke, *CWS*, 316.

76. The use of the designation *She Who Is* derives from the insights of Elizabeth A. Johnson from her book of the same name. See 241–243. Johnson's understanding will be brought to bear on the developments of a female model of the Triune God in the final chapter.

77. Eliot, "Four Quartets 4: Little Gidding."

CHAPTER 6

1. This chapter forms the foundation of the article "A Procreative Paradigm of the Creative Suffering of the Triune God: Implications of Arthur Peacocke's Evolutionary Theology," which first appeared *Theological Studies* 67, no. 3 (2006): 542–566. I am grateful to editor David Schultenover, SJ, for his enthusiastic permission for its use.

2. Portions of this section appear in the article "Midwifery as a Model for Ecological Ethics: Expanding Arthur Peacocke's Models of 'Man-in-Creation,' " *Zygon* 42, no. 2 (2007): 489-501.

3. Recall that *protopathy* is a "primary suffering; pain or other sensation immediately produced, i.e. one not produced by or consequent on another . . . term for a first or original suffering, opposed to sympathy."

4. Peacocke, *PSG*, 139.

5. Peacocke, "Cost of New Life," 38.

6. Johnson, *She Who Is*, 242–243.

7. Ibid., 241.

8. Ibid., 242.

9. Ibid., 240.

10. Cf. Colossians 1:16–17, adapted from the *NAB*.

11. Peacocke, *PSG*, 86-87.

12. Johnson, *She Who Is*, 254.

13. Cf. Isaiah 42:14, in which this is explicitly said of God.

14. Johnson, *She Who Is*, 255.

15. Ibid., 214.

16. Gershom Scholem, "Readings from *On the Mystical Shape of the Godhead: Basic Concepts of the Kabbalah*," trans. Joachim Neugroschel, accessed 1 December 2001; available from http://dhushara.tripod.com.

17. The appellation *Shekhinah* has a number of different spellings, including *Shekinah, Shekhina, Shechina,* and *Schechina.* Unless quoted from a specific source, the spelling used in this essay is *Shekhinah.*

18. Raphael Patai, *The Hebrew Goddess* [1967, 1978], 3rd ed. (Detroit: Wayne State, 1990), 98.

19. "*Shekhina,*" *Encyclopedia Britannica,* accessed 1 December 2001; available from http://www.britannica.com; Patai, *Hebrew Goddess,* 98; and Scholem, Readings from *On the Mystical Shape of the Godhead.*

20. Gershom Scholem, *The Kabbalah and Its Symbolism*, trans. Ralph Manheim (New York: Schocken, 1996), 105.

21. Patai, *Hebrew Goddess*, 96.

22. Scholem, Readings from *On the Mystical Shape of the Godhead*.

23. See my essay "The Power of Divine Presence: Toward a *Shekhinah* Christology," in *Christology: Memory, Inquiry, Practice: Proceedings of the College Theology Society 2002*, ed. Anne Clifford and Anthony Godzieba (Maryknoll, NY: Orbis, 2003). For further discussion of the attributes of the *Shekhinah*, see, inter alia, Moltmann, "*Shekinah*: Home of the Homeless God" and "God's Kenosis in the Creation and Consummation of the World," and Johnson, *She Who Is*, 83–86.

24. Ephraim E. Urbach, *The Sages: Their Concepts and Beliefs*, trans. Israel Abrahams (Cambridge, MA: Harvard University Press, 1987), 38.

25. Ibid., 43–48, and Chanoch Gebhard and Dovid Landesman, *As the Rabbis Taught: Studies in the Aggados of the Talmud—Tractate Megillah*, trans. Dovid Landesman (Northvale, NJ: Aronson, 1966), 301.

26. J. Abelson, *The Immanence of God in Rabbinic Literature* [1912] (New York: Hermon, 1969), 122.

27. Gershom Scholem, *Major Trends in Jewish Mysticism* (New York: Schocken, 1995), 111.

28. Ibid., 98, 106, 143; Patai, *Hebrew Goddess*, 100–110; and Urbach, *Sages*, 42, 63.

29. Max Kadushin, *The Rabbinic Mind* (New York: Jewish Theological Seminary of America, 1952), 227; and Abelson, *Immanence of God*, 104.

30. Abraham Heschel, *God in Search of Man: A Philosophy of Judaism* (New York: Harper & Row, 1955), 21.

31. Kadushin, *Rabbinic Mind*, 224; and Jürgen Moltmann, "*Shekinah*: The Home of the Homeless God," 175.

32. Cf. Matthew 10:40, Mark 9:37.

33. Peacocke, *SCE*, 124–128.

34. Ibid., 127, 128.

35. Susan Cole, Marion Ronan, and Hal Taussig, *Wisdom's Feast* (Kansas City, MO: Sheed and Ward, 1996), 15.

36. Cf. Proverbs 8:27–31 (*RSV*).

37. Wisdom 7:7, 10–12 (*RSV*). Because of its significance for this feminist reconstruction, I have substituted the appellation *Sophia* for its translation "wisdom" as found in the *RSV* and *NAB* in this quote and those that follow.

38. Wisdom 8:1 (*RSV*).

39. Wisdom 7:25, 27 (*RSV*).

40. Wisdom 8:6, 8, translation from Cole et al., *Wisdom's Feast*, 204.

41. Wisdom 7:17b–24 (*NAB*).

42. Proverbs 8:13, 36 (*NAB*).

43. Wisdom 1:5 (*NAB*).

44. Proverbs 1:24–25, 28, 33, 30, 32 (*NAB*).

45. Cole et al., *Wisdom's Feast*, 198.

46. Wisdom 7:30, translation from Cole et al., *Wisdom's Feast*, 203.

47. Wisdom 7:27 (*NAB*)

48. Proverbs 1:20–21, translation from Cole et al., *Wisdom's Feast*, 199.

49. Johnson, *She Who Is*, 177–178.

50. Tricia Sheffield, "Toward a Theory of Divine Female Embodiment," *Journal of Religion and Society* 4 (2002), accessed 21 March 2005; available from http://moses.creighton.edu/JRS/2002/2002-6.html.

51. Johnson, *She Who Is*, 177–178.

52. Peacocke, *CWS*, 281–312. *The Oxford English Dictionary* defines *symbiont* as "either of two organisms living in symbiosis; a commensal." See "Symbiont," *Oxford English Dictionary Online*, accessed 21 February 2005; available from http://dictionary.oed.com.

53. "Midwives Model of Care," Citizens for Midwifery, accessed 12 February 2005; available from http://www.cfmidwifery.org.

54. "What to Expect from a Caregiver Who Provides the Midwifery Model of Care," Citizens for Midwifery, accessed 12 February 2005; available from http://www.cfmidwifery.org.

55. The Earth Charter Initiative, "Earth Charter," accessed 19 May 2006; available from http://www.earthcharter.org.

56. Margaret Wheatley, *Leadership and the New Science: Learning about Organization from an Orderly Universe* (San Francisco: Berrett-Koehler, 1992), 9.

57. Peacocke, *CWS*, 316.

58. The designation "in, with, and under" derives from a Lutheran description of the Eucharistic presence of Christ. It must be noted that the sequence, however, does not follow the Trinitarian sequence of transcendent, incarnate, and immanent that Peacocke himself ordinarily uses. As implied in the first section of this chapter, God-as-Transcendent suffers *with* the cosmos, God-as-Incarnate suffers *in* the cosmos, and God-as-Immanent suffers under the cosmos. Because Peacocke uses both the spatial model of Transcendent-Incarnate-Immanent and the Eucharistic imagery of "in, with, and under," the sequence of presentation in this section of the chapter may need to be reordered at times. For example, for strict conceptual clarity, the sentence should read "transcendent, incarnate, and immanent presence 'with, in, and under' the cosmos."

59. William J. Hill, *The Three-Personed God: The Trinity as a Mystery of Salvation* (Washington, DC: Catholic University of America, 1982), 283.

60. One thinks again of the proposal by Jürgen Moltmann with regard to the suffering of God: "The Son suffers dying, the Father suffers the death of the Son." See *Crucified God*, 243.

61. Psalm 139:1–4, passim, adapted from the *NAB*.

62. "Sympathy," *Oxford English Dictionary Online*, accessed 14 February 2005; available from http://dictionary.oed.com.

63. Cf. Isaiah 49:15 (*NAB*).

64. "Empathy," *Merriam Webster Online Dictionary*, accessed 14 February 2005; available from http://www.m-w.com/cgibin/dictionary?book=Dictionary&va=empathy&x=8&y=16.

65. "Empathy," *American Heritage Dictionary of the English Language,* accessed 14 March 2005; available from http://www.bartleby.com/61/58/E0115800.html.

66. Cf. Isaiah 53:3–4 (*RSV*).

67. "Protopathy," *Oxford English Dictionary Online,* accessed 14 February 2005; available from http://dictionary.oed.com.

68. Johnson, *She Who Is,* 260–261.

Bibliography

Abelson, J. *The Immanence of God in Rabbinic Literature* [1912]. New York: Hermon, 1969.

Aquinas, Thomas. *Summa Contra Gentiles*. Book One: God, trans. A. C. Pegis. Notre Dame, IN: University of Notre Dame, 1975.

———. *Summa Theologiae: Existence and Nature of God*. Vol. 2 (Ia. 2–11), trans. Timothy McDermott. Manchester, England: Blackfriars, 1964.

Atkins, Peter W. *Creation Revisited*. New York: Freeman, 1992.

Augustine. "*Sermo 52*." In "Creeds, Trinity, and Providence." *Catechism of the Catholic Church*. Available from http://www.illinoisknights.org; accessed 8 June 2004.

Barbour, Ian A. *Issues in Science and Religion*. New York: Harper Torch, 1971.

———. *Myths, Models and Paradigms*. London: SCM, 1974.

———. *Religion and Science: Historical and Contemporary Issues*. San Francisco: HarperSanFrancisco, 1997.

———. "Review: *Intimations of Reality: Critical Realism in Science and Religion*." *Religion & Intellectual Life* 2, no. 4 (Summer 1985): 111–114.

Barrow, John D., and Frank T. Tipler. *The Anthropic Cosmological Principle*. Oxford: Oxford University Press, 1986.

Bartholomew, David J. *God of Chance*. London: SCM, 1984.

Behe, Michael J. *Darwin's Black Box: The Biochemical Challenge to Evolution*. New York: Touchstone Books, 1996.

Bohr, Niels. *Atomic Theory and Description of Nature*. Cambridge: Cambridge University, 1934.

Bonhoeffer, Dietrich. *Letters and Papers from Prison*, trans. Reginald H. Fuller. New York: Macmillan, 1962.

Bracken, Joseph A. "Images of God within Systematic Theology." *Theological Studies* 63, no. 2 (June 2002): 362–373.

Brewer, Elmer W. "The Approaches of John Polkinghorne, Arthur Peacocke, and Ian Barbour for the Integration of Natural Science and Christian Theology." Ph.D. diss., Southern Baptist Theological Seminary, 1995.

Brierley, Michael W. "Naming a Quiet Revolution: The Panentheistic Turn in Modern Theology." In *In Whom We Live and Move and Have Our Being: Panentheistic Reflections on God's Presence in a Scientific World*, ed. Philip Clayton and Arthur Peacocke, 1–15. Grand Rapids, MI: Eerdmans, 2004.

Brown, Joanne Carlson, and Rebecca Parker. "God So Loved the World?" In *Violence against Women and Children: A Christian Theological Sourcebook*, ed. Carol J. Adams and Marie M. Fortune, 36–59. New York: Continuum, 1995.

Campbell, Donald T. " 'Downward Causation' in Hierarchically Organized Systems." In *Studies in the Philosophy of Biology: Reduction and Related Problems*, ed. Francisco J. Ayala and Theodosius G. Dobzhansky, 179–186. London: Macmillan, 1974.

Carnes, J. R. *Axiomatics and Dogmatics*. Belfast: Christian Journals, 1982.

Carter, Brandon. "Large Number Coincidences and the Anthropic Principle in Cosmology." In *Confrontation of Cosmological Theories with Observational Data: Copernicus Symposium II*, ed. M. S. Longair, 291–298. Boston: D. Reidel, 1974.

Casaldáliga, Pedro. *Todavia estas Palabras*, trans. Paul Burns and Francis McDonagh. Navarra, Spain: Editorial Verbo Divino, 1990.

Cassell, Eric. "Pain and Suffering." In *Encyclopedia of Bioethics*. Vol. 4, ed. William T. Reich, 1899–1900. New York: Macmillan, 1995.

Chardin, Pierre Teilhard de. *The Phenomenon of Man*, trans. Benjamin Wall. New York: Harper & Row, 1975.

Chaudhuri, Haridas, and Frederic Spiegelberg, eds. *The Integral Philosophy of Sri Aurobindo: A Commemorative Symposium*. London: Allen & Unwin, 1960.

Clayton, Philip. "Emerging God: Theology for a Complex Universe." *Christian Century* 12, no. 1 (13 January 2004): 26–30.

———. *God and Contemporary Science*. Edinburgh, Scotland: Edinburgh University, 1997.

———. *The Problem of God in Modern Thought*. Grand Rapids, MI: Eerdmans, 2000.

Cole, Susan, Marion Ronan, and Hal Taussig. *Wisdom's Feast*. Kansas City, MO: Sheed and Ward, 1996.

Copleston, Frederick C. *Aquinas*. Baltimore, MD: Penguin Books, 1961.

Cox, Harvey. *The Feast of Fools*. Cambridge, MA: Harvard University Press, 1969.

Craig, William Lane. *Divine Foreknowledge and Human Freedom: The Coherence of Theism: Omniscience*. Leiden: E. J. Brill, 1991.

Cross, F. L., and E. A. Livingstone, eds. *Oxford Dictionary of the Christian Church*. 2nd edition. Oxford: Oxford University Press, 1983.

Daly, Mary. *Beyond God the Father*. Boston: Beacon, 1973.

Darwin, Charles. *On the Origin of Species by Means of Natural Selection, or the Preservation of Favoured Races in the Struggle for Life* [book online]. *Online Literature Library*. Knowledge Matters Ltd. Available from http://www.literature.org; accessed 4 May 2004.

Davis, John Jefferson. "Quantum Indeterminacy and the Omniscience of God." *Science and Christian Belief* 9, no. 2 (1997): 129–144.

Dawkins, Richard. *The Blind Watchmaker*. Harlow, England: Longmans, 1986.

Dembski, William. *The Design Inference: Eliminating Chance through Small Probabilities*. Cambridge: Cambridge University Press, 1999.

Denbigh, Kenneth. *An Inventive Universe*. London: Hutchinson, 1975.

Dobzhansky, Theodosius. "Teilhard de Chardin and the Orientation of Evolution: A Critical Essay." In *Process Theology: Basic Writings*, ed. Ewert Cousins, 229–248. New York: Newman, 1971.

Doctrinal Commission of the Church of England. *We Believe in God*. London: Church House Publishing, 1987.

Doye, Jonathan, Ian Goldby, Christina Line, Stephen Lloyd, Paul Shellard, and David Tricker. "Contemporary Perspectives on Chance, Providence, and Free Will." *Science and Christian Belief* 7, no. 2 (1995): 117–139.

Earth Charter Initiative. 2000. "Earth Charter." Available from http://www.earthcharter .org; accessed 19 May 2006.

Edwards, Denis. "The Discovery of Chaos and the Retrieval of the Trinity." In *Chaos and Complexity: Scientific Perspectives on Divine Action*, ed. Robert J. Russell, Nancey C. Murphy, and Arthur R. Peacocke, 157–175. Vatican City State: Vatican Observatory Foundation, 1995.

———. "Original Sin and Saving Grace in an Evolutionary Context." In *Evolutionary and Molecular Biology: Scientific Perspectives on Divine Action*, ed. Robert John Russell, William R. Stroeger, and Francisco J. Ayala, 377–392. Berkeley, CA: Center for Theology and the Natural Sciences, 1998.

Eigen, Manfred. "*Molekulare Selbstorganisation und Evolution*." *Naturwissenschaften* 58, no. 10 (1971): 465–523.

Eigen, Manfred, and Ruthild Winkler. *The Laws of the Game: How the Principles of Nature Govern Chance*, trans. Robert Kimber. New York: Knopf, 1981.

Einstein, Albert. *Out of My Later Years*. Westport, CT: Greenwood, 1970.

Eldredge, Niles, and Stephen J. Gould. "Punctuated Equilibria: The Tempo and Mode of Evolution Reconsidered." *Paleobiology* 3 (1977): 115–151.

Eliot, T. S. "Burnt Norton V." *Four Quartets*. *Art of Europe*. Available from http:// www.artofeurope.com; accessed 7 December 2004.

———. "Four Quartets 4: Little Gidding." *American Poems*. Available from http:// www.americanpoems.com; accessed 4 January 2005.

Evdokimov, Paul. "Nature." *Scottish Journal of Theology* 18, no. 1 (1965): 1–22.

Fatula, Mary Ann. "Suffering." In *The New Dictionary of Theology*, ed. Joseph A. Komonchak, Mary Collins, and Dermot A. Lane, 990. Wilmington, DE: Glazier, 1988.

Fawcett, Thomas. *The Symbolic Language of Religion*. London: SCM, 1970.

Gebhard, Chanoch, and Dovid Landesman. *As the Rabbis Taught: Studies in the Aggados of the Talmud—Tractate Megillah*, trans. Dovid Landesman. Northvale, NJ: Aronson, 1966.

Goetz, Ronald. "The Suffering of God: Rise of a New Orthodoxy." *Christian Century* 103 (April 1986): 385–389.

Gould, Stephen J. *Wonderful Life: The Burgess Shale and the Nature of History*. London: Penguin, 1989.

Hacking, Ian. *Representing and Intervening*. Cambridge: Cambridge University Press, 1983.

Harré, R. M. *Theories and Things*. New York: Sheed & Ward, 1961.

Haught, John. *God after Darwin: A Theology of Evolution*. Boulder, CO: Westview, 2000.

———. "Review of *Science and the Christian Experiment*." *Theological Studies* 33 (1972): 558–559.

Hefner, Philip. "Just How Much May We Intimate about Reality? A Response to Arthur Peacocke." *Religion and Intellectual Life* 2, no. 4 (Summer 1985): 32–38.

Heim, Karl. *The Transformation of the Scientific World View*. London: SCM, 1953.

Heschel, Abraham. *God in Search of Man: A Philosophy of Judaism*. New York: Harper & Row, 1955.

Hesse, Mary. *Revolutions and Reconstructions in the Philosophy of Science*. Brighton, England: Harvester, 1981.

Heyward, Isabel Carter. *The Redemption of God: A Theology of Mutual Relation*. Washington, DC: University Press of America, 1982.

———. *Touching Our Strength: The Erotic as Power and the Love of God*. San Francisco: Harper & Row, 1989.

Hick, John. *Evil and the God of Love*. London: Macmillan, 1966.

———. "An Irenaean Theodicy." In *Encountering Evil*, ed. Stephen T. Davis, 39–52. Edinburgh, Scotland: T. & T. Clark, 1981.

Highfield, Ron. "Divine Self-Limitation in the Theology of Jürgen Moltmann: A Critical Appraisal." *Christian Scholar's Review* 32, no. 1 (2002): 49–71.

Hill, William J. *The Three-Personed God: The Trinity as a Mystery of Salvation*. Washington, DC: Catholic University of America, 1982.

Himma, Kenneth E. "Design Arguments for the Existence of God." *The Internet Encyclopedia of Philosophy*. Available from http://www.iep.utm.edu; accessed 20 December 2004.

Howe, Frederic R. "Review: *God and the New Biology*." *Bibliotheca Sacra* 145 (1988): 459–460.

Huchingson, James E. "Review: *Theology for a Scientific Age*." *Zygon* 31 (1996): 352–355.

Hume, David. *An Enquiry concerning Human Understanding*. La Salle, IL: Open Court, 1958.

Huxley, Julian. *Evolution in Action*. Middlesex, England: Penguin, 1963.

Huyssteen, Wentzel van. *Theology and the Justification of Faith*. Grand Rapids, MI: Eerdmans, 1989.

Jaki, Stanley L. *God and the Cosmologists*. Washington, DC: Regnery Gateway, 1989.

Jantzen, Grace. *God's World. God's Body*. London: Darton, Longman, and Todd, 1984.

Johnson, Elizabeth A. *She Who Is: The Mystery of God in Feminist Theological Discourse*. New York: Crossroad, 1993.

Kadushin, Max. *The Rabbinic Mind*. New York: Jewish Theological Seminary of America, 1952.

Kasper, Walter. *The God of Jesus Christ*. London: SCM, 1983.

Kierkegaard, Søren. *Christian Discourses,* trans. Walter Lowrie. Princeton, NJ: Princeton University Press, 1971.

Klaaren, Eugene M. "Review: *Creation and the World of Science.*" *Zygon* 16, no. 2 (1981): 191–194.

Kreisberg, Jennifer Cobb. "A Globe, Clothing Itself with a Brain." *Wired Magazine.* Terra Lycos Network. Available from http://www.wired.com; accessed 5 May 2004.

Kuhn, Thomas S. *The Structure of Scientific Revolutions.* Chicago: University of Chicago Press, 1962.

LaCugna, Catherine M. *God for Us: The Trinity and Christian Life.* San Francisco: HarperCollins, 1991.

Leplin, Jarrett, ed. *Essays on Scientific Realism.* Berkeley: University of California Press, 1984.

Lewontin, Richard. "Gene, Organism, and Environment." In *Evolution from Molecules to Men,* ed. D. S. Bendall, 273–285. Cambridge: Cambridge University Press, 1983.

Lindbeck, George. *The Nature of Doctrine: Religion and Theology in a Postliberal Age.* Philadelphia: Westminster, 1984.

Lucas, J. R. "The Temporality of God." In *Quantum Cosmology and the Laws of Nature: Scientific Perspectives on Divine Action,* ed. Robert J. Russell, Nancey Murphy, and C. J. Isham, 235–246. Vatican City State: Vatican Observatory Foundation; Berkeley, CA: CTNS, 1993.

——— . *A Treatise on Space and Time.* London: Metheun, 1973.

Macquarrie, John. *In Search of Deity: An Essay in Dialectical Theism: The Gifford Lectures 1983–1984.* London: SCM, 1984.

Mascall, E. L. "Review: *Creation and the World of Science.*" *Religious Studies* 16, no. 3 (1980): 357–359.

McFague, Sallie. *The Body of God: An Ecological Theology.* Minneapolis: Fortress, 1993.

———. *Metaphorical Theology.* Philadelphia: Fortress, 1983.

———. *Models of God: Theology for an Ecological, Nuclear Age.* Philadelphia: Fortress, 1988.

McGrath, Alister. "Old Theology and the New Biology." *Science and Christian Belief* 1, no. 2 (1989): 167–171.

McMullin, Ernan. "The Case for Scientific Realism." In *Essays on Scientific Realism,* ed. Jarrett Leplin, 8–40. Berkeley: University of California Press, 1984.

McPherson, Jim. "The Integrity of Creation: Science, History, and Theology." *Pacifica* 2 (1989): 333–355.

Metz, Johann Baptist. *A Passion for God: The Mystical-Political Dimension of Christianity.* New York: Paulist, 1998.

"Midwives' Model of Care." Citizens for Midwifery. Available from http://www .cfmidwifery.org; accessed 12 February 2005.

Mitchell, B. G. *The Justification of Religious Belief.* London: Macmillan, 1973.

Moltmann, Jürgen. *The Church in the Power of the Spirit: A Contribution to Messianic Ecclesiology,* trans. Margaret Kohl. New York: Harper & Row, 1977.

———. *The Crucified God: The Cross of Christ as the Foundation and Criticism of Christian Theology*, trans. R. A. Wilson and John Bowden. Minneapolis: Fortress, 1993.

———. "God's Kenosis in the Creation and Consummation of the World." In *The Work of Love: Creation as Kenosis*, ed. John Polkinghorne, 137–151. Grand Rapids, MI: Eerdmans, 2001.

———. "*Shekhinah*: The Home of the Homeless God." In *Longing for Home*, ed. Leroy S. Rouner, 170–184. Notre Dame, IN: Notre Dame University Press, 1996.

———. *Theology and Joy*, trans. Reinhard Ulrich. London: SCM, 1973.

———. *Theology of Hope: On the Ground and Implications of a Christian Eschatology*, trans. James Leitch. London: SCM Press, 1967.

———. *The Trinity and the Kingdom: The Doctrine of God*, trans. Margaret Kohl. Minneapolis: Fortress, 1993.

Monod, Jacques. *Chance and Necessity*. New York: Vintage, 1972.

Montefiore, Hugh. *The Probability of God*. London: SCM, 1985.

Mulkay, Michael. *Science and the Sociology of Knowledge*. London: Allen and Unwin, 1979.

Murphy, Nancey C. "Relating Theology and Science in a Postmodern Age." *CTNS Bulletin* 7, no. 4 (Autumn 1987): 1–10.

———. "Review: *Intimation of Reality*." *Zygon* 20, no. 4 (December 1985): 464–466.

———. "Review: *Theology for a Scientific Age*." *Cross Currents* 41, no. 3 (1991): 415–417.

"Neo-Darwinism." *ISCID Encyclopedia of Science and Philosophy*. The International Society of Complexity, Information, and Design. Available from http://www.iscid.org; accessed 5 May 2004.

New American Bible. United States Conference of Catholic Bishops. Available from http://www.usccb.org/nab/bible/index.htm; accessed 17 February 2005.

"Newton." University of Dallas. Available from http://phys.udallas.edu; accessed 4 May 2004.

Newton, Isaac. *The Mathematical Principles of Natural Philosophy*. Trans. A. Motte. *Internet Modern History Sourcebook*. Available from http://www.fordham.edu/halsall/mod/newton-princ.html; accessed 1 April 2007.

Pailin, David. "Can the Theologian Legitimately Try to Answer the Question: Is the Christian Faith True?" *Expository Times* 84 (1973): 321–329.

———. *God and the Processes of Reality*. New York: Routledge, 1989.

———. "Review: *Theology for a Scientific Age*." *Journal of Theological Studies* 42 (1991): 814–819.

Papanikolaou, Aristotle. "Divine Energies or Divine Personhood: Vladimir Lossky and John Zizioulas on Conceiving the Transcendent and Immanent God." *Modern Theology* 19, no. 3 (2003): 357–385.

Patai, Raphael. *The Hebrew Goddess*. Detroit: Wayne State University Press, 1990.

Peacocke, Arthur R. "Articulating God's Presence in and to the World Unveiled by the Sciences." In *In Whom We Live and Move and Have Our Being: Panentheistic Reflections on God's Presence in a Scientific World*, ed. Philip Clayton and Arthur Peacocke, 137–154. Grand Rapids, MI: Eerdmans, 2004.

———. "The Challenge and Stimulus of the Epic of Evolution to Theology." In *Many Worlds*, ed. Stephen Dick, 88–117. Philadelphia: Templeton Foundation, 2000.

———. "Chance and Law in Irreversible Thermodynamics, Theoretical Biology, and Theology." In *Chaos and Complexity: Scientific Perspectives on Divine Action*, ed. Robert J. Russell, Nancey Murphy, and Arthur Peacocke, 123–143. Vatican City State: Vatican Observatory Foundation, 1995.

———. "Cosmos and Creation." In *Cosmology, History, and Theology*, ed. W. Yourgrau and A. D. Breck, 365–381. New York: Plenum, 1977.

———. "The Cost of New Life." In *The Work of Love: Creation as Kenosis*, ed. John Polkinghorne, 21–42. Grand Rapids. MI: Eerdmans. 2001.

———. *Creation and the World of Science: The Bampton Lectures 1978*. Oxford: Clarendon, 1979.

———. *God and the New Biology*. London: J. M. Dent and Sons, 1986.

———. "God as the Creator of the World of Science." In *Interpreting the Universe as Creation*, ed. V. Brummer, 100–112. Kampen, Netherlands: Kok Pharos, 1991.

———. "God's Interaction with the World: The Implications of Deterministic 'Chaos' and of Interconnected and Interdependent Reality." In *Chaos and Complexity: Scientific Perspectives on Divine Action*, ed. Robert J. Russell, Nancey C. Murphy, and Arthur R. Peacocke, 263–287. Vatican City State: Vatican Observatory Foundation, 1995.

———. *Intimations of Reality: Critical Realism in Science and Religion*. South Bend, IN: University of Notre Dame Press, 1984.

———. "The New Biology and Nature, Man and God." In *The Experiment of Life: Proceedings of the 1981 William Temple Centenary Conference*, ed. F. Kenneth Hare, 27–88. Toronto: University of Toronto Press, 1983.

———. *Paths from Science towards God: The End of All Our Exploring*. Oxford: Oneworld, 2001.

———. "Rethinking Religious Faith in a World of Science." In *Religion, Science, and Public Policy*, ed. Frank T. Birtel, 3–29. New York: Crossroad, 1987.

———. *Science and the Christian Experiment*. London: Oxford University Press, 1971.

———. "Theology and Science Today." In *Cosmos and Creation: Science and Theology in Consonance*, ed. Ted Peters, 28–43. Nashville, TN: Abingdon, 1989.

———. *Theology for a Scientific Age: Being and Becoming: Natural, Divine and Human*. Revised and expanded ed. Minneapolis: Augsburg Fortress, 1993.

Pike, Nelson. *God and Timelessness*. London: Routledge and Kegan Paul, 1970.

Polanyi, Michael. *The Tacit Dimension*. London: Routledge and Kegan Paul, 1967.

Polkinghorne, John. *Belief in God in an Age of Science*. New Haven: Yale University Press, 1998.

———. "*Creatio Continua* and Divine Action." *Science & Christian Belief* 7 (1995): 101–108.

———. *One World: The Interaction of Science and Theology*. London: SPCK, 1986.

———. *Science and Christian Belief: Reflections of a Bottom-up Thinker*. London: SPCK, 1994.

———. *Science and Creation*. London: SPCK, 1988.

————. *Science and Theology: An Introduction.* Minneapolis: Fortress, 1998.

————. *Science and the Trinity: The Christian Encounter with Reality.* New Haven: Yale University Press, 2004.

Popper, Karl. *A World of Propensities.* Bristol, England: Thoemmes, 1990.

Prigogine, Ilya, and Gregoire Nicolis. "Biological Order: Structure and Instabilities." *Quarterly Review of Biophysics* 4 (1971): 107–148.

Pugh, Jeffrey C. *Entertaining the Triune Mystery: God, Science, and the Space Between.* Harrisburg, PA: Trinity, 2003.

Rahner, Karl. *Foundations of Christian Faith: An Introduction to the Idea of Christianity.* New York: Seabury, 1978.

Revised Standard Version, The Bible. The Electronic Text Center, University of Virginia. Available from http://etext.virginia.edu/rsv.browse.html; accessed 1 March 2005.

Richard, Lucien. *Christ the Self-Emptying God.* New York: Paulist, 1997.

Rosenzweig, Franz. *The Star of Redemption,* trans. William W. Hallo. New York: Holt, Rinehart, Winston, 1971.

Russell, Robert J. "A Critical Appraisal of Peacocke's Thought on Religion and Science." *Religion and Intellectual Life* 2 (1985): 48–58.

————. "The Theological Scientific Vision of Arthur Peacocke." *Zygon* 26 (December 1991): 505–517.

Salmon, James. "Review: *Theology for a Scientific Age.*" *Theological Studies* 53, no. 4 (1992): 790–791.

Saunders, Nicholas. *Divine Action & Modern Science.* Cambridge: Cambridge University Press, 2002.

Schaab, Gloria L. "The Creative Suffering of the Triune God: An Evolutionary Panentheistic Paradigm." *Theology & Science* 5, no. 3 (2007): in process.

————. "Midwifery as a Model for Ecological Ethics: Expanding Arthur Peacocke's Models of 'Man-in-Creation.'" *Zygon* 42, no. 2 (2007): 489–501.

————. "The Power of Divine Presence: Toward a *Shekhinah* Christology." In *Christology: Memory, Inquiry, Practice: Proceedings of the College Theology Society 2002,* ed. Anne Clifford and Anthony Godzieba, 92–115. Maryknoll, NY: Orbis, 2003.

————. "A Procreative Paradigm of the Creative Suffering of the Triune God: Implications of Arthur Peacocke's Evolutionary Theology." *Theological Studies* 67, no. 3 (2006): 542–566.

Schillebeeckx, Edward. *Christ: The Experience of Jesus as Lord,* trans. John Bowden. New York: Crossroad, 1999.

————. *Jesus: An Experiment in Christology,* trans. Hubert Hoskins. New York: Seabury, 1979.

Schlegel, Richard. "The Impossible Spectator in Physics." *Centennial Review* 19 (1975): 217–231.

Scholem, Gershom. *The Kabbalah and Its Symbolism,* trans. Ralph Manheim. New York: Schocken, 1996.

————. *Major Trends in Jewish Mysticism.* New York: Schocken, 1995.

————. "Readings from *On the Mystical Shape of the Godhead: Basic Concepts of the Kabbalah*," trans. Joachim Neugroschel. Available from http://dhushara.tripod .com; accessed 1 December 2001.

Sheffield, Tricia. "Toward a Theory of Divine Female Embodiment." *Journal of Religion and Society* 4 (2002). Available from http://moses.creighton.edu/JRS/2002/2002-6 .html; accessed 21 March 2005.

"Shekhina." *Encyclopedia Britannica*. Available from http://www.britannica.com; accessed 1 December 2001.

Simpson, George G. *The Meaning of Evolution: A Study of the History of Life and Its Significance for Man*. London: Oxford University Press, 1950.

Sobrino, Jon. *Christology at the Crossroads: A Latin American Approach*, trans. John Drury. Maryknoll, NY: Orbis, 1978.

————. *Jesus the Liberator: A Historical-Theological Reading of Jesus of Nazareth*, trans. Paul Burns and Francis McDonagh. Maryknoll, NY: Orbis, 2001.

Soskice, Janet M. *Metaphor and Religious Language*. Oxford: Oxford University Press, 1984.

Southgate, Christopher. "Different Understandings of Chance." *Meta-Library* of the *Metanexus Online Journal*. Available from http://www.meta-library.net; accessed 10 May 2004.

Sperry, Roger W. *Science and Moral Priority*. Oxford: Blackwell, 1983.

Stapp, Henry P. *Mind, Matter, and Quantum Mechanics*. Berlin: Springer-Verlag, 1993.

Stiver, Danny R. "Review: *God and the New Biology*." *Review and Expositor* 85 (Winter 1988): 167–168.

Surin, Kenneth. "The Impassibility of God and the Problem of Evil." *Scottish Journal of Theology* 35, no. 2 (1982): 97–115.

Swimme, Brian, and Thomas Berry. *The Universe Story: From the Primordial Flaring Forth to the Ecozoic Era—A Celebration of the Unfolding of the Cosmos*. San Francisco: HarperSanFrancisco, 1994.

Swinburne, Richard. *The Existence of God*. Oxford: Clarendon, 1979.

————. "Mackie, Induction, and God." *Religious Studies* 19 (1983): 385–391.

Tan, Seng-Kong. "The Doctrine of the Trinity in John Wesley's Prose and Poetic Works." *Journal for Christian Theological Research* 7 (2002): 3–14.

Tennyson, Alfred. "In Memoriam. A.H.H." *Tapestry: The Institute for Philosophy, Religion, and the Life Sciences*. Available from http://www.tapestryweb.org; accessed 17 November 2004.

Thompson, Curtis L. "From Presupposing Pantheism's Power to Potentiating Panentheism's Personality: Seeking Parallels between Kierkegaard's and Martensen's Theological Anthropologies." *Journal of Religion* 82, no. 2 (April 2002): 225–251.

Tillich, Paul. *Theology of Culture*. New York: Oxford University Press, 1959.

Torrance, Thomas F. *Reality and Scientific Theology*. Edinburgh: Scottish Academic Press, 1985.

Trickett, D. G. "Review: *Creation and the World of Science*." *Journal of Religion* 61, no. 2 (1981): 205–207.

Urbach, Ephraim E. *The Sages: Their Concepts and Beliefs,* trans. Israel Abrahams. Cambridge, MA: Harvard University Press, 1987.

Ward, Keith. *The Concept of God.* Oxford: Blackwell, 1974.

————. *Religion and Creation.* Oxford: Clarendon, 1996.

Ware, Kallistos. "God Immanent Yet Transcendent: The Divine Energies according to Saint Gregory Palamas." In *In Whom We Live and Move and Have Our Being: Panentheistic Reflections on God's Presence in a Scientific World,* ed. Philip Clayton and Arthur Peacocke, 157–168. Grand Rapids, MI: Eerdmans, 2004.

Westhelle, Vitor. "Theological Shamelessness? A Response to Arthur Peacocke and David A. Pailin." *Zygon* 35 (March 2000): 165–172.

"What to Expect from a Caregiver Who Provides the Midwifery Model of Care." *Citizens for Midwifery.* Available from http://www.cfmidwifery.org; accessed 12 February 2005.

Wheatley, Margaret. *Leadership and the New Science: Learning about Organization from an Orderly Universe.* San Francisco: Berrett-Koehler, 1992.

Williams, Daniel Day. *God's Grace and Man's Hope.* New York: Harper, 1949.

————. *The Spirit and the Forms of Love.* New York: Harper & Row, 1968.

Wiseman, James A. *Theology and Modern Science: Quest for Consonance.* New York: Continuum, 2002.

Index